American Narratives

American Narratives

Multiethnic Writing in the Age of Realism

MOLLY CRUMPTON WINTER

 *Louisiana State University Press*

BATON ROUGE

Published by Louisiana State University Press
Copyright © 2007 by Louisiana State University Press
All rights reserved
Manufactured in the United States of America
FIRST PRINTING

Designer: Barbara Neely Bourgoyne
Typeface: Adobe Minion Pro
Printer and binder: Edwards Brothers, Inc.

Library of Congress Cataloging-in-Publication Data
Winter, Molly Crumpton, 1968–
    American narratives : multiethnic writing in the age of realism /
Molly Crumpton Winter.
        p. cm.
    Includes bibliographical references and index.
    ISBN 978-0-8071-3225-8 (alk. paper)
    1. American literature—Minority authors—History and criticism.
2. Realism in literature. 3. Minorities in literature. 4. Ethnic groups
in literature. 5. Immigrants in literature. 6. Group identity in literature.
7. Ethnicity in literature. 8. Multiculturalism in literature. 9. Race in
literature. I. Title.
    PS153.M56W56 2007
    810.9'920693—dc22
                                                    2007003619

The paper in this book meets the guidelines for permanence and
durability of the Committee on Production Guidelines for Book
Longevity of the Council on Library Resources. ♾

To Jarrod

Contents

Acknowledgments

THIS BOOK WOULD NOT have been possible without those scholars whose recovery work and critical consideration of ethnic American realist writers form the foundation of this study. Among them is the incomparable James Nagel, and I am exceedingly grateful to him for his editorial and professional advice, which helped shape this book and guide it to publication. Special thanks to Judith Ortiz Cofer and Barbara McCaskill for sharing their knowledge of multiethnic literature and to Katie Smith for facilitating my development as an academic. I am deeply indebted to Gloria Cronin, whose keen reading of and critical comments on this study helped to give it direction and heart. My appreciation extends to Carol J. Batker for her insightful commentaries as the manuscript developed. I would also like to thank Candis LaPrade for her support along the way, and John Easterly, executive editor of Louisiana State University Press, for his wisdom and kindness.

I am endlessly grateful to my mother, Mimi, and to my late father, Mickey Crumpton, for all they have done for me. I would also like to thank my sister, Claire Baum, and her family, David, Malcolm, Michael, and Stephen. My appreciation also goes out to Beverly and Jeff Winter for their support. Most of all, I would like to express my profound gratitude to my husband, Jarrod, and to my boys, Solomon and Samuel, for their patience and encouragement.

American Narratives

Diversity in the Age of Realism

BETWEEN 1890 AND 1915, an unprecedented number of works by immigrants, African Americans, and American Indians were being published in the United States, but their contributions to American literature are only beginning to be fully recognized. The turn into the twentieth century was a pivotal era in American literature because of the new wave of writing about ethnicity that was appearing as part of the development of realism. At this time, the tradition of African American narrative, which had its roots in the abolitionist literature of the nineteenth century, was expanding to new artistic heights. American Indian voices were gaining power through the writings of the first generation of Native Americans to graduate from missionary and government-sponsored boarding schools, and recent immigrants or children of first-generation émigrés were depicting life in their burgeoning communities. Though much has been written on each of these distinct ethnic literary traditions, very little scholarship exists on the points at which they intersect and their common role in the development of American realism. The works of these ethnic authors have never been collectively evaluated for their contributions to the literature of the nation.

A comprehensive analysis of a cross-section of this group of writers reveals how they expanded the range of realist social writing to include themes of ethnic identity and national belonging and, in so doing, how they expanded the notion of American citizenship. Four writers who worked with these themes were Mary Antin, a Jewish American im-

1

migrant from Russia; Zitkala-Ša, a Sioux originally from South Dakota; Sutton E. Griggs, an African American from the South; and Sui Sin Far, a biracial Chinese American who lived for a time on the West Coast. Though these authors in no way cover all the groups writing in America between 1890 and 1915, they have been strategically selected to represent diverse perspectives and four distinct models of interrogating the status quo. The sample consists of three women and one man. Two were born in America; two were born elsewhere. Their literary production includes autobiography, short stories, essays, and novels. Mary Antin wrote of the Russia of her early youth and of her experiences in Boston, where her family eventually settled after immigrating to America. Born on the Yankton reservation, Zitkala-Ša wrote narratives set there and in boarding schools in Indiana and Pennsylvania. Sutton E. Griggs placed his novels primarily in the South. Sui Sin Far's short stories most often depict the Chinatowns of the West Coast. What unites these writers is their literary focus on how immigrants, American Indians, and African Americans respond to assimilatory forces and situate themselves in the concept of the nation.

Until very recently, these writers' texts, and those by other ethnic American writers as well, were overlooked in the scholarship on American literary realism. However, many of the works that are recognized as the most important of the era—such as those by William Dean Howells, Stephen Crane, Theodore Dreiser, Henry James, and Edith Wharton—have much in common with ethnic realist texts. All deal with contemporary life, explore social dynamics, and consider how individual identity is affected by and constructed within society. The first critics of this era's literature did not give much thought to immigrant writers or authors of color; however, they did construct inclusive paradigms that would help facilitate the reintroduction of writers such as Mary Antin, Zitkala-Ša, Sutton E. Griggs, and Sui Sin Far.

In fact, though the early surveyors of realism—including Fred Lewis Pattee, Vernon Louis Parrington, and Van Wyck Brooks—do not consider issues of ethnicity and nationality or the writers who addressed such themes, they nonetheless must be credited with broadness and diversity. In *The History of American Literature since 1870* (1915) and *The New American Literature, 1890–1930* (1930), Pattee examines a variety of themes and includes both male and female writers from all over the United States. In *Main Currents in American Thought* (1930), Parrington covers a similar range of authors and regions, as well as genres, as does Brooks in *The Confident Years, 1885–1915* (1952). In these four wide-reaching studies, Mary Antin is included in a list of "Fifty Noteworthy Biographies and Autobiographies," Paul Laurence Dunbar is mentioned once and dismissed, Abraham Cahan is named in passing, and Charles W. Chesnutt—the best-known African American writer of realism—is briefly discussed in a chapter devoted to Eugene O'Neill. Part of the reason for literary critics' cursory treatment of immigrant and African American authors, and their apparent dismissal of Native American writers, may have been lack of access. Sutton Griggs sold his novels mainly in the South, while Zitkala-Ša did not collect her essays and stories into a book until 1921, and Sui Sin Far's short-story collection did not have a wide distribution. Antin's autobiography, however, was a bestseller, as was *Iola Leroy* (1891) by Francis E. W. Harper, and the works of Cahan and Chesnutt were promoted by those within the literary establishment, most notably by William Dean Howells.[1]

A better explanation for this early neglect of immigrant authors and writers of color is that scholars failed to identify the themes of ethnicity and citizenship as being central to the era. However, Pattee, Parrington, and Brooks all agree that the literature of the age was unified by its exploration of contemporary America. As Pattee observes, realist writers "wrote without models save as they took life itself as their model. Coarse and uncouth some of their work might be, but teeming it always was with the freshness, the vitality, and the vigor of a new soil and newly awakened nation."[2] These scholars also recognized that attention to social themes was paramount. As Parrington wrote, "In the last decades of the century the problem novel spread swiftly, expanding the field of its inquiry, and seeking to understand the new ways. Making its first essays in the familiar field of the political, it soon turned to consider the economic problems arising out of the new industrialism. . . . The class passions of the time found reflection in its pages, and in consequence the sociological novel became increasingly a repository of the social ideas of a perplexed and troubled generation."[3] These evaluations do not necessarily exclude the consideration of ethnic writers, and in fact most of their works could easily fit within these definitions. Immigrant, Native American, and African American writers represented the contemporary reality of their respective groups, and the social themes that they explored in their works had to do with the state of race relations in the nation. Ultimately, Pattee, Parrington, and Brooks defined the realist era in such expansive terms that they left room for the inclusion of themes and authors that they themselves did not consider.[4]

In *The Ferment of Realism* (1965), Warner Berthoff defines the era from 1884 to 1919 as the age of realism, and he mentions but does not discuss Chesnutt, Cahan, and W. E. B. Du Bois, the better-known writers who wrote about racial issues. Though Berthoff does not specifically consider the themes of ethnicity and citizenship, he expands the types of writing that can be considered realism: "Documentary chronicles of city life and exotic legends of the remote and strange, horrific melodramas and placid genre sketches, works of social criticism and works of psychological analysis, novels written all in dialogue and novels in which the characters are barely capable of consecutive speech, prophecies of a transformed future and haunted daydreams of a visionary past . . . all could be identified as works of realism."[5] This definition allows for the inclusion of ethnic writers of realism who did not necessarily adhere strictly to the tenets of the movement as defined by its early advocates, such as William Dean Howells. Donald Pizer, in *Realism and Naturalism in Nineteenth-Century American Literature* (1984), focuses on the works of seven of the most important writers of the era and does not include any authors of color. However, he too posits a broad definition, writing that realism, "in its ethical idealism and in its exploration of richly diverse experience . . . achieved both its vitality and its promise of future growth."[6] Eric J. Sundquist in *American Realism: New Essays* (1982) also argues that there is room for any number of texts and themes in the realm of American realism. Like Pizer's work, however, the essays in Sundquist's collection focus on a limited selection of authors and do not address themes of ethnicity and nationality.

The close examination of a handful of authors can lead to important revelations that cannot be revealed in sweeping analyses, but there are limitations in coming to conclusions based on a noncomprehensive cross-section of writers. In *The Social Construction of American Realism* (1988),

Amy Kaplan conducts an enlightening examination of the social and material influences on the writings of Howells, Wharton, and Dreiser, but her conclusion, that realism is "a strategy for imagining and managing the threats of social change—not just to assert dominant power but often to assuage fears of powerlessness," does not seem to apply to the works of immigrants or people of color.[7] She sees realists as "constructing a cohesive social world to contain the threat of social change"; yet many ethnic American writers who questioned assimilation as a path to citizenship clearly sought to facilitate—not contain—change through their narratives.[8]

In the last decade of the twentieth century, scholars began to acknowledge the ethnic perspective in American realism in collections such as *Facts on File Bibliography of American Fiction, 1866–1918* (1993), edited by James Nagel and Gwen Nagel; *American Realism and the Canon* (1994), edited by Tom Quirk and Gary Scharnhorst; *The Cambridge Companion to American Realism and Naturalism* (1995), edited by Donald Pizer; and *The Portable American Realism Reader* (1997), edited by James Nagel and Tom Quirk. In these works, texts by black, American Indian, Asian American, and immigrant writers are examined, and racial issues are considered as key themes of the period. The Nagel and Nagel *Bibliography* gives publishing information for many writers of color and is the only book surveying the realist era to include Sutton E. Griggs. *The Portable American Realism Reader* also reflects the diversity of the period, containing stories by Chesnutt, Sui Sin Far, Zitkala-Ša, and other ethnic writers alongside narratives by more established realist writers, such as Howells, Wharton, and Crane. *American Realism and the Canon* is an important collection of essays that considers how authors coming out of different cultural traditions were able to utilize the tenets of realism to tell their stories. Diversity is viewed as a critical subject of the age; as Quirk and Scharnhorst state, "The realist mode was flexible enough and of sufficient range, the realist era hospitable enough, that a multitude of women writers and minority writers produced and published texts that, albeit at times covertly, gave voice to the most urgent concerns of race, ethnicity, gender, class, section, and region."[9] This definition of realism, like Berthoff's, opens up the movement in ways that lead to the consideration of how previously overlooked writers of the era might fit into the tradition. The diverse essays in the *Cambridge Companion* also broaden the study of the realist movement. Perhaps the article that best addresses the multiethnic aspects of the age is "Expanding the Canon of American Realism," by Elizabeth Ammons, who incorporates Sui Sin Far and Zitkala-Ša into her analysis.

In fact, Ammons's scholarship has helped shape the understanding of ethnic American realist writing. Two texts that emphasize the diversity of the era are her *Conflicting Stories: American Women Writers at the Turn into the Twentieth Century* (1992) and *Tricksterism in Turn-of-the-Century American Literature* (1994), edited by Ammons and Annette White-Parks. In *Conflicting Stories,* Ammons reveals that diversity was one of the defining factors of this generation of writers. Each of the essays in *Tricksterism* explores this trope in the writings of authors from different ethnic backgrounds, revealing a common and unifying theme that can be traced through the works of a wide variety of writers.

A more recent work that focuses on ethnicity in American realist literature is *The Culture Concept: Writing and Difference in the Age of Realism* (2002), by Michael A. Elliot, which explores the connection between the rise of realism and the beginning of cultural anthropology. Elliot examines the idea of inclusiveness that was at the heart of both William Dean Howells's notion of realism and Franz Boas's conception of anthropology. Though Elliott primarily focuses on African American and Native American texts, his fundamental premise—that literature of both cultural difference and inclusion grew out of this era—can be expanded to incorporate immigrant writings as well.

Thanks to the work of these and many other scholars, some of the writings of Sui Sin Far, Zitkala-Ša, Mary Antin, and Sutton E. Griggs are back in print, and portions of them are included in anthologies for classroom use. Works by other long-neglected writers of the period—such as Abraham Cahan, Francis E. W. Harper, Alexander Posey, Pauline Hopkins, and Onoto Watanna—also have been reprinted. Some important texts, like most of the novels by Sutton E. Griggs, have been out of print for some time, which hinders the chances of their study and precludes a full understanding of the true diversity of the era.[10] There have always been writers of ethnicity who were included, at least in passing, in discussions of American literary realism, but their centrality to the movement only becomes apparent when the themes of ethnicity and citizenship are recognized as essential elements in the literature of social analysis. With these themes in mind, it is important to take a new and sustained look at multiethnic authors such as Mary Antin, Sutton E. Griggs, Zitkala-Ša, and Sui Sin Far.

Viewing the texts of these authors in association to each other reveals a dialogue about the ways in which mainstream Americans expected conformity and acquiescence from ethnic minorities, yet simultaneously upheld beliefs and systems—such as the segregation of blacks, the exclusion of Chinese, literacy tests for immigrants, and programs of "civilization" for American Indians—that prevented their full political and social participation in civic life. The forces to which each author responds serve to shape his or her narrative. Mary Antin counters nativist rhetoric with a memoir of her assimilation that challenges notions of immigrant inferiority. Sutton E. Griggs responds to the demoralizing oppression of blacks in the South with novels depicting a power and unity among African Americans that ultimately leads to their incorporation into the nation. Zitkala-Ša's narratives reveal the larger culture's fundamental disregard of American Indian cultures even as the U.S. government instituted programs intended to accelerate the assimilation of Native Americans, and her texts express deep-seated ambivalence toward the notion of national belonging. Finally, Sui Sin Far, writing of Chinese immigrants who were denied the possibility of naturalization, develops in her short stories an idea of citizenship in which individual belonging is not dictated by national character.

Together these texts constitute a varied yet unified political critique of the status quo, one that articulates the uneven relationships of both individuals and groups to the existing American system. The complexity of the authors' responses to barriers from citizenship demonstrates how ideas of cultural identity and nation were constantly contested. Often these texts reflect the national discourse at the turn into the twentieth century, as they respond to the obstructions created by mainstream society. For example, African Americans, despite their status, had long been a part of American culture. Segregation and disenfranchisement were based on prejudice of skin color, and so race was the important

issue in most African American texts at the time. The debate about
the incorporation of Native Americans and recent immigrants into the
larger society focused on whether these groups, considered to be from
inferior cultures, would be able to change sufficiently—that is, to shed
their cultural particularity and adopt mainstream American ways—to
allow for their integration. Though biology became part of the rhetoric
of exclusion, it was often ethnicity, not race, that was at the heart of
citizenship issues. It is important to remember, however, that at this
time terminology was blurred, and words such as "race," "culture," and
"nationality" were often used indiscriminately.

Despite changing immigration patterns and increased inequali-
ties between American Indian and African Americans and their white
counterparts at the turn into the twentieth century, a conservative notion of assimilation held sway as the path to national belonging. Paula E.
Hyman gives a useful definition of assimilation as a process that begins
with acculturation—"the acquisition of the basic markers of a larger society, such as language, dress, and . . . 'values'"—followed by the "integration of minority group members into the majority institutions," and
ending with "the dissolution of the minority."[11] In America, this was the
path that earlier immigrant groups from Europe had followed, and by
the late nineteenth century it was established in popular consciousness
as the only way to incorporate people into the nation. The writings of
ethnic Americans during this period, however, complicated and challenged this paradigm as one that would not serve in a multicultural
nation and that in practice was not applied equally to all. In fact, the era
is marked by a national insistence on acculturation without a real commitment to integration.

The notion of assimilation has to do with the idea that there was an
American model and that immigrants and native-born people of color
could become American by conforming to it. Sidonie Smith sees this
model as deriving from the expectations of mainstream America: "The
metaphor through which the country understood the process by which
diverse inhabitants became a part of the corporate 'nation' called America was the metaphor of the 'melting pot' and its desired effect was 'assimilation.' To be truly American one had to assimilate by becoming the
normative American subject, adopting the values, behaviors, dress, and

point of view of the Anglo-American middle-class and shedding differences of language, outlook, dress, demeanor."[12] Mary Antin, in her autobiography *The Promised Land* (1912), interprets the American character as hardworking, patriotic, and democratic. In the course of her narrative she demonstrates how she—and by association other immigrants—embodied these ideals through the process of Americanization. The other writers in this study, however, did not embrace assimilation as Antin did.

One dimension of the mainstream conception of American identity that was problematic for many ethnic Americans was that it was inherently white. This fact complicates the quest for national identity in the works of many writers of color. Some express a sense of reluctance to sacrifice cultural particularity to conform to the dominant American identity when the act of conforming was no guarantee that others would accept that construction. W. E. B. Du Bois, the era's most outspoken advocate for both civil rights and the value of African American culture, stated that the African American "would not bleach his Negro soul in a flood of white Americanism."[13] Sutton E. Griggs, echoing Du Bois, implies in his novels that the best way for black citizens to gain acceptance into American society is by racial cohesion. At the time, the only way for African Americans to integrate was to pass as white, a possibility open to only a small percentage of the population. Those who could do so invariably were estranged from their communities. Griggs's novels suggest that in order for blacks to enter into mainstream American society as an intact culture, they had to be unified. He delineates a dual affiliation that encompasses both complete devotion to one's culture and an unwavering insistence on American citizenship. For Griggs, racial cohesion involves the conscious desire to claim allegiance to race and nation without sacrificing one for the other.

Whereas Griggs depicts the desire of his African American characters for full acceptance into American society, Zitkala-Ša is wary of a nation that has never respected the rights and cultures of American Indian peoples. In her autobiographical essays, she shows how her disdain for what she perceives to be white Christian values prevents her from claiming an American identity, even as she becomes adept at the language and customs of American society. Her ambivalence is fostered by her belief that, due to her education, she can no longer claim her traditional identity because she was removed physically, and to some degree culturally, from Sioux society. Ambivalence and ambiguity signify an inability to claim either an inherited or an American identity. Sui Sin Far, however, embraces the possibility of a multicultural society in which the individual can selectively incorporate both an ethnic and a national identity based on personal choice. Her short stories are populated by Chinese, white, and biracial individuals who choose their own destinies, thereby creating a new America (at least in fiction) in which individuality is not based on prescribed cultural or societal strictures.

When examining ethnic realist literature, it is important to remember that methods of representing American citizenship were not culturally specific, and writers coming out of different ethnic traditions did not necessarily choose one model over another. The works of Antin, Sui Sin Far, Griggs, and Zitkala-Ša are emblematic of specific ways of dramatizing cross-cultural experience in the United States; they are not necessarily representative of the respective groups to which the authors belonged. For example, Mary Antin's *The Promised Land* is a forthrightly assimilationist book. It does not follow, however, that other Jewish-American authors espouse assimilation, or that writers of other ethnicities do not favor it. In 1891, S. Alice Callahan, a Muscogee Indian, published *Wynema: A Child of the Forest,* in which an American Indian girl, after receiving a Western education, integrates easily into the white family with whom she goes to live. Similarly, several of Charles W. Chesnutt's novels demonstrate that there is little difference between black and white Americans except the arbitrary "color line." In contrast, most of the stories by the Jewish American writer Abraham Cahan register a distrust of the Americanizing process. In tone and theme Cahan's works are much more closely aligned with Zitkala-Ša's writings; both express profound ambivalence about dual cultural heritage.

Social cohesion can be found in some very different texts, including *Observations by Mr. Dooley* (1902), by Irish American satirist Finley Peter Dunne, which portrays individuals who are proud of their Irish heritage and comfortable in their American identities. The poems by various unnamed authors in *Songs of Gold Mountain* (1911) articulate a strong allegiance among the Chinese in San Francisco that serves simultaneously as an expression of power and a means of protection in response to the often-hostile American society.[14] Several short-story writers depicted the diversity of America's growing cities. Among these was Myra Kelly, a New York teacher whose *Little Citizens* (1904) and *Little Aliens* (1910) are collections of intimate sketches of life in a racially mixed city school. Jacob Riis, a Danish immigrant famous for his exposé of inner-city slums, treats inhabitants of New York neighborhoods with great sympathy in *Out of Mulberry Street* (1897), and African American writer Alice Dunbar-Nelson explores the various intersections of culture in New Orleans in *The Goodness of St. Rocque and Other Stories* (1899). The themes of assimilation, ambiguity, dual affiliation, and diversity all speak to differing ideas of citizenship.

Though each of these writers can be considered a part of the broad multiethnic spectrum of American literature at the turn into the twentieth century, each is also a part of a particular literary tradition. Zitkala-Ša, as a Sioux, is an important link in the complex history of American Indian literature. In the nineteenth century, Native Americans began to publish English-language biographies and histories of their people. This body of literature would blossom at the turn into the twentieth century, as the first generation to attend Dawes-era boarding schools began to write their stories. Paula Gunn Allen explains that Native American literature encompasses two divisions: the traditional, which consists of ceremonial and popular oral discourse, and the contemporary, which includes the written Western genres of fiction, poetry, autobiography, and "as-told-to narratives and mixed genre works."[15] Far from being separate, these two forms influence each other in intriguing ways. As Allen explains, "The whole body of American Indian literature, from its traditional, ceremonial aspects to its formal literary aspects, forms a field, or, we might say, a hoop dance, and as such is a dynamic, vital whole whose different expressions refer to a tradition that is unified and coherent on its own terms."[16] This "hoop dance" is apparent in Zitkala-Ša's literary production. Not only did she publish a collection of Dakota legends, but her fiction and her autobiographical writing was also informed by the myths, stories, and spiritual worldview of her tribe. The diverse works of Zitkala-Ša and other American Indians served to counter the racist, stereotypical, or romantic depictions that shrouded the reality of Native American existence. Such writers as S. Alice Callahan,

Alexander Posey, John Oskison, Charles Eastman, and Zitkala-Ša were able to negotiate their own space in American letters and to convey their personal and communal visions by writing within popular literary conventions. Their works also indicate an attempt to make room for a new American Indian identity next to, but not in place of, traditional tribal existence. Gerald Vizenor views this generation of writers—the first to graduate from Indian boarding schools—as being at the forefront of a new age of Native American literary thought and achievement. In some cases their ambivalent positionality marks the beginning of a complicated negotiation not only with mainstream America but also with their traditional cultures.

As with the American Indian tradition, black American literature comes out of a culture rich in storytelling. Scholars from W. E. B. Du Bois to Eric Sundquist have been able to detect an African presence in black American folklore and song. The oral tradition was particularly strong because of laws in the antebellum South that prevented slaves from learning to read or write. Despite these prohibitions, the history of African American literature written in English reaches back to the revolutionary period and the poems of Phillis Wheatley. The fight for abolition before the Civil War brought about a surge of slave narratives and novels that influenced generations of writers. At the turn into the twentieth century, a group of writers—including Chesnutt, Dunbar, Harper, Du Bois, and Dunbar-Nelson—wrote fiction, poetry, and essays that would find their way into the mainstream of American society. Sutton E. Griggs, though often overlooked by critics, was no less important.

Jewish American literature written in English had its beginnings in the early nineteenth century with the plays of Mordecai Manuel Noah and the poetry of Penina Moïse. Others were to follow, but Jewish literary production was sparse until the immense immigration of eastern European Jews at the end of the nineteenth century. This influx brought with it an electric cultural and intellectual climate that would foster the advent of "a coherent sense of Jewish American literature in English."[17] The most important English-language authors were Mary Antin and Abraham Cahan, but their writing existed alongside American poetry and plays being written in Yiddish that probably had more influence in urban Jewish communities. Cahan, as editor of the Yiddish newspaper the *Jewish Daily Forward (Foverts)*, was part of this trend; Antin was not. Nevertheless, the fact that stories from the Jewish religious tradition informed Antin's work and her perception of America is evident in the title of her autobiography, *The Promised Land*. Antin and her generation, while articulating the condition of being Jewish in America, were also a part of another important literary tradition—the writing of Jews in the Diaspora.[18]

Like eastern European Jews on the East Coast, Chinese immigrants on the West Coast were quick to establish theaters and newspapers in their native language. Poetry, which was perhaps the most respected literary genre in China, continued to be written by immigrants; the several hundred poems published as *Songs of Gold Mountain* offer a fascinating look into the lives and aesthetics of the Chinese community in San Francisco. The tradition of Chinese American writing in English, however, probably begins with the autobiography *When I Was a Boy in China* (1887), by Lee Yan Phou. The short stories of Sui Sin Far mark the advent of Asian American fiction, as she was the first to write in English about Chinese characters living in the United States. She was able to represent the residents of North American Chinatowns in her stories because of her Asian heritage and her Western education. Raised in England and Canada, Sui Sin Far learned Chinese stories, legends, and songs from her mother. She thus came to America in a unique position, in that she had an intimate knowledge of Chinese life and culture and could write sophisticated prose in English. The Chinese elements that appear in her fiction connect her stories, albeit in a very tenuous way, to the oral tradition of mainland China.

Not only are Zitkala-Ša, Sutton E. Griggs, Mary Antin, and Sui Sin Far important to their respective ethnic literary traditions; they are also part of an exciting time in American literary history. After the Civil War, people across the United States became interested in discovering who was living within their borders, which resulted in the increased popularity of local color and regionalist writing. This fascination with the different regions of the country and the people who lived there—their customs, language, and history—eventually grew into a desire to know about African Americans and Native Americans (who had been there since before the nation was founded), as well as about the new immigrants coming to America. This curiosity is reflected in the un-precedented number of magazine articles and book publications by ethnic Americans at the turn into the twentieth century. Increasing interest in works by immigrants and people of color coincided with a rise in literacy that fueled the demand for reading materials. More books were finding their way to print, and magazine publications grew at an enormous rate at the end of the nineteenth century. At the close of the Civil War, the number of magazines published in America numbered in the hundreds; by 1900, they numbered in the thousands. The cultural standard-bearers to which the educated classes subscribed, such as the *Atlantic Monthly* and *Harper's,* remained vital, but new magazines that relied on newsstand sales, such as *McClure's* and the *Ladies' Home Journal,* served to diversify the material that was being published. The interest directed at the non-traditional writer, combined with new publishing opportunities, allowed ethnic American writing to enter into the public discourse as never before.

Though ethnic writers were something new on the literary land-scape, the kinds of stories that many of them wanted to tell were not out of sync with the dominant literary movement of the day, American realism. Elizabeth Ammons describes this era as "a time in American literary history especially distinguished by three things: topical issues frequently occupied a central position in the literature; formal experimentation was a primary focus for many writers; and women and black men can be seen as the majority, not the minority, of the most important authors."[19] Writers of American realism—ethnic and mainstream, male and female—wrote of the tensions of American society through the lens of individual characters and in the language of everyday lives. In this sense, Antin, Zitkala-Ša, Griggs, and Sui Sin Far are clearly connected to the tradition of realism. But all four were influenced by other literary conventions as well.

Even as American letters moved towards realism, the reading public maintained its Victorian taste for the sentimental, the melodramatic, and the sensational. Sentimental novels were written to induce emotions in the reader, often to lead them to a new way of thinking or to a specific plan of action. Melodrama relied on easily identifiable stock characters to represent good and evil, exciting physical scenarios, and the assurance that justice would be served in the end. Sensational novels were always based on a mystery, often having to do with family relationships. These Victorian modes of narrative were used very effectively in abolitionist texts written by both black and white authors, such as Harriet Beecher Stowe and William Wells Brown, and these methods became a part of the African American literary tradition. It is little wonder, then, that Sutton E. Griggs utilized them. Because he was trying to reach a wide cross-section of people and not the Eastern literary elite, it makes sense that he would gravitate toward popular and familiar forms. The conventions of sentimentalism served their purpose, eliciting emotional responses from Griggs's readers that caused them to sympathize with African Americans faced with injustice and violence. Griggs relied on melodrama to give a clear moral picture of race relations in the country, and he incorporated the sensational to highlight the connection between white and black America, as issues of parentage and color often point to the familial relationship between the races. Indeed, the Victorian use of sentimentalism can be found to some degree in all four writers in this study. Most of their writings had a social dimension and in some sense a political purpose: they were each writing, in part, to educate the reading public about the reality of their respective ethnic groups and to garner support for the rights of those people. The history of protest literature in the nineteenth century had shown that sentimental forms were effective; if writers could gain sympathy for the characters in their books, they could perhaps gain sympathy for the groups that those characters represented.

Another American tradition comes into play in Mary Antin's *The Promised Land*. Antin reaches back to the romantic period of the midnineteenth century, and in particular to transcendentalism, to define her place in the world. According to James Nagel, the literature of that era was "based on a set of philosophic assumptions that regarded reality as fundamentally spiritual in nature"; he argues that transcendentalism "rested on the notion that physical facts were merely an indication of the more important spiritual facts behind them."[20] Antin's transcendentalism lays claim not only to an American literary heritage, but also to a form of spirituality that reiterates the universal rights that are at the heart of democracy. As she writes:

If I had died before my first breath, my history would still be worth re-
cording. For before I could lie on my mother's breast, the earth had to be
prepared, and the stars had to take their places; a million races had to die,
testing the laws of life; and a boy and girl had to be bound for life to watch
together for my coming. I was millions of years away, and I came through
the seas of chance, over the fiery mountains of law, by the zigzag path of
human possibility. . . . Such creatures of accident are we, liable to a thousand deaths before we are born. But once we are here, we may create our
own world if we choose. Since I stood on my own feet, I have never met my
master. . . . However I came here, it is mine to be.[21]

Antin's meditation reflects the organic style of Henry David Thoreau,
the cosmic citizenship of Walt Whitman, and the self-reliance of Ralph
Waldo Emerson. She uses such transcendental passages sparingly but
to great effect. In this quotation she portrays her own creation as emblematic of the divinity of each individual. She states that her right to
be—and to be whatever she chooses—shall not be determined by anyone but herself. These moments lend moral and historical support to
her decision to become an American citizen.

The muckraking tradition that grew out of big-city newsrooms
in the late 1890s and early 1900s may have influenced Zitkala-Ša and
Sutton E. Griggs, whose works include critical exposés of corrupt systems, and Sui Sin Far, who worked as a journalist. According to John T.
Flynn, "The eruption of denunciatory writing constituted a phenomenon in the life of the time and exercised a powerful effect on the public mood."[22] Though most muckraking writers—such as Jacob Riis, Ida
M. Tarbell, and Upton Sinclair—explored the dynamics of wealth and
labor, their methods of exposing corrupt economic systems also could
be applied to the examination of institutional racism. The writers who
took up the cause of their respective ethnic groups may have hoped
that exposing the abuses American Indian children suffered in federal
boarding schools, the damage that southern disfranchisement caused
to black individuals and communities, or the biased immigration laws
targeted at the Chinese would be a first step in national campaigns to
enact enduring social change.

Influenced as they were by other literary methods, ethnic writers
such as Antin, Zitkala-Ša, Griggs, and Sui Sin Far did not always ad-

here as strictly as many of their contemporaries to the tenets of realism. But instead of placing these writers outside the realist tradition, it may be more accurate to describe them as expanding the movement in different directions. What Nagel says of other realists can also be said of them: "Their literature was fundamentally democratic, dealing with average characters in mundane situations, struggling with the social, racial, economic, and moral issues of terrestrial life."[23] Precisely because of their focus on ethnicity and nationality, these writers comprise an important group within the larger paradigm of American realism.

In order to comprehend these writers' commitment to social themes, it is necessary to understand the complicated and heady age in which they wrote. National political movements in the late nineteenth and early twentieth centuries created a perception that average or working-class men and women were important, momentous, and worth writing about. The early 1890s saw the rise of the Populist Party, which gave voice to farmers, women, factory workers, and others who viewed themselves outside of national politics. The influence of the Populists would again be felt in the early twentieth century, when the Progressive movement, bolstered by Theodore Roosevelt's "square deal" in 1910, incorporated the ideas of many reformers driven to improve the lives of workers, women, immigrants, and children. The power of the people was also evident in a series of major labor strikes from the 1890s through 1915—strikes that were not always successful in themselves, but that eventually led to legislation to protect the rights of workers. The public was interested in the plight of the poor and the working class, which was then being examined in newspapers and in books such as Jacob Riis's *How the Other Half Lives* (1890). Americans were also fascinated by the rise to immense wealth of capitalists such as John D. Rockefeller, Andrew Carnegie, William Randolph Hearst, and J. P. Morgan. These figures both repelled and attracted the average reader, as demonstrated by the popularity of both muckraking literature, which sought to expose the corruption of such individuals, and the body of literature, represented best by the Horatio Alger novels, that advanced the notion that through pluck and luck any boy could attain vast riches and influence. Realist and naturalist writers of the day reflected the national focus on the conflict between the haves and have-nots. Many books—

including Stephen Crane's *Maggie, Girl of the Streets* (1893), Theodore Dreiser's *Sister Carrie* (1900), and Frank Norris's *The Octopus* (1901)—explored the centrality of business and economics in American life.

For realist writers who focused on issues of ethnicity and citizenship, issues of race took precedence over issues of economics. Sutton E. Griggs, who does address the plight of the working class, often shows how bigotry limited African Americans in the workforce; in his novel *Overshadowed,* for example, a black character is not allowed to join a labor union. The events that influence or inform the works of these writers, however, are not primarily the battles between capital and labor, but the struggles of different ethnic groups in a society structured to limit their participation in it.

The narratives of Zitkala-Ša, Sutton E. Griggs, Mary Antin, and Sui Sin Far are very much imbedded in the histories of their respective ethnic groups in America. Though each writer has other stories to tell, all comment in some way on the racial atmosphere and governmental policy of the day. Just as they are influenced by the politics of their age, their works are shaped by their personal histories. In their writing and in their lives, these four artists demonstrated a steadfast loyalty to their respective ethnic groups. All worked outside the realm of literature to advance the causes of their people, and all but one eventually abandoned narrative writing altogether to fight their battles in the public sphere. All four were involved in the political and social debates of a multiethnic society. And while all eventually became recognized for their literary production, in their own time they were known, to a greater or lesser extent, for their contributions to their particular ethnic communities and to the discussion of racial relations in America.

Mary Antin was born Maryashe Antin in Polotzk, a town in the Russian Pale of Settlement, in 1881. In the late nineteenth century, Jewish inhabitants of the Pale still lived a very Orthodox religious existence. Because of the many restrictions Russian law placed on Jews, Jewish communities found strength and comfort in their religion and traditions, some of which Antin describes in the early chapters of *The Promised Land.* When Antin was ten years old, her father immigrated to the United States, and in 1894 the rest of the family joined him in Boston. As a result, Antin's life changed dramatically. In Russia she had

had no consistent formal education, but in America she was enrolled in public schools and was able to finish her elementary schooling in four years. She also took advantage of community programs—such as Hale House and the Hebrew Immigration Aid Society—that were established to aid immigrants. She made many influential friends through these organizations, and after a few years she was supported in her studies and literary endeavors by an impressive roster of mentors and benefactors. Among her friends and correspondents at this time were Edward Everett Hale, the founder of Hale House; Josephine Lazarus, a well-known essayist and transcendentalist; and the Anglo-Jewish novelist and playwright Israel Zangwill, whose popular play *The Melting Pot* influenced contemporary ideas about American citizenship. These and other influential supporters were instrumental in Antin's admittance to the prestigious Latin School for Girls in Boston. They also furthered Antin's early literary career, helping her to place several short pieces in newspapers and journals and to publish a short book recounting her migration story, *From Plotzk to Boston* (1899).

While Mary Antin was enjoying academic and literary success, as well as concerts and vacations with her benefactors, her home was always with her family in overcrowded tenement houses in Boston's immigrant neighborhoods. Perhaps because of the stresses of poverty and the need to appease her sometimes controlling patrons, she married before she finished high school. In 1901 she became the wife of Dr. Amadeus Grabau, a professor of geology, a German American, and a Lutheran. That year they moved to New York, where he took up a faculty position at Columbia University. For several years, Antin took classes at Columbia's Teaching College and Barnard College, but she never earned a degree. In 1907 she gave birth to her only child, Josephine, who was probably named for Antin's friend Josephine Lazarus, who encouraged Antin's writing and to whose memory Antin dedicated *The Promised Land.*

In 1911, Antin's literary life resumed with a series of articles in the *Atlantic Monthly* that would become *The Promised Land.* The book, which tells of her life in Russia, her immigration, and her assimilation experience, was an immediate bestseller and remained popular for years. Between 1911 and 1912 Antin published three short stories in the *Atlantic Monthly* and two political essays in *The Outlook.* Her final book, the nonfictional *They Who Knock at Our Gates,* came out in 1914. All of Antin's writings from this era share certain themes. She combines a glowing patriotism with a political stance that strongly favors public education and open immigration. In 1914 Antin also became an advocate of Zionism, reflecting her continuing commitment to Jewish peoples. Her very successful and lucrative career as a public speaker, which took off in 1912 due to the amazing popularity of *The Promised Land,* coincided with her active participation in politics. She considered herself a Progressive and campaigned for Theodore Roosevelt (whom she met in 1912), and in 1916 she became chairman of the Women's Committee of the National Hughes Alliance for Republican presidential candidate Charles Evans Hughes. Between 1912 and 1917, Antin was one of the most recognized women in the country. Her strong and compelling Jewish voice had the ear of the public and of important political figures, and she used that voice to protect the rights of her fellow immigrants.

Antin's life took a drastic turn with the advent of World War I. Her husband expressed German sympathies and as a result lost his professorship at Columbia. These views no doubt caused embarrassment to Antin, whose public persona was based on her devotion to America. She and her husband separated in 1917, and Grabau took a position at the National University in Peking, where he spent the rest of his life. Antin subsequently suffered a debilitating emotional breakdown, from which, it seems, she never fully recovered. After spending time in psychiatric care, she moved to Gould Farm, a residential community run by William Gould, a Protestant minister. This was her home, off and on, until her death in 1949. Although Antin continued to correspond and associate with interesting public figures, she was never again in the public eye. Antin instead began a lifelong spiritual journey that led her to explore Christian universalism, mysticism, and anthroposophy.[24] For several years in the 1930s she became a disciple of the mystic Meher Baba, and at the end of her life she was dedicated to the out-of-body-experience ideas of Rudolph Steiner. Antin's spiritual quest seemed to give her solace from her mental illness. Evelyn Salz, after reviewing Antin's letters and interviewing family members, has come to the conclusion that Antin probably suffered from bipolar disorder.[25]

The direction that Antin's life took after World War I led her away from politics and the public life, but it does not diminish her legacy. As a public speaker, she was able to give a face and a voice to millions of immigrants in America, and *The Promised Land* remains an important book on many levels. It is the first text in English by a Jewish writer to describe both life in the Russian Pale and life as an immigrant in America. The book also forcefully addresses the two issues that lay at the heart of all Antin's efforts: public education and unrestricted immigration. Finally, her portrayal of assimilation reflects an important contemporary reality, as countless Jewish immigrants went through the process themselves.

Like Antin's, Zitkala-Ša's early childhood was radically different from the life she would eventually lead. In 1876, on the Yankton reservation in South Dakota, she came into the world as Gertrude Simmons. Her mother, Ellen, or Tate I Yohin Win ("She Reaches for the Wind"), was Sioux. Zitkala-Ša's father was Ellen's third husband, a white man named Felker who abandoned the family before Zitkala-Ša was born. Ellen decided to retain the surname of her second husband, Simmons, and this name was given to her daughter. Zitkala-Ša lived a traditional Sioux life on the reservation until the age of eight, when she went to White's Manual Institution, an Indian boarding school run by Quakers in Wabash, Indiana. According to Dexter Fisher, the school "adhered to the policy of the Bureau of Indian Affairs that Indian children would more rapidly assimilate into American society if they were kept away from the reservation for long periods of time."[26] Zitkala-Ša stayed at the school for three years before returning to the reservation at age eleven. Once home, she found that the changes she had experienced at school had made her unsuitable for reservation life. She felt profoundly different from her mother, with whom she was once so close, and she suffered a restlessness for which there was no outlet on the reservation. She returned to White's Institute to finish her education, returning home to stay with her mother only during summer vacations.

From 1895 to 1897, Zitkala-Ša attended Earlham College in Indiana, where she won awards as an orator and published poems and essays in the school newspaper. She also studied voice and violin at the New England Conservatory of Music in Boston. From 1898 to 1899 she was a teacher at the Carlisle Indian School, the flagship institution on which most other Indian boarding schools were modeled. She resigned after one year because she did not agree with the school's policies or the way that the Native American children were treated. During this period Gertrude Simmons gave herself the name Zitkala-Ša ("Red Bird" in Lakota) after a dispute with her brother's family; she also began publishing in mainstream American magazines. In her brief literary career, she gained a national audience for her autobiographical essays, short stories, articles on American Indian issues, and book of Sioux legends. Of these works, three autobiographical pieces printed in the *Atlantic Monthly* in 1900 are the most overtly literary, in that they incorporate tropes and forms identified with both Western and American Indian literatures. In these essays, Zitkala-Ša invokes trickster ironies, uses natural metaphors, imbeds the history of removal, allotment, and government schools, recounts the importance and techniques of the oral storytelling tradition, evokes Judeo-Christian mythology, and portrays the ambivalence of living between worlds in the borderlands of a culture. As a whole, the body of Zitkala-Ša's work bridges the several worlds with which she was familiar and reveals the broad spiritual and physical terrain of her experience.

In 1902 Zitkala-Ša's literary career ended when she married Raymond T. Bonnin. He was also Sioux and an advocate for American Indians. The couple moved to the Uintah and Ouray reservation in Utah, where Raymond took up his position as a government employee for the Bureau of Indian Affairs, and Zitkala-Ša, now Gertrude Bonnin, worked to improve the lives of women and children on the reservation. In 1903 she had a son, Raymond O. Bonnin. The family lived on the reservation for fourteen years. Zitkala-Ša's only known work from this period is an Indian opera, *Sun Dance,* upon which she collaborated with William Hanson. The production was staged many times in Utah, and it was also performed in New York City in 1938 after being selected by the New York Light Opera Guild as the American Opera of the Year.[27]

In 1916 Gertrude Bonnin was elected secretary-treasurer of the Society of the American Indian, which, according to Fisher, "provided a collective forum for Indians who sought to redress the multitude of inequities they had suffered."[28] This position prompted the Bonnins to move to Washington, D.C., and marked the advent of Zitkala-Ša's lifelong career as an American Indian activist and advocate. According to Carol J. Batker, she used her political voice to "mediate between the competing demands of integration and separatism," that is, to help Native Americans find a way out of the often-debilitating life of the reservations while still maintaining tribal integrity.[29] Though critical of many government policies, Zitkala-Ša came to believe that full U.S. citizenship was crucial in the fight for American Indian rights—a conclusion she may have come to through wrestling with the idea in her early fiction. From 1918 to 1919 she served as editor of the *American Indian Magazine,* writing articles and editorials on Native American issues. In 1921 she created the Indian Welfare Committee under the auspices of the General Federation of Women's Clubs in Washington, D.C., through which she continued her crusade for both citizenship and the betterment of life for Native Americans. In 1926 she founded the National Council of American Indians, an organization dedicated to fighting for the personal and property rights of Native Americans. She served as president of the NCAI until her death in 1938. Through her life and her writings, Zitkala-Ša opened new perspectives on both American Indian peoples and the nation itself.

Like Zitkala-Ša, Sutton Elbert Griggs actively worked as an advocate for his race even after his literary career ended. He was born in Chatfield, Texas, in 1872. His father, Allen R. Griggs, who had been a slave in Georgia, subsequently became a Baptist clergyman, and in that capacity he was instrumental in establishing churches and schools to serve African Americans in his adopted state of Texas. Sutton E. Griggs was raised in Dallas, where he attended public schools. He then went to Bishop College in Marshall, Texas, graduating in 1890. He studied for the ministry at Richmond Theological Seminary (now Virginia Union University), from which he received a degree in 1893. After graduation he married Emma J. Williams and became pastor of his own congregation, the First Baptist Church in Berkeley, Virginia. During his ministry there, he published his first two novels, *Imperium in Imperio* (1899) and *Overshadowed* (1901). In 1902 Griggs moved to Tennessee to assume the pastorate of the First Baptist Church in East Nashville, where he served for the next eleven years. During this time he wrote his final three novels, *Unfettered* (1902), *The Hindered Hand* (1905), and *Pointing the Way* (1908). He also published the first two of the ten social theory books on race that he would write.

In 1913 Griggs became the pastor of the Tabernacle Baptist Church in Memphis, Tennessee. For next sixteen years he continued to write books on social theory and endeavored to put his ideas into action, with the goal of improving the lives of African Americans in his congregation, the city of Memphis, and the South. He may have hoped that, like the characters in his novels, his actions would eventually influence the nation as well. According to Randolph Meade Walker, from the beginning of his pastorate Griggs was determined to make the Tabernacle Baptist Church an institutional church that would serve its members in many capacities.[30] Under Griggs's guidance, and with the financial aid of black and white patrons and the city government, the congregation constructed an elaborate new church, as well as ancillary facilities that included a swimming pool, a gym, and an employment bureau. Griggs's design was to serve the spiritual, physical, and everyday needs of the people. The facilities gave black citizens a place of recreation in a city where segregation kept them out of most parks and pools. Griggs also founded the Public Welfare League to serve African Americans in Memphis. The goals of this organization were to foster the development of black talent and businesses, to promote cooperation within the community, to cultivate good feelings between black and white citizens, and to aid African Americans, individually and as a group, in any way possible. It was through this agency that Griggs published at least nine books: six on racial and social theory, a religious manual, a biography of John L. Webb, and his autobiography. In 1919 he began publishing a weekly newspaper, *The Neighbor,* that reported on black achievements and issues in Memphis and nationwide and was meant to be distributed in cities with large African American communities throughout the South.

Although Griggs never returned to writing fiction after *Pointing the Way* was published in 1908, some of the themes that he developed in his novels were reflected in his life as a community leader in Memphis. In his narratives he often shows how the work of a unified group of dedicated individuals could change the nation. The core philosophy of his social theory was one of social efficiency, which Walker defines as simply "the ability of people to become socially collected into a whole."[31] Eventually Griggs's political tracts, as well as the achievements of his community in Memphis, began to influence groups and individuals outside of his immediate region. According to Walker, in 1925 "the American Woodman, at the time America's strongest black fraternal organization, voted at a session held in Denver, Colorado, to adopt the philosophy of racial advancement as worked out by Dr. Sutton E. Griggs in his books 'Guide to Racial Greatness' and 'Stepping Stones to Higher Things.'"[32] In the 1920s Griggs frequently traveled as a speaker in various southern cities, which further aided the spread of his social philosophy. Always concerned about the spiritual welfare of his people, he was also instrumental in the founding of the American Baptist Theological Seminary in 1924. He was elected president of the seminary in 1925, and he and his father have a building named after them on its campus.

The triumph of Griggs's ideas and efforts came to a sudden halt with the stock market crash in October 1929. Like many large black congregations at the time, the Tabernacle Baptist Church became insolvent, and it was sold at public auction a year after the crash. Devastated by the collapse of all that he had worked for, Griggs joined his father in Texas, where he became pastor of the Hopewell Baptist Church in Denison. In 1933 he died in Houston, where he had recently moved to start a civic organization run by the Baptist Church. Throughout his life, Griggs worked tirelessly to advance the spiritual and secular lives of members of his church and all African Americans. His novels still stand as compelling works that incorporate a variety of literary styles and depict a wide range of political reactions to the racial problems of his day. Though Griggs has fallen out of favor with critics, he was a pioneering black novelist with a distinctive voice and serves as an important link between nineteenth- and twentieth-century writers in the African American literary tradition.

In contrast, as the first writer of Asian American fiction in English, Sui Sin Far stands at the beginning of a new literary tradition. Although scholars often describe her as a Chinese American writer, her actual national affiliations were much more ambiguous. She was born Edith Maude Eaton in England in 1865 to a British father, Edward Eaton, and a Chinese mother, who was known to her family as Lotus Blossom but who

appears as Grace in government records. The couple had met and married in Shanghai, where Eaton was a silk merchant and Lotus Blossom
was training to be a missionary. The family moved back to Eaton's
hometown of Macclesfield, England, sometime between the birth of
their first child, Charles, and their second, Edith. Over the years the
couple would have twelve more children. During Edith's early childhood in rural England, her mother was the only Chinese resident, and
the biracial children were objects of curiosity, and often cruelty, in the
community.

When Edith was eight, her family moved to North America, finally
settling in Montreal. Edward Eaton eventually gave up the world of
business to return to his first passion, art, and the ever-growing family
seemed always to be in financial straits. After several years of formal
education, Edith was taken from school at the age of eleven to sell her
father's paintings, along with lace that she made herself, door-to-door.
At eighteen she went to work as a typesetter at the *Montreal Daily Star*,
where she taught herself stenography and typing. In the mid 1880s she
had three articles published in small "radical U.S. newspapers," and in
the late 1880s the *Dominion Illustrated* published two of her essays and
six of her short stories, all dealing with white Canadian subjects.[33] The
early 1890s marked a turning point in her life and career: she began to
go with her mother to visit the wives of Chinese merchants who were
beginning to settle in Montreal. In the mid-1890s Edith Eaton started to
publish articles and stories on Chinese subjects under the pen name "Sui
Seen Far" and then "Sui Sin Far," which in translation means "Water Lily."

In 1898 Sui Sin Far moved to San Francisco, where she befriended
Chinese women in the community and published six more stories. In
1900 she relocated to Seattle, where she again worked as a stenographer
and became acquainted with the city's small Chinese community. That
year several more of her tales of immigrant life appeared in newspapers
and magazines. She also spent time in Los Angeles and wrote a series of
articles on Chinatown for the *Los Angeles Express*. Sometime between
her last publication of 1905 and her next, which appeared in 1909, a
significant shift occurred in her writing. Sui Sin Far continued to write
on Chinese American subjects and to address themes of identity and
ethnicity, as she had done in her earlier stories, but there was a new

emotional and aesthetic depth in her writing. This is first evident in "Leaves from the Mental Portfolio of an Eurasian," an engaging and insightful autobiographical essay that appeared in the *Independent* in January 1909. White-Parks describes the appearance of this essay as a type of rebirth, in which Sui Sin Far's "voice came bursting forth—publicly, nationally—signaling unprecedented recognition and a cycle of writing and publishing energy."[34] At about this time Sui Sin Far moved to Boston. In the following three years she would place thirteen stories and essays in major periodicals. The height of her literary career was her collection of short stories, many of them new, in *Mrs. Spring Fragrance,* which was published by McClurg in 1912. Sometime after her last essay appeared in the *Independent* in July 1913, Sui Sin Far moved back to Montreal, probably because of failing health; she died in that city in 1914. Her grave is marked by a striking obelisk that was erected in her memory by the local Chinese Canadian community.

In many ways Sui Sin Far's life was not an easy one. She suffered from persistent ill health, most likely due to an early bout with rheumatism. She was raised in poverty, and during most of her adulthood she had to worry about making ends meet—especially given the fact that when she was doing well, she would send money home to her always-struggling family. Moreover, it was often difficult for her as a biracial individual in a society that held prejudices against her mother's people. Yet Sui Sin Far experienced a type of freedom that was not available to most women in her day. As an intelligent, articulate, and skilled person, she was able to make some sort of living for herself, and, as an unmarried woman, she was free to move from place to place and to associate with whom she pleased. She took advantage of this autonomy to live and work near Chinatowns, where she could both learn about the Chinese and their culture and help them through her writing. The downside to her independence was the necessity of fending for herself, and the business of making a living often took precedence over her true passion of writing. Nevertheless, her literary output stands as an important beginning to what would become the rich tradition of Asian American literature.[35]

Most of Sui Sin Far's stories dealing with North American Chinese subjects are set in the United States, and almost all of them were published in America, as was her one book. Moreover, most of this writing was done during the fifteen years she lived in the United States. There is little doubt, however, that she considered Canada her home. She lived there from the age of eight until she was thirty-two, and even while she resided in America, she would go to Montreal to visit her family whenever she had the time and money. In terms of nationality, she should probably be considered a British citizen, as that was the country of her birth. However, she did not choose to identify herself with any particular country, saying, "I have no nationality and am not anxious to claim any."[36] Despite this reluctance, the United States cannot but claim her, for the literature of the era would be incomplete without her compelling stories of Chinese American life.

The turning of a century brings with it the promise of a new age, a fresh page on which to write an original story. At the turn into the twentieth century, many ethnic American writers raised their voices in print to inform the nation of their existence, their humanity, and their talents. In their works, these artists moved into new, unexplored territory, generating ideas and establishing themes that would be revisited throughout the twentieth century. Homi Bhabha describes the literary areas that nontraditional writers create as "'in-between' spaces" that "provide the terrain for elaborating strategies of selfhood—singular or communal—that initiate new signs of identity, and innovative sites of collaboration, and contestation, in the act of defining the idea of society itself."[37] In their attempts to redefine society, community, and self, ethnic American authors found it necessary to reflect accurately their own new realities. As they situated themselves and their respective groups in relationship to the nation, they also changed the definition of what it meant to be an American. Though these artists were of different ethnicities, were born in different areas of the United States (or even different countries), they were all participants in a wave of writing that sought to redefine American citizenship. Because of their similar concerns, Mary Antin, Zitkala-Ša, Sutton E. Griggs, and Sui Sin Far, along with other writers who focused on issues of cultural identity and nationality, can be considered a unified group within the larger tradition of American realism. For several generations their literary productions were overlooked or forgotten by scholars, but their importance to American letters began to be recognized at the end of the twentieth century, and now many of their works are back in print. With the current renewal of interest in early immigrant, Native American, and African American writers must come new and thoughtful criticism. The inclusion of their narratives in the scholarship about the realist era serves to expand the understanding of the age and of the centrality of themes of ethnicity and citizenship to the national literature.

CHAPTER TWO

Mary Antin and Assimilation

SINCE THE PUBLICATION of her autobiography *The Promised Land* in 1912, Mary Antin has been both commended and disparaged for her adamant belief in Americanization. However, her book contains a much more complex depiction of the process than critics have assumed. While pro-American rhetoric and Antin's joy in regard to her acculturation dominate the book's tone, Antin also carefully delineates her reasons for transforming herself into a U.S. citizen, and she includes some of the pressures and difficulties she experienced in her new country along her path to citizenship. Some contemporary scholars have rejected assimilationist texts because they express currently unpopular ideas such as allegiance to the dominant culture and rejection of one's traditional heritage, but this wholesale dismissal overlooks the very real allure of American citizenship that was experienced by many immigrants. *The Promised Land* is an important work of realism because it reveals the social forces behind the powerful pull of assimilation while focusing on the individual as the locus of cultural transformation. And even though Antin declares herself a completely acculturated citizen, her residual ties to her community and Jewish culture reflect a more accurate account of how integration often works. To decry the subject of assimilation in American literature as objectionable is to misunderstand one of the prevailing realities of immigrant life in America. *The Promised Land* portrays the tension of negotiating a path to citizenship in a society that often gave immigrants conflicting signals, and Antin's positive tone comes from her pride in having come through this process to gain success in her adopted country.

From 1890 to 1915, over 10 million immigrants from southern and eastern Europe came to the United States; about one-third of them were Jewish. Most came because America seemed to offer more opportunity and freedom than was available to them in their native countries. In 1881 Czar Alexander of Russia severely restricted the lives of Jewish citizens by levying discriminatory taxes, limiting their access to education, and restricting where they could live and the types of jobs they could take. The May Laws of 1882 drove Jews from the countryside and, in 1891, from Moscow and other Russian cities. In 1881 government-authorized pogroms began against Jewish settlements throughout the Pale. Jews in Austria-Hungary and Romania were not victims of the same type of organized violence as their Russian counterparts, but they were subjected to deep-rooted anti-Semitism and similar restrictions on their livelihood. These conditions prompted the mass migration of eastern European Jews, who started to come to America in great numbers in the summer of 1881. Most of these immigrants settled in the big cities in the northeastern United States, creating ethnic enclaves and finding work in factories, doing piecework for the garment industries, or selling goods and services in their neighborhoods. In 1905, after the failure of the first Russian Revolution, an increasing number of political activists, professionals, and intellectuals also began to arrive in the States.

Some old-stock Americans were unsettled by this influx of "new immigrants," both because of their great numbers and because they represented cultures unfamiliar to American society. Nativist attitudes began being expressed in the press, and in 1894 Henry Cabot Lodge and other young Boston Brahmins founded the Immigration Restriction League. This small but socially influential group argued that America should retain the white, Anglo-Protestant characteristics of its Revolutionary forebears, that the descendants of "real" Americans were losing their majority in the country due to immigration, and that the new arrivals (Italians, Jews, and Slavs) were mentally, socially, and culturally inferior and would therefore lead to the corruption of the nation.[1]

Though Jewish immigrants were not welcomed by many Americans, some took up their cause and attempted to ease their transition into the new culture. Jewish American descendants of an earlier migration from Germany, who were more established in American society, set up associations to tend to the needs of the wave of Russian Jews. They created organizations that offered free medical care, relief services, and classes to teach English and prepare immigrants for citizenship. These established Jewish Americans were working both to give much-needed aid to the newcomers and also to Americanize them so that others in society would not develop the negative impression that Jewish people were altogether alien and inassimilable. These early efforts were followed by the work of progressive reformers, who sought to improve the lot of inner-city immigrants through a variety of programs. The education of Jewish children became a matter of public policy. As Glenn C. Altschuler notes, "Most Americans insisted that immigrant pupils be taught the English language, Protestant prayers, and the catechism" in order to "ensure the transmission of American values."[2]

Another movement led to the discovery by some white Americans that close association with their international neighbors could be a mutually enriching experience. Starting with Hull House, which was founded by Jane Addams in Chicago in 1889, the settlement house movement spread to big cities with large immigrant populations throughout the eastern United States. These institutions were created not just to give aid to individuals but also to create a sense of community and to offer classes and cultural experiences that would enrich the lives of the people they served. Many settlement houses also became forums for political debate. Most of the staff in settlement houses were young, college-educated, white women. While these workers tended to impose their middle-class American values and expectations on the people they served, some of them—such as Jane Addams, who won the Nobel Peace Prize in 1931—learned to respect the cultures of their new acquaintances. Though anti-Semitism was deeply rooted in America at this time, through the support of their families, communities, teachers, and social workers, many children of inner-city Jewish immigrants eventually found success in business and in the professions. According to Arthur Hertzberg, "By 1910 Jews were already roughly one-quarter of all the students in American medical schools," and a great many young Jewish women were graduating with teaching degrees from college.[3]

Even as those fearful of the new arrivals continued to fight for a national closed-door policy, pro-immigration groups began to form, such as the multiethnic National Immigration League in 1906. One of the most outspoken figures to address these issues was Mary Antin, who captured the nation's attention with her own story of immigration.

The sentiments of patriotism were perhaps stronger in the early twentieth century than in any other non-war era. The catchy showmanship of George M. Cohan, whose Broadway productions included fireworks, American flags, and many popular pro-American songs (such as "Yankee Doodle Dandy") played to sold-out audiences between 1904 and 1918. Antin, too, embodied for many the inclusive ideals of a democratic America. One reason for the overwhelming popularity of *The Promised Land* might have been its theme of national pride, which reflected the patriotism popular at the time. In response to the virulent anti-immigration sentiments that were being expressed in the press, Antin extols the superiority of the American way of life. The activities of the outspoken Boston-based Immigration Restriction League might have been especially motivating to her, since she not only considered Boston her home but also aspired to become the type of educated person of letters that comprised the group's membership.

Antin's autobiography posits assimilation as the best model for ethnic American identity and as the key to entry into full American citizenship. The story of her systematic, rapid Americanization can be clearly traced in the text, and its telling won her much admiration and acclaim. There are other dimensions to Antin's narrative, however, that belie her claims that the process of assimilation is ever easy or complete. These elements connect Antin's autobiography to other texts in the twentieth century, in which the desire for integration is often met with social, economic, and cultural barriers. Antin's exploration of her ethnicity and the history of her people also aligns her book with multiethnic literary themes later in the century. Antin was one of the first writers to portray the division that immigrants experience between the world of their past and their new American lives. She structures her autobiography in two parts. The first eight chapters depict life in the Settlement of the Pale in Russia, where she was born and where she lived until her family's immigration. The following twelve chapters chronicle her arrival in the United States and her life through high school. Despite the fact that nearly half the book portrays her early years in Russia, the text is centered on her account of her Americanization.

The Promised Land tells the familiar and cherished story of becoming an American. This story has been a staple in the American literary tradition at least since Hector St. John de Crèvecoeur published his *Letters of an American Farmer* in 1782.[4] In its basic form, the narrative of the process of assimilation reaffirms the value of democracy and the potential inherent in a free country. Antin's autobiography embodies the unspoken contract that America makes with its newcomers: if they adopt its ways and values, they can enter into full U.S. citizenship with all its rights and privileges. Antin marvels at such an offer: "I was an ignorant child of the ghetto, but I was admitted to the society of the best; I was given the freedom of all America" (92).[5] This sense of limitless possibility permeates the text.

The story of Antin's successful assimilation begins with this promise of freedom, which in her case means access to an education that serves both to satisfy her desire for learning and to acculturate her into the American way of life. Her new country offers liberation from traditional restraints; its public educational system offers the possibility for advancement. She tells her readers that "the public school has done best for us foreigners, and for the country, when it has made us into good Americans. . . . You should be glad to hear of it, you born Americans; for it is the story of the growth of your country; of the flocking of your brothers and sisters from the far ends of the earth to the flag you love; of the recruiting of your armies of workers, thinkers, and leaders" (175). Antin reinforces the progressive movement to foster assimilation through public education by attributing much of her success to the school system that welcomes the immigrant. Perhaps the most important consequence of her American education is a knowledge of English. Antin is unequivocally proud of her English language skills. In her "public declaration of my love for the English language," she exclaims, "I am glad that American history runs, chapter for chapter, the way it does; for thus America came to be the country I love so dearly. I am glad, most of all, that the Americans began by being Englishmen, for thus did I come to inherit this beautiful language in which

I think" (164). English becomes a sign of Antin's assimilation: she not only learns to read, write, and speak the language of the nation, but also adopts it as her primary tongue. Once she has mastered English, she is able to discover, among other things, the history and values of her new country. The young immigrant, hungry for knowledge and a sense of belonging, quickly adopts American ideals as her own. Antin is drawn especially to the quintessential American icon, George Washington. After she learns about him in school, she writes, "I could not pronounce the name of George Washington without pause. Never had I called upon the Most Holy, in such utter reverence and worship as a I repeated the simple sentences of my child's story of the patriot" (175). She embraces Washington as her American cultural forebear, as the father of the country in which she is now a citizen.

In the story of her success, Antin aligns herself not only with George Washington but also with other American icons, such as Ben Franklin (the father of American autobiography), Ralph Waldo Emerson (whose views on self-reliance and transcendentalism echo throughout her text), and Horatio Alger (whose books she read as a girl after coming to America). She describes her growing attachment to the United States and its values, icons, and symbols as inevitable. She had the right qualities to be an American, and her new country offered her all the freedom and opportunity that she desired. She postulates that any immigrant child with similar sensibilities "who was set down in a land of outspoken patriotism . . . was likely to love her new country with a great love, and to embrace its heroes in a great worship. Naturalization, with us Russian Jews, may mean more than the adoption of the immigrant by America. It may mean the adoption of America by the immigrant" (179). This reciprocal relationship stands as the culmination of the melting-pot experience.

Antin often positions herself as representative of other Russian Jews to show how their immigration stories were not so different from those of newcomers of generations past. As with former settlers, according to her model, a time of hardship would be followed by complete acculturation and integration into America. Immigrants' pre-American lives would be important only as signifiers of what had been escaped, adding to the nation's glory by comparison. Antin's own understanding of the relationship between her past and present is emblematic of this

process: "When I passed as an American among Americans, if I was
suddenly made aware of the past that lay forgotten. . . . I thought it
miracle enough that I, Mashke, . . . born to a humble destiny, should
be at home in an American metropolis, be free to fashion my own life,
and should dream my dreams in English phrases" (156). Antin links her
experience and that of her fellow immigrants to the life and history of
America, thereby claiming kinship to all who live within its borders.
Her text is appealing for the passionate way she claims her American
identity: "For the country was for all the citizens, and *I was a Citizen.*
And when we stood up to sing 'America,' I shouted the words with all
my might. I was in very earnest proclaiming to the world my love for
my new-found country" (177). Such affirmative declarations serve as
powerful testimonies to the Americanizing process.

When viewed as a story of unhindered assimilation—in which freedom, education, the English language, and American history and values are successively acquired—Antin's narrative reinforces the type of
Americanization that has long been celebrated in the nation's history.
The popularity of *The Promised Land* attests to the fact that its reaffir-
mation of America's assimilationist ideals was appealing to both native-
born and newer Americans. It was the best- selling nonfiction book of
1912, and it remained a best seller for years.[6] In his introduction to the
book, Werner Sollors writes of its positive reception, particularly in the
libraries that served a variety of readers, including many immigrants.
Ethnic American interest in the book is also revealed by the fact that it
inspired immigrants from many groups to write their own autobiographies. Sollors also points out, as do several other critics and historians,
that parts of the text were included in textbooks for decades.[7] Antin
obviously struck a chord with Americans in the way that she described
her new country and her experiences in it.

Despite the overwhelming and sustained popularity of *The Promised Land,* or perhaps because of it, the book has also been the target of
criticism. At the time of its publication, some Jewish reviewers resented
Antin's self-aggrandizing tone and secular message. Since then, scholars
have taken issue with her choice to write in English, her portrayal of
immigrants, and her failure to disclose fully the patronage she received.
A dislike for Antin's assimilationist message seems to underlie most of

the late twentieth-century criticism about the book. Antin is faulted for her unquestioning acceptance of all things American, as well as her lack of loyalty to her Jewish heritage. Some critics' antagonism toward the text reflects their resentment that any aspect of ethnic culture should be sacrificed to claim an American nationality that one rightfully holds as a native-born or naturalized citizen.[8]

While the concept of assimilation is now slighted in favor of diversity and the preservation of cultural heritage, it is important to read Antin in a pre-modernist context. In her day, Antin was influenced by two schools of thought. One, coming from liberal social reformers, was that assimilation was the key to American citizenship; the other, coming from nativists, was that newcomers from eastern Europe had no rights to American citizenship and were, in fact, inassimilable. Pressure to limit foreigners' entry into the United States came from such outspoken groups as the Immigration Restriction League, which was formed the very year Antin came from Russia to Massachusetts. In their efforts to convince the public that the new wave of arrivals was detrimental to the American national character, this group and other nativists set out to "prove" and publicize the inferiority of peoples from southern and eastern Europe. In an 1896 essay in the *Atlantic Monthly,* Francis Amasa Walker twice refers to the new immigrants as an "ignorant and brutalized peasantry."[9] In a similar vein, the forty-two volume Dillingham Report, submitted to the Senate in 1911, described their biological inferiority. This document, which is a compilation of studies conducted throughout the United States, contains useful statistical information. Unfortunately, its overall bias is obvious. For example, it includes a 1909 study of newly arrived schoolchildren that was conducted "as an effort to ascertain some of the causes of retardation or backwardness and the relation to the races."[10] Between 1897 and 1917 the Immigration Restriction League was able to push four bills through Congress that would have established an English literacy test for foreigners wishing to move to the United States.[11] It is thus little wonder that Antin chose not to emphasize difference in her text. Considering the discourse of the day, the most persuasive response to the claim that immigrants like her were inferior and inassimilable would be the evidence of her own successful acculturation and first-generation integration into American society.

Antin also tries to disprove inherent difference between the new immigrants and their native-born critics by linking the journey and progress of her people with the history of the United States. She places her story in the context of a nation that was founded by immigrants, making her heir to a tradition that goes back to the Pilgrims and that encompasses the ancestors of all Americans of European descent.[12] Antin's transformation into an American is rapid, the text implies, because she had a head start. She was in the process of becoming a U.S. citizen even before she came to America's shores. Her narrative advances the idea that certain types of people are drawn to America: freethinkers, hard workers, tough individuals who love the nation and its values. These "true" Americans are willing to sacrifice anything, including their native language and culture, to become a part of the national way of life. Either consciously or intuitively, Antin answers the perennial complaint of nativists who fear that the newcomers are going to change, in some profound way, the essence of American society. She assures her readership that the recent arrivals from eastern Europe are not so different from their American-born neighbors or from immigrants of generations past. She insists that they share the same values and are willing to make the same sacrifices for the nation. In short, they are both willing and able to discard "old world" ways in order to assimilate into mainstream American society.

Antin's autobiography stands as a counter-narrative to claims that Russian Jews were inassimilable. It is also a model of the type of wholesale assimilation that was being advocated by teachers, social workers, and politicians at the time. Theodore Roosevelt rejected the nativist agenda, but he was also against the idea of immigrants maintaining allegiance to their former lands and cultures.[13] In *Jews in America*, Arthur Hertzberg notes that "Roosevelt thundered, again and again, against 'hyphenated Americans,' by which he meant anyone who did not sever ties with his past and assimilate into American society."[14] For many American citizens, there was something suspect in newcomers who sought cultural syncretism in their new land. The then-dominant metaphor for ethnic American identity was the melting pot. In this conceit, immigrants' old world characteristics gradually melt away as they take on the flavor of their new surroundings, emerging as new Americans.

In the early twentieth century this paradigm was advocated by Antin's teachers and mentors, social reformers, and politicians like Theodore Roosevelt. It was the theme of the popular 1908 play *The Melting Pot* by Anglo-Jewish playwright Israel Zangwill, who had been a friend and literary mentor to Antin since 1898. In fact, many of Antin's well-established patrons were American Jews whose ancestors had come from Germany half a century earlier. They were ready examples of the social and economic benefits that came with cultural assimilation.[15]

Though some writers at the time, including Sui Sin Far, were envisioning a multicultural society, the fact remains that the ideology of cultural pluralism would not become a staple of the American vocabulary until at least 1915, when Horace Kallen, another Jewish American, would publish his insightful and controversial "Democracy versus the Melting Pot" in *The Nation*.[16] This essay, written three years after Antin's autobiography, marks a shift in the assimilation debate to, as Glenn Altschuler puts it, "whether immigrants *should* Americanize, rather than whether they *could*."[17] In *The Promised Land,* Antin makes it clear that she can assimilate, and that she should goes without question. Michael P. Kramer is correct in his assessment that "*The Promised Land* does not offer hybridity as an answer," but the truth is that hybridity was not an option for Antin.[18] Her American identity had been shaped by the public school system and the patriotic traditions it espoused, by the Progressivist ideology of Theodore Roosevelt, and by the assimilated Jewish Americans who supported and encouraged her as a young woman. She had also been influenced by nativist rhetoric that disparaged immigrants and held that they could never be truly American.

In Antin's narrative of the evolution of her American self, she first recreates the world from which she came and then depicts what elements of the past she chose to shed in order to conform to her conception of an ideal American citizen. She easily rejects some facets of her culture and religion, and more often than not she is glad to do so. Superficial trappings of her newly "old country," such as her clothing and her Russian name, are changed so that she can begin her new life. The social pressure on Antin and her siblings to acculturate, and the potential rewards to be gained by doing so, become apparent with their first transformation. As she remembers: "We exchanged our hateful home-made European costumes, which pointed us out as 'greenhorns' to the children on the street, for real American machine-made garments, and issued forth glorified in each other's eyes" (149). The shame of being a "greenhorn" and the excitement of encountering a new culture were strong incentives, especially for younger immigrants, to fashion new American selves.

In another rite of passage, each member of the Antin family receives an "American" name. As Antin writes: "With our despised immigrant clothing we shed also our impossible Hebrew names. . . . As for me, I was simply cheated. The name they gave me was hardly new. . . . My friends said that it would hold in English as *Mary;* which was very disappointing, as I longed to possess a strange-sounding American name like the others" (149–50). The pleasure she gains from abandoning her Russian name, "Mashke," is instantly replaced by disappointment that "Mary" is so similar to the name she has just discarded. To throw off an identity marker that signifies association with one's origins indicates a rejection of the past. However, the eagerness with which Antin takes on a new American name, and her regret that it is not more different from her former one, is also indicative of many common traditions with which she can be associated. In many cultures (then as now), a woman is expected to adopt her husband's name after marriage to indicate her new position in society and her new association with her husband's family. The passage to America is, according to Antin, the most important transition in her life. This crossing, which divides her narrative, separates her former subjugated self as a woman and a Jew in Russia from her new "free" American self. To mark the beginning of a new identity with an adopted signifier is a part of the rite of passage common to many immigrants to America.

Another important name-changing convention is the *nom de plume.* In the American literary tradition, some writers, such as Mark Twain, have taken on pen names that reflect the culture and region from which they came and about which they wrote. This pattern of adopting a new name to reflect one's cultural allegiance is even more important in the history of ethnic American women's writing. Both Zitkala-Ša and Sui Sin Far opted to write under names they invented for themselves, rejecting their Western birth-names and choosing new names that reflect their respective ethnic heritage. Antin, in contrast, identifies herself throughout her life by her American name and uses it even after her marriage to German American Amadeus Grabau. Perhaps the American name that was bestowed on her during her first days in the United States became symbolic of the new life she was determined to lead.

The taking of new clothes and names is common for immigrants, particularly for those who do not intend to return to their homeland. Other immigrants, such as many Chinese or Italians, saw themselves mainly as sojourners. Both these groups came to the United States primarily for economic reasons. The Chinese, who were barred from seeking U.S. citizenship, had a high rate of return home, and even many Italians, who were eligible to become U.S. citizens, chose to return to Italy after a period of labor in America.[19] Russian Jews, persecuted for their ethnicity, were both economic and political refugees. Though the first half of *The Promised Land* contains some engaging memories of her homeland, Antin is not at all reluctant to abandon her allegiance to Russia because, as she explains, it is a country that never claimed her. Its Jewish residents (never really citizens) were disenfranchised both socially and economically. Antin explains how this rejection enables her to embrace her new country so quickly and so fully: "Where had been my country until now? What flag had I loved? What heroes had I worshipped? . . . Well I knew that Polotzk was not my country. It was *goluth*—exile" (178).

Antin's relationship to her traditional religion is not as clear-cut as her attitude toward Russia, however. Her apparent dismissal of Judaism— the faith that infused her childhood and sustained her people for thousands of years—is not as easy or complete as some critics make it out to be. What complicates the exploration of this theme is the nature of Judaism itself, which is at once a religion, an ethnicity, and a culture. Jewish American writers, including Antin's contemporary Abraham Cahan, have described the loss of religious devotion and attachment to Jewish culture that results from Americanization and the void this loss leaves in the individual psyche; yet the rejection of elements of Jewish beliefs and culture does not necessarily mean that the immigrant becomes any less Jewish. Many different types of Jewish communities and ways of being Jewish exist in America. Orthodox Judaism exists alongside Reform and Conservative Judaism (which developed in the United States to fit the needs of American-born Jews), which in turn exist alongside a great number of people who consider themselves Jewish but who only practice their faith sporadically, if at all. The truth is that in America, freed from adherence to the rigid Orthodoxy that existed in eastern Europe—where opportunities in education and business were closed to most Jews—many Jewish immigrants and their children gravitated to more secular ways of life.

Antin's description of the shift in her religious beliefs begins in the first section of the book, so it is not accurate to attribute the evolution of her cultural and spiritual consciousness exclusively to the process of or desire for Americanization. Despite the teachings of her family and community, Antin as a child begins formulating her own personal belief system. She recalls that "in those days my religion depended on my mood. I could believe anything I wanted to believe. I did believe, in all my moods, that there was a God who had made the world, in some fashion unexplained" (101). Antin's young musings stand in contrast to the strict Orthodoxy of her community. As Antin begins challenging the tenets of her religion, she sees her father doing the same. Her father, "never heartily devoted to the religious ideals of the Hebrew scholar," is attracted to the more lax religious attitudes he has observed in "the large cities" he visits on his business travels (62). The young Antin is influenced by her father's attitudes and actions, finding in them a validation for her own rejection of some of the more Orthodox beliefs and practices.

One element of the Judaic system under which she had bridled in Polotzk, and which she was more than happy to do without in America, was the patriarchal culture that considered girls inferior to boys and that circumscribed the lives of women. She explains that "in the mediaeval position of the women of Polotzk education really had no place. A girl was 'finished' when she could read her prayers in Hebrew, following the meaning by the aid of the Yiddish translation especially prepared for women. If she could sign her name in Russian, do a little figuring, and write in Yiddish to the parents of her betrothed, she was called *wohl gelehrent*—well educated" (90). Throughout the text, Antin describes her development as an American New Woman, which is clearly at odds with the Polotzk community's expectation that she become a traditional Jewish wife and mother. Antin emphasizes her intelligence and portrays herself as hopelessly undomestic, with a personality un-suited for a society in which "woman's only work was motherhood" (30). Most restricting of all for the bright and curious child in Russia is the limited education afforded to girls. This, perhaps above all else, con-tributed to her perception of "the narrowness, the stifling narrowness, of life in Polotzk" (128). Antin's retreat from the Orthodox Judaism of her ancestors has much to do with the position of women within the religion.[20]

In *The Promised Land,* Antin's father embodies both the patriarchy of their native culture and the apostasy that gives her license to move away from their traditional religion. In America she sheds the trappings of her creed more easily, perhaps, than other immigrants because her father has done the same thing. He uses his conventional role of head of the family to encourage his children to cast off the conventions they had learned in Polotzk: "He could do all the thinking for the family, he believed; and being convinced that to hold to the outward forms of orthodox Judaism was to be hampered in the race for Americanization, he did not hesitate to order our family life on unorthodox lines" (194). Her father's attitude, which affords Antin a great deal of freedom in her new country, was difficult for her mother, who found structure and comfort in the traditional Jewish faith and customs. As Antin explains, "Individual freedom, to him, was the only tolerable condition of life; to her it was confusion" (194). Though Antin recognizes that her father's position on Judaism has contributed to her own accelerated assimila-tion, she also admits that the process of becoming an American, which she values, is not viewed the same way by all who immigrate.

As the confusion of Antin's mother demonstrates, the loss of reli-gion and culture can pose a threat to a Jewish immigrant moving into a predominantly Christian culture, but Antin seems comfortable and not overconcerned with the decisions she makes in regard to her personal belief system. As she distances herself from the Orthodox religion of Polotzk, she does not gravitate toward American incarnations of orga-nized religion, like Reform Judaism, that would be more in line with her secular tendencies. According to Norma Fain Pratt, few religious options existed for an immigrant Jewish woman of Antin's generation if she chose not to practice Orthodox Judaism. Fain Pratt states that "very few Eastern European women joined the Reform Temples" that had been established by descendants of German Jews who had arrived in America in the middle of the nineteenth century. Fain Pratt continues, "For nearly forty years, after 1880, Jews who were no longer orthodox and yet could not accept Reform Judaism had no form of Judaism through which to express their changing mode of behavior."[21] Antin was thus not dissimilar from many other Russian Jewish women in America. In some ways, her description of her move away from Jewish Orthodoxy represents a part of a larger social reality.

With the freedom to disassociate herself from the religious traditions of her ancestors, Antin at times seems to abandon Judaism as an identity marker altogether. However, though the narrative chronicles her rejection of the religion of her early youth, it also reveals how formative its teachings were to her development. The ways in which Judaism inform her text suggest how central it is to her worldview. In fact, her American self is firmly rooted in her traditional Jewish upbringing:

> I was fed on dreams, instructed by means of prophecies, trained to hear and see mystical things that callous senses could not perceive. I was taught to call myself a princess, in memory of my forefathers who had ruled a nation. Though I went in the disguise of an outcast, I felt a halo resting on my brow. Sat upon by brutal enemies, unjustly hated, annihilated a hundred times, I yet arose and held my head high, sure that I should find my kingdom in the end, although I had lost my way in exile; for He who had brought my ancestors safe through a thousand perils was guiding my feet as well. God needed me and I needed him, for we two together had work to do, according to an ancient covenant between Him and my forefathers. (35)

Antin's confidence, her sense of destiny, and her construction of herself as a new kind of prophet in the New World all have their origin in the stories of her childhood. Michael Kramer also sees Antin's American identity as growing out of the Judaism of her youth. He explains, "In evolutionary terms, to move from 'the heritage of the children of Jacob' to 'the full inheritance of American freedom and opportunity' is both abandonment and fulfillment. Fulfillment *through* abandonment."[22] In the course of her narrative, Antin's new kingdom becomes America; in the course of her life, the work she does for her people is writing and public speaking in order to defend their right to be there.

Antin's history and heritage infuse her book with an ethnic particularity that is not completely replaced by the dominant American identity. At the beginning of *The Promised Land,* she hopes that she can abandon her old memories and find "release from the folds of [her] clinging past," but it is clear from the depth of emotion with which she writes about her early life that the old country has stayed with her (3). Though she repeatedly defends her choice to dispense with what she views as the restricting dogma of Judaism, she also remembers rituals and celebrations that brought her family together in enriching ways. She recalls how "the year, in our pious house, was an endless song in many cantos of joy, lamentation, aspiration, and rhapsody" (61). One component that Antin portrays as being central to the Jewish community in Polotzk is reverence for education. Yet the scholarship that was valued was religious in nature, and girls were not welcome in the Talmudic schools. As a bright and dedicated student in America, she broadens the traditional Jewish love of learning to encompass her secular education.

Antin claims that she remains faithful to the core beliefs of her religion, but the lack of religious alternatives for women who did not want to practice Orthodox Judaism drives her search for her own spiritual system. The spirituality expressed in *The Promised Land* is a personal form of American transcendentalism, in the mode of Emerson, Thoreau, and Whitman, which is connected to the "golden truth of Judaism" (190). Transcendentalism may have been a way for Antin to enter into an American spiritual and philosophical system without converting to Christianity. She was friends with and dedicated her book to the well-known transcendentalist Josephine Lazarus, who may have served as a religious guide.[23] Antin's transcendentalist leanings, however, seem to come from an innate belief system that can be glimpsed in her first book, *From Plotzk to Boston,* which is a translation of a letter written soon after she came to America at the age of thirteen.[24] Antin's quest for new spiritual vistas would be her most prolonged journey; after retiring from public life, she explored forms of religion and mysticism for several decades.

Another major cultural shift that Antin describes, and what might really lay at the heart of *The Promised Land,* is her adoption of the English language. To comprehend her relationship to her new language, it is important to understand that all of her success in America, and much of the approval and recognition she received, came from her language skills. Antin remembers with pride how she was praised while a child in Polotzk for demonstrating a remarkable aptitude in Hebrew, though working with inferior teachers, and for teaching herself Russian at a very young age. These early rewards for her language skills, however, are nothing compared to the benefits and acclaim she receives after coming to America. Antin distinguishes herself in her family, school, and even her community by learning to read and write English very quickly, and her writing arouses the interest of others. Her first publication was a short essay titled "Snow," which one of her teachers sent to an education journal to demonstrate the remarkable progress that was possible with immigrant students. For a girl who had been studying English for only four months, the essay is striking, and its sentiments are indicative of an active young mind. It is no wonder that Antin captured the interest of those around her and continued to captivate a wide audience for many years. This first publication was followed by two other literary successes. A poem on George Washington appeared in the *Boston Herald,* and *From Plotzk to Boston,* with a preface by playwright Israel Zangwill, was published when Antin was only seventeen years old.[25] The English language became Antin's ticket to legitimacy and success in America.

Antin admits to abandoning her native tongue gladly; when her success is assured and her assimilation complete, she says she has learned to "think without an accent" (282). Because her language skills earn her praise, she apparently never considered the possibility of making her way in the world of American Yiddish literature.[26] When evaluating Antin's relationship to her two languages, however, it is important to consider her circumstances. She came to America as a child and was soon enrolled in English-only schools, which accelerated her English-language acquisition. Because of her young age, her attachment to Yiddish may not have been as strong as it was for adult immigrants. In *The Promised Land,* Antin reveals two aspirations—one personal and one social—that were to influence her writing and guide her life. The personal goal was to find acceptance in the established American literary community. As Susanne Shavelson recognizes, Antin's aspiration was entrance into the Boston literary elite, and it is testimony to her drive and determination that, as a young immigrant girl, she was able to find friends among the class that she admired. She begins by befriending her teachers and branches out to include businessmen, philanthropists, and writers in her circle of friends. Her social aim, inextricable from her personal ambition, was to act as mediator between native-born Americans and immigrants. From the publication of *The Promised Land* in 1912 to the eve of World War I, Antin lectured tirelessly against anti-immigration laws and nativist attitudes. Her final book, *They Who Knock at Our Gates* (1914), is both an emotional and a rational plea for American citizens to look at immigrants both as part of the nation's heritage and as a valuable resource. If Antin wrote her most important work in her adopted language, it was because the audience she sought was not the immigrant but established, English-speaking Americans. It is clear that through her books and lectures she succeeded in finding a wide audience: her autobiography became a best seller, and for several years she was one of the most famous lecturers in the country.[27]

Though *The Promised Land* is overwhelmingly positive in its tone and optimistic in its message, a close look at Antin's narrative reveals that the process of assimilation is a much more individual and complicated process than she allows. While she delineates the context of and reasons for the myriad changes and substitutions she makes in order to become an American, one particular scene is fraught with complications. In it, Antin goes to luncheon at the house of her favorite teacher, Mrs. Dillingham. Because of her language skills and her sheer will, she has entered the society of which she longed to be a part. She is finally a guest in the home of a friend and educator, and she is determined to fit into this society of elite, educated, Anglo-Protestant company. Antin's presence at this table can be read metaphorically in terms of her assimilation into American society. She has been invited to the table, and it is her desire to be there. However, she is clearly uncomfortable and unsure of herself among this crowd. She is careful to follow others in the use of utensils and manners, just as she has been able, since coming to America, to imitate the language, values, and behavior of those around her. Things are going well until the culture of the native-born Americans comes into direct conflict with her own traditional culture. In this instance, Mrs. Dillingham serves pork.[28] Antin, both shockingly and predictably, makes the decision to eat the forbidden food: "I ate, but only a newly abnegated Jew can understand with what squirming, what protesting of the inner man, what exquisite abhorrence of myself" (196). Not only does she eat the ham, but she also makes a point of devouring as much of it as she can. Her act is shocking because it is a direct rejection of one of the most clear and basic rules of the Jewish religion, to not partake of *Trefah,* that which is unclean. It is predicable because Antin's narrative journey has been leading toward a rejection of the rigid elements of Judaism. That the two paths of her life, the inherited and the self-determined, should converge in this one symbolic gesture is fitting, and it becomes the climax of the book. The ham obviously represents the point at which the demands of assimilation become invasive on personal, inherited, and private levels. Antin has a few options: she could decline the meat without explaining or drawing attention to herself; she could decline with a polite explanation; or she could eat. That Antin consumes a great deal of the meat shows the extent to which she is willing to go to prove her "Americaness." This act most clearly marks *The Promised Land* as an assimilationist text.[29]

Yet Antin's patriotic rhetoric often obscures the reality of a less than perfect America and a less than satisfying acculturation experience. It is not accurate to say that things are repressed in the text—in fact, Antin includes some distressing experiences in her narrative—but it is fair to say that she diminishes the effects of those experiences and in some ways protects her audience from their negative implications. *The Promised Land* contains many moments of slippage in the façade of a fluid and benevolent transition to American life, but Antin is careful to describe these episodes in ways that both explain and minimize the impact that these experiences had on her. Despite the fact that she downplays the more painful elements of her life, their inclusion in her narrative gives it depth, as they connect her to the difficulties with which most other immigrants were confronted.

One facet of American society that seems glaringly absent in Antin's text is anti-Semitism. The years depicted in her narrative, 1894 to

1899, were marked by increasing nativism, and many Americans were committed to protecting "their country" from what they perceived as growing Jewish influences. However, only a very few instances in the American section of *The Promised Land* can be interpreted as revealing the prejudice of other Americans against Jewish immigrants. It may be that Antin, because of her intellectual gifts, gender, age, language skills, or circumstances, was actually not a direct target of resentment. Her father, who never seemed to find success in his new country, or her sister, who did not have the opportunity to go to school but who began working in factories as a teenager, may have had a different perspective on prejudice in America.

Though anti-Semitism is all but absent in the American section of *The Promised Land,* the first half of Antin's narrative describes the psychological effects of Russian anti-Semitism on the Jews in Polotzk. These chapters include depictions of injustice and the damage it does to both the individual and the community. The Polotzk chapters give Antin a chance to speak to her American readers on an important subject that they might be resistant to if the same topic were discussed in an American setting. Reading about prejudice that occurs at a remove, in Russia, allows Antin's audience to contemplate its implications without feeling that America is being criticized. When considering anti-Semitism from this distance, Antin can be direct and forceful in her criticism: "Perhaps it was wrong of us to think of our Gentile neighbors as a different species of beings from ourselves, but . . . it was easier to be friends with the beasts in the barn than with some of the Gentiles. The cow and the goat and the cat responded to kindness, and remembered which of the housemaids was generous and which was cross. The Gentiles made no distinctions. A Jew was a Jew, to be hated and spat upon and used spitefully" (21). Antin demonstrates how prejudice does not allow much room for communication. She does not, however, depict all Christians as antagonistic towards their Jewish neighbors, for to do so would allow little hope for cross-cultural understanding in the latter part of her text. She remembers that "there were wise Gentiles who understood. Those were educated people"; but "most of the Gentiles were ignorant and distrustful and spiteful" (15–16). Anti-Semitism, the narrative conveys, is the response of the stupid, the insecure, and the mean, not the enlightened individual, the American. Antin implies that race hatred would be harmful in America because it impedes the goal of the nation to assimilate successfully all who come to her shores.

Another reality of American immigrant life that Antin glosses over in *The Promised Land* is the debilitating poverty of the slums. Despite her own shining success, Antin's household is not spared from the economic struggles faced by thousands of other immigrant families. She bluntly states that her father cannot sustain employment, that her sister is obligated to go to work in a factory shortly after their arrival in the States, and that her mother continues to have children despite the family's poverty and cramped apartments. She depicts her younger self, during her first few years in America, as unaffected by economic concerns, but by the time she enters high school they weigh heavily on her mind. The chapters that most vividly describe the family's condition—such as "Manna" and "Dover Street"[30]—reveal an adolescent consciousness repulsed by the poverty surrounding her and embarrassed by the inhabitants of her neighborhood who are unable to rise out of it. Antin also remembers her longing to be removed from such misery. Buried in these chapters are troublesome episodes that counterbalance the rosy assimilationist vision of much of her book.

However, Antin isolates and to a great extent neutralizes her descriptions of poverty in *The Promised Land*. She masks the more painful realities revealed in these chapters by concluding them with an optimistic transcendentalism that assures her audience that, in the process of assimilation, poverty and anxiety are merely transitory. In "Manna," Antin describes the crowded and dirty life of Wheeler Street, the breakdown of her family (which she sees as "part of the process of Americanization"), and her own sense of her "shabbiness and lowliness" (213, 215). Yet in the last paragraph of the chapter she attributes her perception of the sordid conditions of her life to common adolescent angst. She explains that, as a teenager, "for some years . . . I must weep and laugh out of season, stand on tiptoe to pluck the stars from heaven, love and hate immoderately, propound theories of the destiny of man, and not know what is going on in my heart" (216). The chapter thus ends with the image of the young Antin reaching up in her dreams and out with her intellect, while the negative feelings she revealed earlier are attributed to the normal mood swings of puberty. Still, the fact that she does not know what is going on in her own heart speaks to the confusion of a young woman who is growing away from her family and her culture in the process of assimilation.

The chapter "Dover Street" contrasts Antin's home in a tenement house with her schooling in the prestigious Latin School for Girls in Boston. Antin describes filth, hunger, the inability of her father to find and hold jobs (sometimes because of his poor English skills or "Jewish appearance"), and "the familiarity of her vulgar neighbors" (229, 233). She reveals how the conditions of life in the tenement touch the psyche when she says that "I felt myself defiled by the indecencies I was compelled to witness" (233). Yet she immediately backs away from this statement, isolates it. A walk outside the neighborhood, or a look at the sunset or the stars, lifts her out of the grim poverty of her surroundings. The chapter ends with another transcendent vision. This time Antin watches the sunrise from the tenement rooftop and sees the "distant buildings . . . massed like palace walls with turrets and spires lost in a rosy cloud." She thinks, "I love my beautiful city spreading all about me. I love the world. I love my place in the world" (236). Once more the confined conditions in which she and her family must live are diminished as she reaches out and beyond them; once more the painful realities and emotions revealed in the chapter fade as it closes.

The harsher realities of the chapters describing the Antin family's poverty are further buried by their position in the structure of the book. The chapter immediately preceding this group is entitled "A Child's Paradise" and lightly tells of Antin's access to the Boston Public Library, her love of reading of all sorts—including American literature and Yiddish newspapers—and the sense of connection to her community that she felt as a child. The chapter after the exploration of her poverty is entitled "The Burning Bush" and discusses the Hale House, where she made influential friends, attended lectures, and developed a love for the natural sciences. The revelation of her poverty is framed by accounts of public institutions that provide opportunities for learning, growth, and escape, effectively limiting the suffering that Antin expresses. The public library in "A Child's Paradise" and the settlement house in "The Burning Bush" provide her with an alternative to the slums and tenement houses and in a sense contain them in the narrative.

The uncompromising optimism of *The Promised Land* also masks an undercurrent of solitude and alienation. In America, the newcomer, the pioneer, has the opportunity to reinvent an identity with every relocation. The peril inherent in establishing a new self is that its creator must be vigilant not to let any inconsistencies appear in the façade. In Antin's case, the outwardly simple progression of her American success is occasionally interrupted by cracks that appear in her ostensibly smooth story of assimilation. These cracks offer glimpses of the disconnection she experiences in her quest for acceptance. Depictions of breaks with family, culture, and religion are familiar in immigrant narratives, but in *The Promised Land* the most profound disassociation arises from things that Antin must deny about herself—including her isolation. While she hints at the friendships she cultivates with older, influential people, there is little mention of close relationships with boys or girls her own age. The only young person for whom Antin expresses any affection is her sister, Frieda. However, circumstances, and a very important decision their father makes, ultimately divide the lives of the two girls. Frieda, who is fifteen when they arrive in America, goes off to work in the factories and is soon married. Mary, always adept at her studies, goes to school. Moreover, when her father fills out her school forms, he lies about her age in order to gain for her a few more years in the American educational system. Antin is thirteen when she enters public school; her father tells the authorities that she is eleven. This lie, told for the best of reasons, is not mentioned in the text.[31]

In light of her letters, Antin's reasons for this omission become clear. From the very beginning of her schooling in America, her teachers had taken her to be a girl who was wise and talented beyond her young years. In 1899 her first autobiography, *From Plotzk to Boston,* was published with a preface written by the internationally famous playwright Israel Zangwill, who gives her false age in his introduction. From that point on, Antin must have sensed that to reveal her real age would be tantamount to exposing herself as a fraud. It would also embarrass all the people who had been kind enough to support, mentor, and promote her. In effect, she was forced into playing the role of adolescent as she entered womanhood. The conflict of her situation is revealed not in so many words but in the loneliness that permeates *The Promised Land.*

Antin's one real confidant, the one girl who knows everything about her—her sister—is living in a completely different world. Antin's Latin School classmates, younger and more privileged than she, could not know her secret and did not share her history. Assimilation with her peers was all but impossible in Antin's high school years.

The picture that finally emerges is of a character who embodies all the promise of the new world but who experiences all the loneliness of the pioneer and the exile. In the chapter "Dover Street," Antin most clearly reveals the fissure between her academic and social life and the condition of living in the tenements among other immigrants. She explains that when "the confusion of the house" became too much for her, she would go at night to the South Boston Bridge, which overlooked a massive tangle of railroad tracks. Returning home, she would sit up late into the night listening to the sounds of Dover Street. This moment of stillness reveals a glimpse of the troubled girl, alone with her thoughts, trying to decipher meaning in the world. The chapter ends with the coming of dawn, with new platitudes, reaffirmations, and optimism; but the shadows of the previous evening reveal that even the most gifted, enthusiastic, and hopeful "new American" has doubts and worries about how to make her way. These dark moments enrich the unabashed assimilationist message of Antin's book.

Antin's narrative is a testimonial to Americanization, but it also a testament to the true complexity of assimilation. It is possible to go through the text and excerpt a narrative of her seamless progression from "greenhorn" to American, but there are moments of trial and doubt in her story that give a more complex model of citizenship than the one she explicitly advances. She believes wholeheartedly in the melting pot, and yet the end result of her own journey through the process of Americanization does not yield an uninflected American type, even though she claims to have learned "to think without an accent." She tries to depict her traditional culture as fully falling away as she steps into her new American identity, but she cannot fully do so. Her history, her past, and her religion still stay with her; her Jewish heritage and her childhood in the Russian Pale are indelibly imprinted upon her work and her life. In *The Promised Land*, these things inform her new life, whether she overtly acknowledges it or not. She emerges from her journey through the melting pot as a Jew and an American, as well as a writer of realism who represents her people's struggles both in the Russian Pale and in the promised land of America.

The compromises and negotiations that Antin makes in *The Promised Land* show how precarious a proposition assimilation can be, even for one who is able to take advantage of free public education, who attains English proficiency early and easily, and who accepts wholeheartedly America's history and ideals. This complexity, finally, may be the most valuable thing about Antin's work. It may be the element that keeps the text alive. Her book represents the broader reality of assimilation and citizenship, not as she preaches it but as she depicts it, and as it was and would be practiced by millions of immigrants before and after her. Her story reveals that a transformation occurs in becoming an American, but that it is not as complete as she proclaims it to be. Antin represents herself as the unhyphenated American—the ideal of teachers, social reformers, and politicians—but in fact the model of the assimilated ethnic American that emerges in her text is more useful. *The Promised Land* represents how the desire to shed cultural particularism and to become a mainstream American is often countered by a lingering connection to tradition and by an indifferent new society. Although Antin hints at what was lost on her path to Americanization and alludes to some difficult passages in her life, her text is ultimately a celebration of what she gained by becoming a citizen of the United States. The concept of assimilation as the ideal model for ethnic American identity found its highest expression in *The Promised Land*. In academic discourse this concept would fall out of favor as the twentieth century advanced, to be replaced with models that stressed the value of traditional inheritance. Though later writers would focus more on the psychological difficulties inherent in acculturation, the assimilationist drive that Antin depicts in *The Promised Land* would become a recurring theme in twentieth-century American literature.

CHAPTER THREE

Ambiguity and Affiliation:
The Stories and Essays of Zitkala-Ša

I N THE WRITINGS OF Zitkala-Ša, a rejection of American identity coexists with a sense that a traditional tribal identity is no longer viable once the process of assimilation begins. What emerges is a profound ambivalence: the record of an individual who does not want to become an American but feels that she can no longer claim her ethnic identity once she is separated from her tribe. This is different from the modern concept of a hybrid individual, described by Gloria Anzaldúa as "la consciencia de la mestiza," which signifies a conscious acceptance and integration of all one's cultures.[1] The protagonists of Zitkala-Ša's narratives do not embrace the borders; instead, they are portrayed as alienated from both their native communities and the nation in which they live. The stories and essays of Zitkala-Ša suggest that the quality of life is diminished for American Indians who enter into the Americanizing system, both in terms of their spiritual lives and their sense of themselves. Most of her texts employ a sharp realism in order to cut through mainstream romantic notions of American Indian life and to reveal the real toll of government policies and public attitudes. Overall, her works stand as a critique not only of the failures of the assimilating process, but also of the long history of tension between Native Americans and the imperial culture that surrounds them.

Zitkala-Ša was born on the Yankton reservation in South Dakota. Though her band never directly engaged in warfare against the U.S.

government, other Sioux were participants in the last, and one of the bitterest, Indian wars in American history.[2] The Great Plains was one of the final areas in the continental United States to be settled by white Americans, and for this reason the conflict that began in 1862 and continued for nearly thirty years is still deeply rooted in American cultural memory. The attacks and counterattacks between American Indians and whites on the Plains came to a head with the battle of the Little Bighorn in 1876, the year that Zitkala-Ša was born. In this encounter a force of Sioux and Cheyenne warriors, led by Crazy Horse and Sitting Bull, killed General George Armstrong Custer and over two hundred of his men. The end of open warfare between the United States and Native Americans was the massacre at Wounded Knee on the Pine Ridge reservation in 1890. On that day, government troops, sent out to stifle the religious practice of the Ghost Dance among Plains Indians, murdered about three hundred unarmed men, women, and children.[3]

Perhaps even more demoralizing in the long run than the bloody conflicts on the Plains were the social and psychological changes that were affecting American Indians all over the country. By the late nineteenth century, the American public had certain ideas about what Native Americans were and what their fate should be. The U.S. government, ethnologists, and writers of popular literature all vigorously propagated the idea that American Indians were an anachronistic and dying race, and a majority of Americans embraced this conceit. It was increasingly obvious to many—in particular to Native Americans themselves—that predictions of their ultimate doom were premature at best; nonetheless, it was true that a long history of battling Europeans and the diseases they brought, the loss of traditional means of sustenance due to diminishing resources, and forced removals to inhospitable lands had devastated the American Indian population in the United States. The same events and policies had also served to weaken tribal cultures. By the second half of the nineteenth century, most Native Americans lived on reservations far from the centers of mainstream America.

In the early 1880s social reformers and government officials began to construct a policy that would profoundly shape the future of Native American peoples. Claiming that reservations and tribal systems led to savagery and dependence, self-proclaimed friends of the Indian developed a comprehensive program that was intended to break up reservations, dissolve tribal loyalties, and indoctrinate American Indians into the American way of life. The General Allotment Act of 1887—also called the Dawes Severalty Act after its designer, Senator Henry Dawes—was the federal legislation around which this movement coalesced. The U.S. government reasoned that reservations served to segregate American Indians and thus postponed their inevitable assimilation, so it moved to do away with communally held land on reservations. Under the Dawes Act, when a people on a reservation were considered sufficiently civilized, each family was to be allotted 160 acres of land, while single adults were to receive eighty acres of land. The idea was that individual ownership of property would encourage independence from the tribe. Lands that were not allotted were sold by the government to white settlers, whose nearby presence was further supposed to civilize the American Indians.[4] In effect, this paved the way for the large-scale transfer of property from Native Americans to whites.

Even as this legislation was being enacted, however, some officials in Washington—including the authors of a minority report of the House Indian Affairs Committee—believed that the goal of acquiring American Indian lands for white settlement was being hidden behind humanitarian rhetoric.[5] Despite the protests of these officials and the resistance of many Native Americans, the rush to sell off any unalloted land was swift, and many reservations were devastated. According to James Wilson, "By 1891 the commissioner of Indian Affairs was able to report that more than twelve million acres—11.5 per cent of all reservation land—had been 'restored to the public domain' in just two years." Moreover, "in the first thirteen years of the Dawes Act alone, the government forced through 33,000 allotments and released some 28,500,000 acres of 'surplus' land."[6] By the time the Dawes Act was repealed in 1934, many reservations were a fraction of their pre-1887 size.[7] The Yankton reservation experienced an all-too-common fate. In a treaty made with the U.S. government in 1858, the Yankton Sioux agreed to cede over 11 million acres of their traditional lands on the condition that the remaining 430,000 acres be reserved for their use alone. The land, however, was allotted under the Dawes Act, and in 1895 the government opened up the reservation to homesteaders. Today the Yankton reservation has less than 37,000 acres in trust.[8]

The breakup of the reservations was a crucial element in what Wilson calls "a breathtakingly ambitious experiment in social engineering."[9] Another part of this experiment was the Christianization of the American Indians. To this end, reservations were divided up among various denominations, which sent missionaries and clergy to establish schools and churches. American Indians were discouraged from practicing their native religions, and in 1884 and 1904 religious crime codes were written by the Department of the Interior, prohibiting certain aboriginal religious customs. The most effective means of Christianizing Native Americans and disengaging them from their traditional ways of life, however, was education—specifically, the system of boarding schools that removed children from the influence of their families and attempted to acculturate them into American society.

The first of these schools was the Carlisle Indian School, which was founded by Captain Richard Henry Pratt in 1879. It was run according to a strict military style. Upon entering the institution, boys and girls were divested of their traditional clothing, their hair was cut, and they were forbidden from speaking their native languages. During the Dawes era, numerous schools were established to educate and assimilate American Indian children, and most were based on the Carlisle model. Over three hundred Indian schools existed by 1900, and about 18,000 children were boarding away from their families.[10] Zitkala-Ša was a student at one of these schools, White's Manual Institution in Indiana, which was run by Quakers. This institution was not as coercive or dogmatic as other Indian schools, but the demoralizing effects of Zitkala-Ša's experiences there are evident in her writings nonetheless.

The removal of children from their homes and the resulting division of families exacerbated the process of cultural loss, which is why the period between 1887 and 1934 is considered by some people to be one of the darkest in Native American history. The Dawes-era boarding school system had both positive and negative results. The education of American Indian children led to Native American doctors, educators, and government employees, who often came back to serve their native communities. However, the insensitivity and even cruelty of the boarding school system also left many Native Americans psychologically scarred, as everything they loved and believed in was devalued. While recognizing that the Dawes era was a painful time, Gerald Vizenor notes that it was also the beginning of a regeneration of American Indian cultural and political power. Vizenor describes the era as a middle period in Native American history. The children who attended the Dawes-era boarding schools and who learned to read and write in English became the generation to fight for the rights of their tribes, both locally and on a national level. In spite of the hardships these individuals faced, they became the locus for what Vizenor calls the "tribal enlightenment" at the turn into the twentieth century.[11]

In 1899, after over a decade of Dawes-era policies, some reformers began to question whether the harm done to Native Americans was not greater than the progress they had made. Henry Dawes himself responded to this criticism by claiming that America had only two choices with regard to the Indian: "Either he must be endured as a lawless savage, a constant menace to civilized life, or he must be fitted to become a part of that life and be absorbed into it."[12] Such rhetoric left little room for alternatives that would have been more respectful of Native American people and their cultures.

This, then, was the era in which Zitkala-Ša came of age. These public attitudes and national policies shaped her life and informed her writing. Zitkala-Ša is representative of many American Indian children during this period of change; she spent her first eight years living a traditional Sioux life and spoke no English before she went to White's Manual Institution. By the time she was a teenager, she had become proficient in English and had decided to make her life off of the reservation. Her early experiences and the problems of the Native American people stayed with her, however, and from her first job as a teacher at an Indian school to her last position as founder and president of the National Council of American Indians, her life was dedicated to educating and defending American Indian people. She was one of many in her generation who, according to Frederick E. Hoxie, "believed indigenous values and traditions gave them the strength to resist federal policies and restore the confidence of Native people in their cultures without retreating into the past."[13]

Though Zitkala-Ša had a rich and varied career as a Native American advocate, she may be best known today for her literary endeavors. These include *Old Indian Legends* (1901), a collection based on stories she had heard as a child, and a series of essays and short stories that appeared in popular journals between January 1900 and December 1902, which were collected, along with a few additional pieces, in *American Indian Stories* in 1921. *Old Indian Legends,* one of the first collections of folklore to be written by a Native American woman, is an engaging work of literature and an important anthropological text. Its Iktomi trickster tales, though written in English, are otherwise free from Western signification; the book's temporal and physical space is a Sioux world that exists only in tribal memories and legends. Zitkala-Ša's essays and stories, in contrast, speak to the condition of living as an American Indian at the turn into the twentieth century. Her national literary career began with a sequence of remarkable autobiographical essays that appeared in the *Atlantic Monthly* in January, February, and March of 1900. These essays—"Impressions of an Indian Childhood," "The School Days of an Indian Girl," and "An Indian Teacher among Indians"—chronicle her life from her early youth on the reservation through her experiences at boarding school to her short-lived career as a teacher at an Indian school. The following year she published two short stories in *Harper's Monthly,* "The Trial Path" and "The Soft-Hearted Sioux," that touched on the changes occurring on reservations. In 1902 another short story, "A Warrior's Daughter," appeared in *Everybody's Magazine.* Her final publication in a national mainstream periodical, "Why I am a Pagan," appeared later that year in the *Atlantic Monthly.*

These works marked the appearance of a new voice on the literary scene. Zitkala-Ša was female, American Indian, and well-educated, and her prose was critical, lyrical, and uncompromising. She offered the American public a glimpse inside a traditional culture that their government was attempting to eradicate, as well as a view of some of the discouraging results of that attempt. Zitkala-Ša's works also reveal a complicated relationship with American identity. In one of the great ironies in history, Native Americans were not officially recognized as U.S. citizens until the Indian Citizenship Act of 1924. Before this act was passed, American Indians—unlike any other individuals born within the nation's borders—had to take specific actions before being considered citizens of the United States. Citizenship was gained by receiving an allotment, officially separating from one's tribe, or gaining special permission of the Secretary of the Interior, and later by service in World War I. However, the works of Zitkala-Ša do not address the right of American Indians to U.S. citizenship as often as they question the value of entering into American society at all. Her narratives are not particularly concerned with the willingness (or unwillingness) of American society to accept Native Americans into its fold. What is at issue is whether American Indians should want or seek such entry in the first place.

Several of Zitkala-Ša's prose pieces are set in a traditional Sioux world, exclusive of white America, and at first they seem to have little relationship to issues of national affiliation. Two short stories, "A Warrior's Daughter" and "The Trial Path," are set before white contact; but when read in their historical context, and in relation to Zitkala-Ša's other literary productions during this period, they reveal an anxiety related to identity and post-contact cultural changes. "A Warrior's Daughter" begins with a father—the "chieftain's bravest warrior"—who is teaching his eight-year-old daughter, Tussee, to dance (346).[14] The scene reveals two elements that become important to the plot. The first is the close relationship between the father and the daughter, and the second is the fact that the girl has learned the language of a neighboring rival tribe from a member of their household, who had come to them several years before, when he was captured in warfare.

The action of "A Warrior's Daughter" revolves around Tussee as a young woman. Her beloved goes into battle and is taken prisoner, but Tussee—using her wit, her language skills, and the bravery she has inherited from her father—is able to sneak into the enemy camp and rescue him. The plot of the "Indian maiden" acting bravely to save her lover is a familiar one. What is original here is the way in which Tussee comes to embody several different tribal roles. When the story begins, she is a spirited and devoted daughter; next, she is a beautiful maiden doing her traditional beadwork; as the warriors ride off to fight, she fulfills the duty of a wife, taking the place of her mother among the "brave elderly women" who follow the war party with food and deerskins (349).

Once the battle is over and she hears that her beloved has been captured, she becomes a warrior, sneaking into the enemy camp and killing
her lover's captor. Near the end of the night, she disguises herself as an
old woman to avoid suspicion, and in this guise she carries out the rescue. This depiction of one female taking on many roles in her tribe can
be interpreted as reflecting anxiety in a changing world. In the story,
set before European contact, the family and the tribe are intact. The girl
has a mother and a father, and tribal members of all ages are fulfilling
their traditional roles. By the early twentieth century, and particularly
in Zitkala-Ša's tribe, this societal wholeness was no longer the case. Her
own family had suffered loss due to illness and removal. Her father had
abandoned the family before she was born, and she and her siblings
had been sent to different boarding schools and separated from their
mother and each other. There was a widespread sense that traditional
roles were disappearing, and "A Warrior's Daughter" may reflect a desire to maintain those roles in some way. The pressure on the individual
to sustain a culture is further exemplified by Tussee's final action. Her
lover is too weak to walk, so "Tussee lifts him upon her broad shoulders," and "with half-running triumphant steps she carries him away
to the open night" (352). This task—emblematic of carrying the culture
into the future—is not a burden but an act of triumph, as Tussee finds
the strength to do the unexpected and the seemingly impossible.

Because Tussee had learned the language of the rival tribe as a child,
she is able to eavesdrop on the members of the band and to lure the
young man who had captured her lover away from camp to kill him.
She learns the language of the enemy only to use it against them. As
she says to her foe, "I am a Dakota woman!" right before she plunges a
knife into his heart (350). It is significant that "A Warrior's Daughter"
was Zitkala-Ša's last short story to be published at the turn into the
twentieth century. Her story ultimately is about a Sioux woman taking
on any role necessary to rescue her tribe, carrying the future of her
people triumphantly on her own shoulders, and using her enemy's language against them in the process.

Another short story set apart from white influence is "The Trial
Path." This story opens in a tepee, as do all of Zitkala-Ša's narratives that
invoke a tribal setting. Gerald Vizenor has noted that for thousands

of years, many North American tribes lived in round, communal dwell-
ings, which inevitably shaped the worldview of their inhabitants. He
connects the relatively sudden move from these circular homes to more
Western-style houses with a shift in perspective that served to distance
American Indians from their traditional ways of life.[15] In "The Trial
Path," the characters are "a maid of twenty years" and her grandmother,
who are lying down to sleep for the night (741).[16] The intervening generation, notably, is absent. As the old woman begins to tell of an important chain of events that occurred when she was a maiden, the story
reaches back another generation, to a time very similar to that of "A
Warrior's Daughter." The grandmother recounts how, before she was
married, the man that she loved had killed his best friend. Again, the
plot of this story is not as important as the world the tale reveals. The
grandmother's narrative depicts the tribe as vital and intact. In it, a
very structured and particular way of life emerges, with its material
objects, customs, and values. The respect with which people are expected to treat each other is obvious in the way that her father invites
the messenger bearing bad news into their home as a guest. The Native
American system of justice, which honors victims and their families
above all, is revealed in the fact that the slain man's father is allowed to
decree the appropriate punishment for the crime; the tribe's emphasis
on harmony and solidarity is evident when the family adopts their son's
killer as their own son after he survives his punishment. The end of the
grandmother's tale imparts details about burial customs and, perhaps
more importantly, beliefs about what happens in the Dakota afterlife.[17]

After the woman shares this story—in which is imbedded the history, worldview, and spirituality of her community—she finds that her
granddaughter has fallen asleep. Though the young woman heard some
of the tale, she did not get the story in its entirety. The grandmother
is frustrated; she says to herself, "Hinnu! hinnu! Asleep! I have been
talking in the dark, unheard. I did wish the girl would plant in her
heart this sacred tale" (744). The grandmother's vexation reflects the
precarious nature of culture and tradition. Every generation is crucial
to cultural continuance, and so a story (or any part of a story) that
does not get conveyed to the younger generation is in danger of being
lost. It is significant, however, that the granddaughter hears most of her

grandmother's story, which is clear from her many interruptions and questions. But the grandmother calls her story "a sacred tale," strongly implying that all the elements are important to the whole. The part of the story that the young woman does not hear, having to do with the spirituality and afterlife of the tribe, is just as crucial as the values and customs she learned about in the earlier part of the tale. The end of the grandmother's story involves "the spirit-trail" to "the next camp-ground" that her husband traveled after death (744). Because this sacred information has been lost, someday, after her own death, the granddaughter may not know where to go and may not be able to join all the generations of her tribe that have come together at "the next camp-ground." Metaphorically, if the young woman does not receive the information her grandmother passes down in her stories, she may never learn the traditional ways and someday may lose connection with her tribe's heritage. Although "The Trial Path" is set in a traditional Sioux world and is infused with its customs, beliefs, and traditions (including the centrality of storytelling), in the end it touches on the ramifications of the loss of American Indian identity.

"The Soft-Hearted Sioux," in contrast, is set in Zitkala-Ša's own time. The main character, this time a young man, recounts his story in the moments before he meets his death. This narrative, too, opens in the circular dwelling of the tepee, where the narrator at the age of sixteen, his parents, and his grandmother sit around the fire. Each member of the family has a vision for the young man's future. The grandmother, perhaps conscious of the passing of generations, hopes the boy will marry soon. His mother suggests that he concentrate on developing his hunting skills and advises him to "learn to provide much buffalo meat and many buckskin" (505).[18] His father encourages him to become a warrior, as he himself became at sixteen. The narrator remembers that "my heart was too much stirred by their words, and sorely troubled with a fear lest I should disappoint them" (505). With these fears in mind, the young Dakota leaves the tent and the family circle to "hobble his pony," for, as he says, "it is now late in the night" (505). This sentence foreshadows the rest of the story. It is the boy who becomes hobbled by new ways of thinking; moreover, it is late at night—a dark time for the tribe, which was about to be divided.

The story picks up again ten years later, and the narrator has been studying at "the mission school" for nine years (505). He admits that he "did not grow up to be the warrior, huntsman, and husband" that he would have been if he had stayed in his community. Rather, he has been taught that "it is wrong to kill," and he has come back to the tribe as a missionary "to preach Christianity to them" (505–06). Upon his return, he sees himself as "a stranger," wearing Western clothes and clutching "the white man's Bible" (506). His transformation is not merely external, for he also brings the "white man's tender heart in [his] breast" (506). Though the narrator depicts himself as drastically changed, at least two elements connect him to his origins: he still speaks the language of his tribe, and he still cares for his parents. He admits, however, that "he did not feel at home" even in his family's tepee. During his long absence, his grandmother has passed away, and his father is now very ill.

The narrator's estrangement from his family and his traditional culture is evident in the psychological differences between his grief and that of his mother. Even as he and his mother cry for the once-brave warrior who now lies sick before them, he recognizes a divide between them: "Far apart in spirit our ideas and our faiths separated us. My grief was for the soul unsaved; and I thought my mother wept to see a brave man's body broken by sickness" (506). The son has become so involved in the religious concepts he has been studying that he does not empathize with the man in front of him. In fact, throughout his father's illness, the narrator seems more concerned with his father's soul than with his health. He is most anxious about the influence of the medicine man, who visits frequently. Finally, he becomes so frustrated that he cannot change his father's "faith in the medicine man to the abstract power named God" that he bars the traditional healer from his father's dwelling. After the medicine man leaves, the narrator's father pleads, "My son, I cannot live without the medicine man!" (506). The narrator has one more encounter with the spiritual leader, and that is when he begins to proselytize to the tribe. His hopes that the men will "wash off their war-paints and follow" him are dashed when the medicine man stands up to declare him a traitor to the tribe and a poor son to his father (506). The medicine man also pronounces the ground where he preached to be tainted, and the tribe packs up and moves on, leaving the narrator's father to suffer away from the community that had always sustained him.

As the next scene opens, the narrator steps out of the isolated tepee to find that "the light of the new day is cold" (507). This is a new beginning for him; he is starting to undergo another transformation. He becomes, in a sense, born again into Sioux culture as the teachings and trappings of his life in white America fall away. The cold of the morning is emblematic of the difficulty of these changes, which are not easy for one who has developed the "soft heart of the white man." Outside the tepee, observing the "snow-covered land and the cloudless blue sky," the narrator reflects on the space that separates him from his tribe and "wonder[s] if the high sky likewise separated the soft-hearted Son of God from us" (507). Although he was formerly sure of his faith, his questioning here marks an initial disconnection from the white culture he had adopted. His return to his native culture is further indicated by his hair, which "had grown long" in the traditional style. Still, at this point the narrator continues to pray to his Christian god, despite the indifference of his father.

Unable to fulfill his family's spiritual needs, the son is also unable to provide for them physically. It is the dead of winter, and all three are starving. Distanced as they are from the tribe that would support them, they have no one but the "soft-hearted" son to hunt for them, who returns day after day empty-handed. In desperation, he finally proceeds to kill one of "the white man's cattle" (508). But he is apprehended as he rushes home with his plunder, and he kills his pursuer in the struggle, only to find his father dead when he returns home. A sad irony permeates the story. Only when the narrator is separated from the tribe does he fulfill the traditional roles that would identify him as a worthy son and valuable member of the tribe. His last acts as a free man are to provide meat for his family, kill an enemy, and return his mother to the tribe; he then gives himself up. In a way he has become the hunter, warrior, husband, and father that his relatives had wished for a decade earlier. He has proven that his true allegiance lies with his family, as he violates the tenets of Christianity in his attempt to provide for them. Whereas he initially referred to a Euro-American as the "white man," he calls the person he killed a "paleface" (508).

Though the narrator has proven his commitment to his family and native traditions in spirit, intellectually he is unsure of where the truth really lies: "I wonder who shall come to welcome me in the realm of the strange sight. Will the loving Jesus grant me pardon and give my soul a soothing sleep? or will my father greet me and receive me as his son? Will my spirit fly upward to a happy heaven? or shall I sink into the bottomless pit, an outcast from a God of infinite love?" (508). Despite these vacillations, he goes to the gallows reflecting the ethos of a Sioux warrior: "Serene and brave, my soul awaits the men to perch me on the gallows for another flight. I go" (508). In this narrative, Zitkala-Ša writes of the ambiguous position of the American Indian who has become distanced from his own people but who ultimately cannot trust the mores of white America. At the end of the story, the narrator's ambivalence is accompanied by a calm that coincides with a new righteousness. Though he is never again to be reunited with his tribe in this world, he has at least freed himself from the Christian ideology that had "hobbled him" and disconnected him from his tribe. According to Jace Weaver, for American Indians "the closest approximation of 'sin' in the Christian lexicon is a failure to fulfill one's responsibility to the community. Conversely there is no concept of 'salvation' beyond the continuance of the community."[19] The narrator of "The Soft-Hearted Sioux" has sacrificed himself while trying to fulfill his responsibility to his tribe; in the end, he no longer rejects his traditional beliefs nor accepts without question his adopted religion. For him, ambivalence is a triumph.

In both the governmental and privately run Dawes-era boarding schools, the education of Indians was an inherently Christian endeavor. Conversion of Native Americans had long been seen as an essential part of the assimilation process. In "The Soft-Hearted Sioux," the narrator's questioning of the religious tenets he had learned at his mission school can be read as tantamount to a rejection of both his education and American society at large. Even nine years of Western education were not sufficient to supplant the indigenous worldview with Christian-American values.

As Susan Bernadin notes, "The Soft-Hearted Sioux" "questions the very core of the Euro-American values taught at Indian schools."[20]

Some of Zitkala-Ša's acquaintances saw the story as an affront that criticized their own endeavors to educate Native American children. Members of the faculty at the Carlisle Indian School, where Zitkala-Ša had taught from 1898 to 1899, were especially offended. Their indignation is evident in an evaluation of her writing that appeared in the school's newspaper, *The Red Man and Helper:* "All that Zitkala-Ša has in the way of literary ability and culture she owes to the good people who . . . have taken her into their homes and hearts and given her aid. Yet not a word of gratitude or allusion to such kindness on the part of her friends has ever escaped in any line of anything she has written for the public. By this course she injures herself and harms the educational work in progress for the race from which she sprang."[21] This statement demonstrates the ideological divide between some of the faculty at Indian schools and the population that they served. According to this editorial, criticism of the system threatens to hinder its progress. Zitkala-Ša, however, demonstrated that the Indian schools needed to be disrupted, examined, and reconsidered so that they could serve Native American children better in the future.

Zitkala-Ša's response to this criticism by her former employer was a short essay, "Why I Am a Pagan," which appeared in the *Atlantic Monthly* in 1902. It is an unequivocal denunciation of the religious education she had encountered, both in boarding school and as an adult American Indian living among white Americans. The essay opens with the narrator, this time Zitkala-Ša herself, alone on her reservation, experiencing "the loving Mystery" of nature that surrounds her (802).[22] The landscape triggers a meditation on inherited spiritual beliefs and legends that are associated with the natural environment. She imparts some information about her traditional spirituality, like the "subtle knowledge of the native folk which enables them to recognize a kinship to any and all parts of this vast universe" (802), but she does not reveal the meaning behind any of the specific traditional figures—such as Stone Boy and Inyan—that she contemplates as she wanders. When she returns to her mother's cabin, she reflects on her relationship with other people, feeling the same connection to them as she does to the rest of the natural world. She explains that "racial lines, which were once bitterly real, now serve nothing more than marking out a living mosaic of human beings" (802). Her equilibrium thus also comes from her balanced consideration of all of humanity.

The tranquility of the essay is disrupted when a "solemn-faced 'native preacher'" comes to visit. Zitkala-Ša "listen[s] with respect . . . though he mouth[s] most strangely the jangling phrases of a bigoted creed" (803). The Christian visitor tells her, "Cousin, I was taught long years ago by kind missionaries to read the holy book. These godly men taught me also the folly of our old beliefs" (803). The preacher is reminiscent of the young man in "The Soft-Hearted Sioux," who has an "honest heart" as he proselytizes among his people but who does not recognize his own role in the disruption of Native American culture. The success of missionary efforts on Zitkala-Ša's reservation is perhaps most evident in the fact that her mother is also "now a follower of the new superstition" (803). It is no longer a matter of generational divisions, with the older tribal members maintaining their traditional spirituality and the younger Sioux embracing Christianity; the parents have been influenced by their children as well as by the missionaries in their community. Zitkala-Ša, however, rejects Christianity outright, even though it seems to have permeated her tribal world: "I prefer to their dogma my excursions into the natural gardens where the voice of the Great Spirit is heard in the twittering of birds, the rippling of mighty waters, and the sweet breathing of the flowers. If this is Paganism, then at present, at least, I am a Pagan" (803). In this personal essay, Zitkala-Ša takes a stand as an individual who will determine her own system of beliefs, regardless of whether it conflicts with mainstream American ideology or with the shifting associations of her home community. In her defiance of contemporary opinion, she pointedly refers to her spirituality as "paganism," a then-disparaging word used to describe non-Christian religions.

One sentence in "Why I Am a Pagan" clearly positions the essay as a response to the criticism that had appeared in the Carlisle School newspaper several months earlier. Zitkala-Ša specifically mentions "a missionary paper . . . in which a 'Christian' pugilist commented upon a recent article of mine, grossly perverting the spirit of my pen" (803). To refer to a Carlisle School editor as a "Christian" (in quotation marks) and to call Christianity "a bigoted creed" and a "new superstition" stand as bold criticism of Christianity.[23] In rejecting this religion, moreover, Zitkala-Ša by association rejects the culture that has attempted to impose it upon her. She reaffirms her devotion to her indigenous religion, even though the tribal people that surround her seem to have gone over to the other side. Once again, she seems to be at odds with her surroundings, unwilling to identify with mainstream America and more comfortable with the traditional Sioux perspective—even as that worldview seems to be shifting.

By far the best and most complex of Zitkala-Ša's publications at the turn into the twentieth century are her three autobiographical essays that appeared in the *Atlantic Monthly.* These works—"Impressions of an Indian Childhood," "The School Days of an Indian Girl," and "An Indian Teacher among Indians"—trace her childhood on the reservation, her experiences at a Quaker boarding school for American Indian children, and her own brief stint as a teacher at a similar institution. These essays play on tropes and themes that are common to American autobiography, such as education, literacy, and the eventual rise to success of the author. In contrast to works such as Mary Antin's *The Promised Land,* however, a persistent ambivalence undermines Zitkala-Ša's narrative of a steady rise from humble origins to mainstream American success. Even as Zitkala-Ša describes her apparently willing participation in the Americanizing process, she questions the worth of the American identity that the system is attempting to impose upon her. Indeed, a fundamental premise of her three essays is that, while Dawes-era policies were ostensibly established to give American Indians a better life, traditional native culture is preferable to that of mainstream American society. Because Zitkala-Ša privileges the Sioux culture that her teachers would wrest from her, she ultimately resists an American identity. Yet it is also clear that the drastic changes she undergoes at boarding school fill her with a profound sense of alienation from her origins and prevent her from viewing herself as fully connected to her tribe. What emerges in these essays is a telling ambivalence, one that will be articulated in the works of many writers of color throughout the twentieth century. Zitkala-Ša is nonetheless different from the familiar biracial character, the "tragic mulatto" or "half-breed," found in the works of American writers up to her era. Although she expresses the anguish of living between two worlds, her pain does not come from society's unwillingness to accept the ethnic individual. Rather, it is born from what she believes is the inability of the Native American to return to his or her traditional culture, as well as her antipathy towards mainstream American culture.

"Impressions of an Indian Childhood" is set in a world removed from, but not untouched by, Euro-Americans. The narrative opens, as do Zitkala-Ša's fictional stories, in a round dwelling, here called a wigwam. She depicts her seven-year-old self as completely free and at one with her surroundings. This sense of unboundedness and peace is disrupted only by the sadness she senses in her mother. While the young Zitkala-Ša finds enjoyment in the environment, her mother reminds her that they came from another place: "We were once very happy. But the paleface has stolen our lands and driven us hither. Having defrauded us of our lands, the paleface forced us away" (38).[24] This forced removal entailed more than the loss of ancestral lands and cultural associations; many in the tribe died as they were "driven like a herd of buffalo" to their present location (38). Among those who did not survive were the mother's brother and first-born daughter. From the very beginning, the essays are informed by tribal history and the knowledge of white American betrayal. But these events happened before Zitkala-Ša's birth, and so all she knows is the reservation and its community. Despite the tragic history of their displacement, she sees both the place and her people as nurturing.

As the essay progresses, a compelling portrait of life on the reservation emerges. Zitkala-Ša recreates the rhythm of her younger days, weaving subtle details about work and play into the story that infuse it with a sense of a particular world. She also vividly depicts the ubiquity of humor, the importance of storytelling, and the close relationships between family members and between the individual and the community. Through her description of the customs of everyday life, Zitkala-Ša reveals the values of her tribe, which are, above all else, hospitality, respect, and sensitivity.[25] These values are evident in the way her mother teaches her to do traditional beadwork, which, Zitkala-Ša says, "enabled me to feel strongly responsible and dependent on my own judgment" (40). As she learns by observation, practice, and patient instruction, she is "treated . . . as a dignified little individual" (40). The lengths to which tribal members will go in order to preserve these values, and the manner in which children are instructed in them, is revealed when the young Zitkala-Ša, in her mother's absence, makes coffee for an old man of the tribe. She pours unheated muddy water over used coffee grounds. The old man politely sips the "coffee" (or pretends to do so) until Zitkala-Ša's mother returns. Zitkala-Ša remembers that "neither she nor the warrior . . . said anything to embarrass me. They treated my best judgment, poor as it was, with the utmost respect" (42–43). The adults encourage her attempt at hospitality and reinforce by their own actions the respect and sensitivity that are the tribe's most valued virtues.

These moral imperatives contrast sharply with the treatment Zitkala-Ša's people have endured at the hands of white America. Her mother had taught her to have "no fear, save that of intruding myself upon others," but she also warned her of "the paleface" who had had forced their tribe from their land (37). These teachings and, more importantly, her mother's actions also stand in sharp contrast to the treatment that Zitkala-Ša will receive from whites when she later goes off to a missionary boarding school.

Until the last segment of the essay, white America is only present in the mother's warnings and memories. Yet Zitkala-Ša writes in English and in the Western genres of autobiography and essay, signifying her connection with the Euro-American education system. Her knowledge of Western discourse is employed most effectively in allusions to the biblical story of mankind's fall from grace and exile from the garden of Eden. Zitkala-Ša's use of the familiar Genesis myth has multiple significations. It is not evident that she is referencing Genesis at all until the last segment of the essay, which is entitled "The Big Red Apples." In this section, the young Zitkala-Ša, now eight years old, is lured off the reservation to a missionary boarding school by the promise of unlimited access to red apples. This detail not only shapes the story of her departure from the reservation, but it also provides an interpretation for the essay as a whole. If the red apples allude to the fruit of the tree of knowledge of good and evil, then the reservation becomes equated with the garden of Eden. Indeed, despite her mother's stories of how they came to be on the reservation, Zitkala-Ša portrays it as Edenic, a place where people live in harmony with the natural world and with each other. Accepting the forbidden fruit, as she eventually does, also means initiation into knowledge that will broaden her perspective but will come at a very high price.

In "The Big Red Apples," various figures clearly correspond to figures in the biblical story. Zitkala-Ša's little friend Judewin, who also desires to eat from the tree of knowledge, represents Eve: "Judewin had told me of the great tree where grew red, red apples; and how we could reach out our hands and pick all the red apples we could eat" (46). Judewin, like Eve, is motivated by her own desires and curiosity; she tempts Zitkala-Ša into following her lead. Also like Eve, Judewin is yet an innocent, with no way of knowing what the consequences of her decision will be. In this recasting of the Fall, the missionaries represent the serpent (45). Zitkala-Ša's mother tries to warn her about "the white men's lies" (46), telling her, "Don't believe a word they say! Their words are sweet, but, my child, their deeds are bitter" (46). In fact, the missionaries are shrewd in their attempts to lure the children. One tells Zitkala-Ša that not only will she receive "nice red apples" but that she will also get to ride on "the iron horse" if she goes with them. Zitkala-Ša underscores the cunning of this temptation: "I had never seen a train, and he knew it" (46). This encounter with the missionaries marks the beginning of her exile from the Eden of her childhood, for even before her mother agrees to let her leave, her desire to go East breaks the harmony of the home. This is the first time she has ever purposely imposed her will on her mother and "refused to hearken to [her] mother's voice" (46). The young Zitkala-Ša gets her way, but as soon as she is separated from her mother, she immediately becomes aware of her exile. She remembers that "a sense of regret settled heavily upon me. I felt suddenly weak, as if I might fall limp to the ground. I was in the hands of strangers whom my mother did not fully trust. I no longer felt free to be myself, or to voice my own feelings" (47). This initial separation is portrayed as the beginning of Zitkala-Ša's loss of her Sioux identity.

The allusions to Genesis at the end of the essay also shed light on a curious section in the middle of the text, which is entitled "The Dead Man's Plum Bush." This segment contains another tale of forbidden fruit that links it thematically to the one from the Bible. However, important differences between the legends highlight the divergence between Christianity and the author's native spirituality. The tribal legend is revealed to the young Zitkala-Ša as she is walking with her mother. She begins to "pick some purple plums that grew on a small bush" but is prevented from doing so by her mother (44). When she protests, her mother tells this story: "Never pluck a single plum from this bush, my child, for its roots are wrapped around an Indian's skeleton. A brave is buried here. While he lived, he was so fond of playing the game of striped plum seeds that, at his death, his set of plum seeds were buried in his hands. From them sprang up this little bush" (44). Zitkala-Ša's reaction is as important as the story itself: "Eyeing the forbidden fruit, I trod lightly on the sacred ground. . . . . After that time, I halted in my ramblings whenever I came in sight of the plum bush. I grew sober with awe, and was alert to hear a long-drawn-out whistle from the roots of it. Though I had never heard with my own ears this strange whistle of departed spirits, yet I had listened so frequently to hear the old folks describe it that I knew I should recognize it at once" (44). From then on, the young Zitkala-Ša meditates on three things each time she encounters the plum bush: the tale her mother told her, the young man buried there, and the tribal belief in "the whistle of departed spirits," which she had learned from her elders.

Comparison of the "forbidden fruit" legends reveals some significant differences between Dakota spirituality and that of Christianity. The Genesis myth is one of separation and loss; it is set in a mythical location. The story now exists in the Bible, for that is where it is recorded and how it gets disseminated. The plum bush tale, in contrast, is one of connection and continuance; it is embedded in the natural environment of the tribe. The brave's life, represented by his favorite activity, becomes rooted in the earth but also reaches out to the living inhabitants of the tribe, who can look to the physical bush to remember him. The ground becomes sacred with this association, and there is an eternal blooming from the bones. The young Zitkala-Ša comes to understand the divinity of the place, which triggers not only memories of the legend but also the associated information about the "whistle of departed spirits" that she has learned from listening to the older members of her tribe.

This simple story of connection, continuance, and remembrance is markedly different from the Christian tale of deception, accusations, and exile. In fact, Zitkala-Ša's treatment of the Genesis legend turns the American Christianizing process on its ideological head. In "The Big Red Apples" section of "Impressions of an Indian Childhood," the missionaries themselves become the serpent, known as the devil in Christian mythology. The children's removal from the reservation is tantamount to their fall from grace; they become exiled from their native religion and the things that sustain it—namely, the natural world and their community. If the Genesis and plum bush stories are viewed as synecdoche, each standing as representations for their respective religions, then Christianity comes across as a punitive religion, one that is grounded on separation and deceit. The chain of events in the Adam and Eve tale, when viewed from this perspective, seems to be based on everyone imposing their will on everyone else. It is the antithesis of the spiritual and cultural system revealed in Zitkala-Ša's portrayal of tribal life.

Though "Impressions of an Indian Childhood" is informed by the Bible, Zitkala-Ša does not privilege Western discourse over that of her traditional culture. She may position herself as the original human in a prelapsarian environment, but the echoes of Genesis in her essay only serve to underscore the sense of wholeness and harmony she felt before going to school. The impression of peace and a connection to the natural world exist in the text before the introduction of the biblical allusions. Furthermore, though she includes allusions to Genesis near the end of the essay, she most frequently depicts herself in relation to the natural world. In fact, the essay is framed by two images that come from nature. At the beginning of the narrative Zitkala-Ša describes herself as "free as the wind that blew my hair, and no less spirited than a bounding deer" (37). In the last sentence of the essay she describes her young forlorn self in a train station, as "frightened and bewildered as the captured young of a wild creature" (47). These descriptions not only serve to connect her to the natural world; they also express the great change she undergoes as soon as she leaves her home and community.

"The School Days of an Indian Girl" begins where "Impressions of an Indian Childhood" left off. The eight-year-old Zitkala-Ša and several other Sioux children are on a train heading east to an Indian boarding school. The children had been looking forward to their trip on "the iron horse," but the journey is spoiled as "the throngs of staring pale-faces disturbed and troubled" them (185).[26] This is their introduction to mainstream America, which appears to Zitkala-Ša to have values that differ wildly from her own. She has learned from her mother and her community always to observe the rules of compassion, courtesy, and respect. The greatest wrong one could do was to impose oneself upon others. For a child who had always been treated with consideration by both the young and the old alike, the rudeness and insensitivity of the white passengers are upsetting. Zitkala-Ša describes "fair women" who "stopped their haste and scrutinized the children of absent mothers," as well as "large men" who "halted nearby, and riveted their glassy blue eyes upon us" (185). She tries to hide from their view by sinking into her seat, but, she says, "directly in front of me, children who were no larger than I hung themselves upon the backs of their seats, with their bold white faces toward me. Sometimes they took their forefingers out of their mouths and pointed at my moccasined feet. Their mothers, instead of reproving such curiosity, looked closely at me, and attracted their children's further notice to my blanket. This embarrassed me, and kept me constantly on the verge of tears" (185). From her point of view, she has entered a culture very unlike her own, a culture that has no respect for her feelings and does not treat others with the dignity she was taught all people deserved. Moreover, the core lesson she has learned from her own mother—not to intrude upon others—does not seem to be a part of white Americans' value system, as the behavior of the mothers on the train reveals. In fact, the mothers reinforce their children's rude behavior by further embarrassing the Sioux children. Another gloss on their behavior, one unavailable to the young Zitkala-Ša, is that the white passengers do have rules of etiquette that normally prevent them from staring at strangers and making them feel uncomfortable, but that these guiding principles do not apply when the object of curiosity is an American Indian child. Because of her age and ethnicity, Zitkala-Ša is "odd" and thus not afforded the same sensitivity that white Americans would give one another. Jane Tompkins has described this attitude, which she identifies as being common throughout U.S. history, as "a certain colonial point of view, a point of view from which

Indians, though present, do not finally matter."[27] Once so free and unself-conscious, Zitkala-Ša finds herself shamed by the combination of curiosity and indifference on the part of the passengers around her.

The young girl's dignity is further violated when she gets to the school. She is already confused when she is grabbed and "tossed high in midair" (186). Zitkala-Ša recalls that "a rosy-cheeked paleface woman caught me in her arms. I was both frightened and insulted by such trifling. I stared into her eyes, wishing her to let me stand on my own feet, but she jumped me up and down with increasing enthusiasm. My mother had never made a plaything of her wee daughter" (186). This is her initiation into the white world inside the school: the discovery that the white Americans do not treat her as an autonomous being, as had the adults in her own culture. Zitkala-Ša's later depiction of her initial contact with this new society reveals that she had entered a culture not only different from her own but, from her perspective, quite inferior to it.

What Zitkala-Ša first portrays as cultural idiosyncrasy becomes a part of her everyday life. A lack of respect for her traditional background is deeply rooted in the educational system into which she enters. She is aware that the goal of this system is broader than just academic instruction; its enterprise is to strip the children of their native culture and instill in them a knowledge of and allegiance to the American way of life. She calls this system a "civilizing machine" and reports that "it was next to impossible to leave the iron routine" of this machine once it was started (190). A statement made by an agent on the Yankton reservation at the very time Zitkala-Ša was in boarding school gives a clear picture of the ideology behind her schooling: "Education cuts the cord which binds them to a pagan life, places the Bible in their hands, and substitutes the true God for the false one, Christianity in place of idolatry, civilization in place of superstition, morality in place of vice, cleanliness in place of filth, industry in place of idleness, self-respect in place of servility, and, in a word, humanity in place of abject degradation."[28] The two main goals of Indian education, according to this agent, are to convert and civilize the children, or, in other words, to Christianize and Americanize them. The repetition of the phrase "in place of" clearly shows that another important goal was to obliterate traditional belief systems. The agent also indicates his opinion of Native American children before they are introduced to American education: they are foolish, sinful, filthy, lazy, servile, and less than human. This is not to say that all who were involved with Indian education shared his point of view, but it is an example of the kind of lack of respect for American Indian children as individuals that Zitkala-Ša describes in "School Days of an Indian Girl."

In fact, the world of boarding school seems in every way to be the antithesis of the life that Zitkala-Ša had led before. The round home of the tepee has been replaced with a room where "many narrow beds were in one straight line down the entire length of the wall" (186). The tranquil flow of the rhythm of life with her mother has been replaced by a series of "loud clamoring" bells that direct the children when to wake up, when to go to meals, and when to stand and sit. The "crashing" of the bells bothers the newly arrived children, as does the "annoying clatter of shoes on bare floors" and "the many voices murmuring an unknown tongue" (186). The biggest shock of the first day at boarding school, however, comes when the new students are to have their hair cut.

Part of the national project to prepare Native American children for American citizenship was the attempt to eradicate their cultural particularity, or, in the words of Carlisle Indian School founder Richard Henry Pratt, to "kill the Indian and save the man."[29] In Zitkala-Ša's experience, this process begins with changing the children's appearance so that they look less traditional. While the young Zitkala-Ša is at first embarrassed and uncomfortable in her Western clothing, the moccasins and blanket that are taken from her do not hold as much significance as her long hair. Perhaps because the American Indian girls' long braids are a cultural marker that connects them to the traditions of their tribes, they are cut off on the first day. Zitkala-Ša writes that her and the other children's sense of themselves was intimately connected to their long hair: "Our mothers had taught us that only unskilled warriors who were captured had their hair shingled by the enemy. Among our people, short hair was worn by mourners, and shingled hair by cowards!" (187). Instead of instilling in the children a sense of independence and self-respect, the system coerces them into capitulation and shame. When the adults first attempt to cut Zitkala-Ša's hair, she declares, "I will not submit!" and runs and hides. They finally catch her, tie her to a chair, and cut her braids off. The effect on her is profound. She remembers: "Then I lost my spirit. Since the day I was taken from my mother I had suffered extreme indignities. People had stared at me. I had been tossed about in the air like a wooden puppet. And now my long hair was shingled like a coward's! . . . Now I was only one of many little animals driven by a herder" (187).[30] The cutting of the children's hair is emblematic of the school's mission to cut them off from their cultural values. The indifference with which the act is performed points to an atmosphere of cultural supremacy. Because the faculty assumes that mainstream American culture is superior to all others, these educators are unable to recognize the value or importance of inherited traditions.

The hair-cutting scene emphasizes both the cultural insensitivity of the white American system at the school and the dehumanizing nature of its practices and policies, which did not consider the individual. Zitkala-Ša acknowledges at one point that the intentions of the people who ran the school were probably good, but that fact does not mitigate the sense of imposition and lack of respect the children experienced. Zitkala-Ša depicts a world in which an established regime and its myriad regulations are more important than the students, whose psychological pain and physical illnesses are often ignored or regarded as disruptions to the system. Martha J. Cutter describes "School Days of an Indian Girl" as "a scathing indictment of a dominant ideology which forces acculturation at the expense of self."[31] Zitkala-Ša depicts the educational process, the "civilizing machine," as overwhelming, and yet she remembers finding the willpower to resist its imperative to capitulate. Though separated from the family and community that would have normally reinforced her Sioux identity, she nonetheless steadfastly refuses to assume the new identity that the school wishes to impose upon her.

Part of the cultural and personal struggle with which she has to contend has to do with the issue of discourse. In "Impressions of an Indian Childhood," Zitkala-Ša recalls that when she left the reservation, "I knew but one language, and that was my mother's native tongue" (45), but she quickly learns that knowledge of English is necessary in her new foreign world. The impetus to learn English is depicted not as a desire for knowledge, but as a fear of the repercussions of not learning it. This fear is illustrated in a scene in which one of her little friends is physically punished for saying "no" to a woman in authority when she should have said "yes." The girl does not know English, and so she does not understand the woman's questions. Zitkala-Ša writes that "misunderstandings as ridiculous as this one . . . frequently took place, bringing unjustifiable frights and punishments into our little lives" (188). Again, the educational system is shown to be punitive and insensitive in comparison to the methods of instruction she received from her mother and her tribe.[32]

Faced with this negative incentive, Zitkala-Ša says that "within a year I was able to express myself somewhat in broken English" (188). As soon as she develops some mastery of the language of her perceived enemies, she, like the Indian maiden in "Warrior's Daughter," contrives to use it against them. In a scene that demonstrates her ability to subvert the language of dominance, when she is told "to mash the turnips for dinner," she proceeds to mash with all her weight and energy until she pounds through the bottom of the jar. Though she receives a scolding, she remembers that "I felt triumphant in my revenge" and "whooped in my heart for having once asserted the rebellion within me" (188). Most of the time Zitkala-Ša expresses her defiance by silent resistance, and even in the turnip-mashing scene she does not say anything; still, it is emblematic of her understanding that she can manipulate the English language to fight her battles. The assertion of defiance that she experiences on a small scale as a child is magnified in the publication of these essays criticizing the Indian education system, which were printed in the *Atlantic Monthly,* the foremost magazine of her day.

The manner in which mainstream American life and culture are introduced to Zitkala-Ša explains why she resists the process of assimilation and declines to embrace an American identity. The restrictive environment of the boarding school only motivates her to fight against her confinement; she writes of "actively testing the chains which tightly bound my individuality like a mummy for burial" (190). The longing for the freedom of her former life becomes complicated, however, when, after three years at school, she comes home to the reservation. Zitkala-Ša conflates the summers she spent at home from age eleven to age fifteen in the section "Four Strange Summers." The title suggests a narrative about four consecutive breaks from school, but the section reads as if she is describing just one summer. In it, she explores her emerging ambivalent identity. Although she defined herself as Indian at the boarding school, at home she feels out of sync with her mother and the life of the tribe: "During this time I seemed to hang in the heart of chaos. . . . My mother had never gone inside of a schoolhouse, and so she was not capable of comforting a daughter who could read or write. . . . I was neither a wee girl nor a tall one; neither a wild Indian nor a tame one" (191). Though Zitkala-Ša has not lost her native language, her acquisition of English differentiates her from her mother. The changes she encounters are both internal and external, as the world of the reservation is changing as well. Her mother has moved from the traditional round dwelling to a cabin, and the young men and women of the tribe "were no more young braves in blankets and eagle plumes, nor young Indian maidens with prettily painted cheeks" (192). They, too, had been to school and had "become civilized," and while Zitkala-Ša returns to wearing traditional dress at home, others wear Western-style clothes and at "gatherings they talked in English" (192). She describes "an unrest gnawing at my heart" that makes her angry and restless (192). Formerly so respectful of the natural world and the members of her tribe, the adolescent Zitkala-Ša is the cause of suffering to both a pony and a wolf by conducting an unnecessary chase; she then becomes annoyed with an "old warrior" who visits to tell of it.

Her four summers of "turmoil" on the reservation convince the teenaged Zitkala-Ša that she no longer belongs there, but in fact she is not happy anywhere (192). Against her mother's wishes, she decides to go to college, and for the first time she disparages her own culture when she dismisses her mother's objections as a desire for her to "roam over the prairies and find my living upon wild roots" (193). Her entry into college, which comes near the end of the essay, is depicted not as a great achievement but as a continuation of her fruitless encounter with white America. As she says, "Homeless and heavy-hearted, I began anew my life among strangers" (193). Zitkala-Ša still feels homesick and longs for her mother, but she elects to live "among a cold race whose hearts were frozen hard with prejudice" (193). It is clear that even as she works through her scholarship for "the white man's respect," she does not consider herself assimilated into mainstream society.

She is friendless, though "several classmates were courteous to me
at a safe distance" (193). Her peers are very supportive when she wins
her school's oratory contest, but when she goes to compete at another
college, her perception of white Americans as cruel and insensitive is
again reinforced when a banner is unveiled with a drawing of "a most
forlorn Indian girl" and the word "squaw" drawn on it. She remembers,
"Such worse than barbarian rudeness embittered me. . . . I gleamed
fiercely upon the throngs of palefaces" (194). In a way, she defeats the
enemy again through her use of the English language by winning one
of the two prizes awarded. But later, alone in her room, the ambivalence of her position reemerges: "The little taste of victory did not satisfy a hunger in my heart. In my mind I saw my mother far away on
the Western plains, and she was holding a charge against me" (194).
This is the final line in the essay. Although "School Days of an Indian
Girl" thus ends with a seeming success story—entry into college and
an award in a statewide collegiate oratory contest—these accomplish-
ments are diminished by the way they are represented. Though Zikala-
Ša fulfills a certain drive and ambition—one that is valorized in white
America—she cannot escape the imperatives of family and culture. The
"charge" her mother "holds against her" may be her willful separation
from tribe and family, or it may be the fact that Zitkala-Ša has had her
dignity publicly compromised by whites at the competition. Her mother's charge itself is as ambiguous as her position between the world of
her mother and that of white achievement.

Zitkala-Ša's final autobiographical essay, "An Indian Teacher among
Indians," is about the year she teaches at the Carlisle Indian School,
which she refers to only as "an Eastern Indian School" (382).[33] Half the
essay, however, is set on the reservation. Through these two locations,
Zitkala-Ša makes a connection between white encroachment onto reservation lands and the mainstream attitude toward American Indians
that lies beneath the ideology of their education. She returns to the
reservation "to gather Indian pupils for the school," and when she ar-
rives at her mother's cabin she learns of many changes that have taken
place (383). The essay describes events that take place in the academic
year 1898–99, and by this time the policies of the General Allotment
Act of 1887 have taken their toll. Her mother tells her that their land has

become "a refuge for white robbers" and that her brother, Dawee, who was "a government clerk" on the reservation, had lost his job when he had "tried to secure justice for our tribe" (384). That night, as mother and daughter sit out under the stars, they can see can see lights along the river of "a tribe of broad-footed white beggars [that] had rushed hither to make claims on those wild lands" (385). In a powerful image of American Indian resistance, Zitkala-Ša's mother stands up and curses the settlers: "She sprang to her feet, and, standing firm beside her wigwam, she sent a curse upon those who sat around the hated white man's light. Raising her arm forcibly into line with her eye, she threw her whole might into her doubled fist as she shot it vehemently at the strangers" (385). That night her mother also gives her a warning that echoes and elaborates on the one she had given her before she left home for the first time: "My daughter, beware of the paleface. It was the cruel paleface who caused the death of your sister and your uncle, my brave bother. It is this same paleface who offers in one palm the holy papers, and with the other gives a holy baptism of firewater. He is the hypocrite who reads with one eye, 'Thou shalt not kill,' and with the other gloats upon the suffering of the Indian race" (385). These words are sharp reminders of a history that continues to affect the tribe and of a past that cannot be erased by the assimilation process.

Her mother's anger and resistance influence Zitkala-Ša when she goes back East: "I slowly comprehended that the large army of white teachers in Indian schools had a larger missionary creed than I had suspected" (385). This doctrine "included self-preservation quite as much as Indian education" (385). She discovers that a variety of white degenerates are allowed to work at Indian schools as a sort of charity operation, regardless of how their presence negatively affects the children in the institutions. She mentions a teacher who is an opium addict, a drunken doctor whose "patients carried their ailments to untimely graves," and a sadistic "teacher who tortured an ambitious Indian youth" by constantly calling him a "government pauper" (385). Zitkala-Ša admits to knowing of a "few rare ones who have worked nobly for my race," but they have little effect on the overall "shameful" conditions she has observed (385). Susan Bernadin notes the significance of these revelations, coming directly after the scene of Zitkala-Ša's mother's curses and warnings: "Zitkala-Ša calls her eastern colleagues an 'army of white teachers' whose verbal and intellectual intimidation of students are implicitly linked with the territorial and physical subjugation of American Indians by the U.S. military and settlers in the West."[34] In fact, the American program of Native American assimilation had many military overtones. From Pratt's philosophy that it was necessary to "kill the Indian within" to the very structure of the Indian schools, the education system seemed to be at war with Native American culture.

It is little wonder, considering all that Zitkala-Ša experienced and observed regarding white America's treatment of American Indians, that she consistently resists an assimilated American identity in her narratives, even as she makes use of her education to find her way in the world off the reservation. Her disgust with the system of Indian education turns her against the American society that supports it, but she admits that she has lost touch with the things that could connect her to her Sioux identity. As she says, "In the process of my education I had lost all consciousness of the nature world around me. . . . I unknowingly turned away from my one salvation. . . . For the white man's papers I had given up my faith in the Great Spirit. For these same papers I had forgotten the healing in trees and brooks. On account of my mother's simple view of life, and my lack of any, I gave her up, also. I made no friends among the race of people I loathed" (386). In her despair, she feels that she has become disconnected from her original community and worldview, and she finds she does not like what she sees in mainstream America. In fact, she blames white society and her attraction to it for her rift from her original community. Even as she describes this profound ambivalence, however, she associates her disconnected self with the Sioux world. She compares herself to a figure in a tribal legend—"I sat like the petrified Indian woman of whom my mother used to tell me"—and then depicts herself as an image connected to the natural world, "a slender tree" that has been "uprooted from my mother, nature, and God . . . shorn of my branches, which had waved in sympathy and love for home and friends" (386). Ultimately, Zitkala-Ša portrays herself as a Sioux woman at a crossroads, entering a new territory of identity that had not yet been explored in Native American literature. Though her heart remains connected to her heritage and community, she believes that her physical distance from her tribe and the effects of her American education have negated her claims to Sioux authenticity.

"An Indian Teacher among Indians" does not end with images from nature or the Sioux life, but with a coming together of white and Native America. This meeting of two cultures is not representative of cultural clash or of common ground; instead, it shows the great silent divide between the two worlds, a rift that she cannot cross because of the colonial gaze of white America. Having been both a student and a teacher at institutions of Indian education, she recalls: "From morning to evening, many specimens of civilized peoples visited the Indian school. The city folks with canes and eyeglasses, the countrymen with sunburnt cheeks and clumsy feet, forgot their relative social ranks in an ignorant curiosity. Both sorts of these Christian palefaces were alike astounded at seeing the children of savage warriors so docile and industrious" (386). In describing this everyday event, Zitkala-Ša reveals the way in which whites used the image of the American Indians to help define themselves. Here, figures from very differing walks of life are unified in their status as "civilized" Christian Americans. Zitkala-Ša's ability to interpret and critique the visitors also suggests that her years in the educational system have given her insight into the workings of the white mind, while the whites who visit have no real understanding of the individuals they come to observe. According to Jace Weaver, "The Indian as subaltern knows quite a bit about the mindset and psychological makeup of those in the dominant culture; only the reverse remains untrue."[35] The visitors' inability or unwillingness to get to know the American Indian children or to learn about the conditions of the schools is self-serving and ultimately detrimental to the students, whom they think they are helping: "As to their shallow inquiries they received the students' sample work to look upon. Examining the neatly figured pages, and gazing upon the Indian girls and boys bending over their books, the white visitors walked out of the schoolhouse well-satisfied: they were educating the children of the red man!" (386).[36] The scene is emblematic of the self-deception of the nation as a whole. Mainstream America adheres to assimilationist policies in order to advance American Indians but does not consider any damaging effects those policies might have on cultures and individuals. The final sentences of "An Indian Teacher among Indians," and so the concluding word of the series of essays, resonates both on a personal and national level: "In this fashion many have passed idly through the Indian schools during the last decade, afterward to boast of their charity to the North American Indian. But there are few who have paused to question whether real life or long-lasting death lies beneath this semblance of civilization" (386). These lines stand as a challenge to Zitkala-Ša's mainstream readership to look deeper into national policies and to try to see the world from the perspective of Native Americans.

In the final scene of "An Indian Teacher among Indians," Zitkala-Ša offers readers of the *Atlantic Monthly* a view of her experiences both on the reservation and in the Indian schools, experiences that had never before been portrayed in print. In doing so, she presents a clear critique of the nation's policy regarding Native Americans, particularly of its method of assimilation though education. In this scene, where white Americans take a "shallow" look at the work produced by the American Indian children, Zitkala-Ša seems to anticipate one possible reaction from her audience. From what she knows of American society, here represented by the "ignorant" observers who pass through the schools, she anticipates that many people will read her essays and come only to the conclusion that she writes very well and that the Indian education system is therefore a success.

The personas that Zitkala-Ša creates in her narratives always seems to exist between "real life or long-lasting death" after they enter into the "semblance of civilization" (386). Even the stories that portray a traditional Sioux world—such as "The Trial Path" and "A Warrior's Daughter"—reflect on the influence of historical change and the desire to preserve cultural identity in the face of it. The protagonist in "The Soft-Hearted Sioux" represents the boarding-school conversion experience, which entails not only an acceptance of Christianity but also the conviction that "Indianness" must be sacrificed for the Western ways that are inextricably connected to Christianity in the American education system. This character suffers and dies because of his between-world status, but his death is not untriumphant; in the end, at least, he relinquishes his allegiance to his transplanted worldview.

The ambivalent identity of a person of color who does not feel at home in her traditional culture but who refuses to accept assimilation into mainstream society is an issue most fully explored in Zitkala-Ša's three autobiographical essays. The lack of respect for Native American children and their cultures that she experienced in Dawes-era boarding schools precludes her acceptance of the model of American citizenship that those institutions sought to impose on their students. Her discussion in the essays of her tribe's recent history of removal, as well as their ongoing loss of land, further justifies her strong resistance to the Americanizing process. She articulates a perspective from which the adoption of a mainstream identity was nothing short of subjugation. However, because she no longer feels at home on the reservation, she also believes that she must abdicate, to some measure, her traditional identity. She has to make her way in the world without a national affiliation, for she leaves her tribe and yet cannot accept herself as an American citizen.

Zitkala-Ša and others of her generation, coming from the boarding schools, had few models of American Indians who had successfully integrated their American education with their tribal inheritance, so her expressions of disconnection and isolation stand as an especially insightful examination of both personal and historical ambivalence. Jace Weaver explains that in many Native American religious worldviews, spiritual wholeness is achieved when one is in harmony with one's place in the world, which "involves right relations not only between the human self and human others but between self and place."[37] In her autobiographical essays, Zitkala-Ša depicts herself as out of sync with her world once she moves from her reservation to boarding school. Her decision to leave her mother, her community, and the land she grew up on is portrayed as a fall from grace. The fact that she has lost the "right relations . . . between human self and human others" is evident in the conflicts she has with her mother and her sustained antipathy for most of the white people around her. The loss of the "right relations . . . between self and place" is evident in the fact that she feels she has no place in the world at all.

The short works that Zitkala-Ša published between 1900 and 1902 are important antecedents to twentieth-century Native American literature. Later authors—such as N. Scott Momaday, Louise Erdrich, and Sherman Alexie—would expand the theme of ambivalence to examine ways in which Native Americans could become reconnected with a tribal identity despite the transformation of indigenous cultures. Weaver notes that "the self is the locus where tribal values become concrete," and in all of Zitkala-Ša's autobiographical essays it is clear that she never abandons her allegiance to traditional Sioux values.[38] Perhaps the most confident expression of this is found in "Why I Am a Pagan," which was her last publication to appear in a mainstream periodical. Though she still patiently derides Christianity and still expresses a feeling of disconnection from the life of the reservation, she is comfortable with her native spirituality and draws strength from it. Dexter Fisher sees Zitkala-Ša's writing "as a model of ambivalences, of oscillations between two diametrically opposed worlds, but it is also a model of retrieved possibilities, a creative, human endeavor that stands at the beginning of many such endeavors eventually to culminate in the finely crafted work of contemporary American Indian writers."[39] Though she foregrounds the ambivalence of the Native American individual at the crossroads of culture, Zitkala-Ša's texts are informed by elements of resistance, maintenance of core cultural values, and a continuing connection to the natural world that will help future generations construct new American Indian identities. The fact remains, however, that in her writings, the figures who move between the American world of Dawes-era boarding schools and the tribal world of the reservation are simultaneously troubled by a sense of disconnection from their traditional culture and proud of their resistance to assimilation. They are not paralyzed by ambiguity, but they are disconnected because of it. In her writings, Zitkala-Ša depicts American Indians who endure despite their ambivalence and who, strengthened by their cultural inheritance, go forward in isolation to ensure the continuance of Native American life. Their relationship to American citizenship, however, remains unresolved.

CHAPTER FOUR

Race and Nation in the Novels
of Sutton E. Griggs

I N THE POST-RECONSTRUCTION ERA, many African American writers were calling for social justice in the face of widespread disfranchisement, increased lynchings, and the creation of segregation laws throughout the South, but only one writer, Sutton E. Griggs, had the creative power to imagine alternatives to the status quo. His five novels—*Imperium in Imperio* (1899), *Overshadowed* (1901), *Unfettered* (1902), *The Hindered Hand* (1905), and *Pointing the Way* (1908)—stand as important critiques of a nation in profound conflict. Though writing at the height of American realism and embedded in the tensions of his time, Griggs moves past the reality of his historical context to envision a scenario in what cultural critic Homi Bhabha calls "the beyond."[1] Griggs's novels, written in the interstices of American history and literature, serve to "innovate and interrupt the performance of the present" and to create new possibilities for black citizens and the nation. In Griggs's fiction, the realms of race and nation are addressed as new territory, full of possibility and potential danger, not as settled, uncontested areas. He offers innovative ways of defining both blackness and America as he struggles with the task of representing an African American solidarity that can coincide with an American identity. In his novels, he articulates a vision of citizenship in which it is possible for individuals to have a dual affiliation with their ethnicity and their nation. In his narratives, only this model of cohesion serves to resist the forces that tear apart African American communities, families, and individuals.

The turn into the twentieth century was a grim time for most African Americans, especially those living in the South. The end of Reconstruction in 1877 signaled that the nation's sentiments had shifted. Where once Republican politicians strove to assure the rights of freedmen, now the political focus was on reconciliation between the North and the South. Unfortunately for African Americans, the southern states were increasingly trusted to work out issues of race without intervention from the North or the federal government. The Civil Rights Act of 1875, based on the Fourteenth Amendment, forbade the exclusion of African Americans from hotels, railroads, and other accommodations; but after 1877, public establishments began systematically to deny service to blacks or to segregate them from white customers. The provisions of the Civil Rights Act were successfully challenged several times, and in 1883 the Supreme Court finally invalidated the act altogether by reasoning that the Fourteenth Amendment declared that no state "shall make or enforce any laws which shall abridge the privileges or immunities of citizens of the United States" or "deprive any person of life, liberty or property."[2] The amendment, they noted, had nothing to say about individuals invading the rights of citizens. The court subsequently came to the same conclusion regarding voting rights, thereby limiting the power of the Fifteenth Amendment., which clearly stated that "the Right of citizens of the United States to vote shall not be denied or abridged . . . by any state on account of race, color, or previous condition."[3] The justices decided that states could not make laws restricting voting rights, but that nothing could be done if individuals prevented blacks from voting. It was up to the states themselves to enact laws preventing such abuses. The states, of course, had other things in mind. As Rayford W. Logan notes, the nullification of the 1875 Civil Rights Act "virtually assured the subsequent development of Jim Crow laws and other forms of race discrimination and the passivity of the Federal government in the face of this discrimination."[4] The South began to enact laws to disfranchise and segregate black citizens, in direct violation of the Fourteenth and Fifteenth Amendments. By 1900 segregation was a way of life in the South, and virtually every southern state had added poll taxes, literacy tests, property requirements, or grandfather clauses as amendments to their constitutions, which effectively denied suffrage to black citizens.

In terms of federal legislation, the landmark case of the era was *Plessy v. Ferguson*. In this 1896 case, an African American man, Homer Plessy, was denied a seat in a white railroad car in Louisiana, where racial segregation on public transportation was required by law. Plessy sued the state of Louisiana, claiming that, by definition, mandatory segregation was discriminatory and hence prohibited under the Fourteenth Amendment. In a stunning decision that would have repercussions for decades to come, the Supreme Court stated that it was fair for Louisiana to make laws according to its "established usages, customs, and traditions." Moreover, the court affirmed that segregation does not imply the superiority or inferiority of any one race; if blacks believe that they are made to use separate facilities because whites feel they are inferior, it is "solely because the colored race chooses to put that construction on it."[5] Ultimately, the court concluded, it is not the role of legislation to solve society's ills. Justice John Harlan, in his dissenting opinion, sharply cut through the disinterested naiveté expressed in the decision. Harlan plainly stated that he believed the Louisiana law to be unconstitutional and predicted that the court's decision would have long-lasting negative effects: "What can more certainly arouse race hate, what more certainly create and perpetuate a feeling of distrust between these races, than state enactments, which, in fact, proceed on the ground that colored citizens are so inferior and degraded that they cannot be allowed to sit in public coaches occupied by white citizens? That, as all will admit, is the real meaning of such legislation as was enacted in Louisiana."[6] This court-sanctioned prejudice seemed to authorize both institutional and individual acts of cruelty. At the turn into the twentieth century, African Americans in the South thus were not only limited politically and socially, but they were also subject to physical violence. It has been estimated that around one hundred lynchings a year occurred in the South during this period.[7]

These conditions led Logan to label this era "the nadir" of African American life and history.[8] Yet despite the oppression black Americans faced—often in the North as well as the South—the age was not without its achievements. Schools that had been established during Reconstruction, as well as institutes of higher learning (such as the Tuskegee Institute, which was founded in 1881 by Booker T. Washington), continued their mission to educate black southerners. Literacy rates of African Americans, which stood at 18.6 percent in 1870, rose to 42.9 percent in 1890.[9] The numbers of black professionals also rose during that era, which meant more doctors, teachers, and lawyers to serve their communities. And writers such as Frances E. W. Harper, Charles W. Chesnutt, Paul Laurence Dunbar, and Sutton E. Griggs were publishing works that shed new light on African American life, ushering in a new era of black literary achievement.

Griggs used the genre of the novel to create a multitude of scenarios that examine possible solutions to what was then being called "the Negro problem." In his testing of ideas, ideologies, and theories, he seemed always to return to one approach to creating a better life for blacks in America. He believed that the form of citizenship that would best serve African Americans would be a kind of dual citizenship, one in which individuals would align themselves with the black community first but would never give up the fight for full participation in the life of the nation. His five novels suggest that African Americans would only gain full equality in the United States by standing together as a unified people, cooperating across lines of class and color. Yet his themes are not separatist, and the ultimate goal of most of his heroes and heroines is always complete acceptance into American society.

Griggs begins his exploration of this sort of racial cohesion in his first novel, *Imperium in Imperio* (1899), or "nation within a nation."[10] In the book, the entire African American population secretly unifies to become a complete underground federation, the Imperium in Imperio, with a government parallel to that of the United States.[11] In a dramatic decision, members of the group resolve to take Texas and Louisiana by stealth and force, establishing their own nation in Texas and giving Louisiana to the international powers that help them achieve their mission. This plan does not come to fruition because the narrator's apocalyptic fears compel him to reveal the plot. This last-minute turn of events, however, does not diminish the revolutionary nature of the narrative as a whole. The novel explores the idea of a black coalition within America that negotiates with other countries and considers the possibility of military action against and separation from the United States. This was a highly imaginative response to the current racial and political climate, and it certainly did not reflect other ideas being considered in the public discourse of the time. For all its innovation, however, the separatist plot is dissolved in the text, and Griggs implies that the powerful unity achieved by African Americans had not been put to the best use. By vowing to separate from the United States, the Imperium had lost sight of its goal, which was to "secure . . . the full enjoyment and privileges due American citizens" (183); it had subsequently lost the moral force that had unified its members.

As members of the Imperium debate how best to alleviate the current plight of black Americans, they present evidence of lynching, hypocrisy, and injustice, all perpetrated in the nation that claims to be a democracy. One dissenting voice, that of educator and activist Belton Piedmont, reveals patriotic sentiments and makes a claim for American citizenship despite the crimes of white Americans. In Piedmont's voice lies another notion of a "nation within a nation," one in which black Americans could organize themselves in order to attain their rights as Americans. To claim fully one's identity as a black person and as an American citizen is here represented as the attainment of wholeness and completeness. To divide into factions or to come into an American identity by denying an African American identity is tantamount to defeat. The achievement of this state of wholeness is not simple, however. There are many barriers to its realization that serve to fragment the nation, the community, the family, and the individual. In all Griggs's novels, the most overwhelming obstacle to the full realization of the ideal of dual citizenship is the political climate of the day. Central to the splintering of blacks from American society was the disfranchisement of the majority of African Americans. Their exclusion from politics enabled the white electorate to pass or uphold other laws that denied justice to African Americans. Not only were blacks denied the vote, but they often were not permitted to sit on juries or testify in trials. This made them easy targets for unjust punishment and forced many into convict lease programs.

The relation of African Americans to American systems of justice is a central theme in all of Griggs's novels. As his works reveal, black

Americans were subjected to three kinds of judicature: mob law, decisions of local courts, and rulings of the Supreme Court. Each had its own codes that effectively circumscribed the lives of blacks. Griggs's novels strongly suggest that this systemic repression was destructive to the entire nation. Black participation in civic life, not their segregation or disfranchisement, was crucial to America's future. Nor was Griggs alone in this conviction. For both Frederick Douglass before him and his contemporary W. E. B. Du Bois, the very notion of America as a free and democratic nation was severely undermined by its treatment of the black citizens living within its borders.[12]

The most immediate form of white control experienced by southern blacks at the turn into the twentieth century was mob law, and this method of "justice" was primarily enacted in the form of lynching. Griggs's works, which reflect the anxiety of black southerners, are laced with memories, threats, and brutally graphic descriptions of vigilante executions. While Griggs carefully delineates the reality of mob law and its psychological effects on individuals, he also deconstructs white southern justifications for racial violence. The myth perpetuated in the South was that there was a "one crime" rule for lynching a black man, and that was in retaliation for an assault on a white woman. In Griggs's novels, however, the circumstances behind most of the lynchings have nothing to do with white women, reflecting the fact that the "one crime" lie that the South telegraphed to the rest of the country was nothing but a smokescreen for or pretext to outright barbarism. As one white participant explains after the mutilation and murder of a black couple in *The Hindered Hand,* "That's all rot about one crime. We lynch niggers down here for anything. We lynch them for being sassy and sometimes we lynch them on general principles. The truth of the matter is the real 'one crime' that paves the way for a lynching whenever we have the notion is the crime of being black" (136).[13] In fact, the vulnerability of white women at the hands of black men is shown to be the inverse of reality. In the opening pages of *The Hindered Hand,* a porter is slipped a note by a white woman on his train.[14] This simple act terrifies the porter and triggers in him an immediate sense of danger. His knowledge of the way mob law works in the South—that even a fleeting communication with a white woman is a threat to his very life—is signaled by a simple gesture: "he put his hand on his collar as though it was already too tight" (16).

Later in the novel, the porter is approached again by the same woman, who threatens to accuse him of impropriety unless he follows her orders to stop the train: "The perturbed porter canvassed in his mind that stock of alleged facts circulated secretly among the Negroes setting forth the manner in which some white women used their unlimited power of life and death over Negro men, things that may in some age of the world's history come to light" (84). Raymond Hedin has argued that "the power of established [white] stories or myths made it all the more essential for a black writer to try to preserve his own sense of story, at least to slip into print . . . the beginnings of a countermyth, in the hope that it would somehow begin to exercise its subversive power."[15] The porter's meditation on mob law reflects the hypocrisy and brutality behind lynching. This is an example of how Griggs's novels act as interventions, as he inserts another southern voice, a black one, into the story of lynching.

The second system of justice that circumscribes the lives of black citizens is the local judicial system, which is represented in Griggs's texts by the local trial. The courtroom scenes, which pit innocent black characters against hardhearted white juries, read like melodrama. The dramatic nature of these scenes reflects the fact that local trials involving African Americans were little more than staged events. The results of these trials were scripted before they even began. There is no expectation that a white jury and judge will rule in favor of a black man, woman, or child. In *Imperium in Imperio,* for example, Belton Piedmont kills a man who sought his death; but the "men who were in the mob that attempted Belton's murder were on the jury. In fact, the postmaster [the ringleader of the lynching] was the foreman" (159). In this case, the jury sentences not only Belton but also the entire family he lives with to be hanged. In *Pointing the Way,* Baug Peppers, an African American lawyer, tries to explain to a white colleague the nature of the local judicial system: "Sheriffs sometimes connive at lynchings. Police often murder wantonly. . . . If you knew the extent of the maltreatment of all classes of colored people by some members of the police force, it would amaze you. Brutal assaults, and wanton, wanton, wanton murder of man after man has been committed and yet not even a reprimand has ever been given to those who have done the killing, though witnesses of character, white and colored, have endeavored to bring the accused to trial" (120–21).[16] Law at the local level is depicted as hopelessly biased and dramatically flawed, a place where those in control thoughtlessly act out, without variation, their roles as "repressionists."

The third system of justice portrayed by Griggs involves the highest court in the land, the Supreme Court. Griggs's treatment of the court and its rulings is two-part. His characters frequently denounce the court, which is often described as being the source of all the injustice to which African Americans are subjected. This criticism stems from the court's many decisions that effectively nullified the 1875 Civil Rights Act, chief among them being the *Plessy v. Ferguson* ruling, which legalized the concept of "separate but equal." Moreover, the Supreme Court had taken no steps to rectify the widespread disfranchisement of southern blacks and, in fact, had upheld prejudicial state suffrage laws in its 1898 *Williams v. Mississippi* ruling. The politically minded characters in Griggs's texts find the Supreme Court inherently responsible for the perversion of law at the state and local level, as Belton Piedmont states in *Imperium in Imperio:* "Remember this, that the Court of last resort has set the example which the lower courts have followed. The Supreme Court of the United States, it seems, may be relied upon to sustain any law born of prejudice against the Negro and to demolish any law constructed in his interest. . . . If this court . . . sets such a terrible example of injustice, it is not surprising that its filthy waters corrupt the various streams of justice in all their ramifications" (237). By denying African Americans their rights to legal recourse, the Supreme Court not only splinters blacks from the full rights of American citizenship but also separates the nation from its highest ideals.

Even though Griggs repeatedly portrays the Supreme Court as grievously deficient in its regard for African American rights, the plots of his novels often culminate in a hearing before the court. In every case, the black litigants emerge victorious. Despite the acknowledgment of Bernard Belgrave, president of the Imperio, that "the highest court in the land is the chief bulwark of caste prejudice in democratic America" (*Imperium* 213), the federal court is imagined by Griggs in the narratives as a place divorced from local and even federal prejudices and politics, a place where justices weep at the truth and beauty of the words of African American lawyers and acquit black defendants who have been accused and convicted in local courts. Here is where the "tragic mulatto,"[17] so familiar in both black and white fiction and often the victim in Griggs's lower courts, becomes the courageous trial lawyer who wins the case and not only saves his client but also redeems the nation.

In Griggs's fiction, the Supreme Court is a realm of reason and right emotion, a purified world. Griggs does not describe this world with any clarity (in fact, the Supreme Court trials are often glossed over in his novels), but it symbolizes hope and the potential for change. If, as Belton Piedmont states in *Imperium in Imperio,* the highest court in the land is the "filthy waters" that contaminate the "streams of justice," its purification can, in turn, wash clean the impure and corrupt judicial system. In Griggs's aptly named *Pointing the Way,* for example, the Supreme Court's decision to rule against restrictive southern suffrage laws leads to the spread of a new "movement throughout the South" (231). The novel's characters devise a "peaceful adjustment of the race question," which gains national acclaim and becomes "a model of procedure for other communities" (231). In this instance, the high court's support of the unified black struggle leads to a new level of peace for all Americans.

Griggs depicts several scenarios in which justice prevails because of a coalition of African Americans from all walks of life and the participation of black lawyers in the legal process. Ultimately, a safe and peaceful society is realized only through cooperation between blacks and whites. In his passages about Supreme Court cases, Griggs envisions, through African American intervention, a healing for both black and white America. In effect, his novels serve as a mediation of history, an attempt, through fiction, to demonstrate not only how defiled American systems of justice have become but how they can be cleansed, redeemed, and rectified. Imbedded in the texts are both reflections of the present and a transformation of that present into the future. The writings of Griggs become, as Homi Bhabha says of other writers who occupy literary space in the beyond, "a meditation on the disposition of space and time from which the narrative of the nation must *begin.*"[18] The true power of Griggs's law motif comes not from his brutal representations of lynching and mob law, nor from his dramatization of the farce that local justice has become, but from his ability to reinvent the Supreme Court in his fiction. Griggs moves beyond the questioning of other contemporary texts and begins to supply answers, and his novels are notable for the way they depict a national healing through black inclusion.

In all of his novels, Griggs is highly critical of the restrictions placed on African Americans, of officially sanctioned violence, and of a Supreme Court that echoes and supports the most racist impulses of society; but he is also critical of black leadership that does not effectively address those problems. Just as he imaginatively heals the nation in his narratives, Griggs uses various methods to depict the inconsistencies of certain political positions held by African Americans. Although most of his rhetorical power is aimed at revealing the injustice of white America, he occasionally finds room to analyze the role of black complicity in this injustice.[19] In almost every novel Griggs wrestles with the figure and ideas of Booker T. Washington, who had a virtual monopoly on the public stage when it came to African American issues.[20] The event that had propelled Washington into the center of the discussion of race relations was his speech at the Atlanta Exposition of 1895. This speech, which came to be known as the "Atlanta Compromise," reassured white southerners and the nation as a whole that African Americans in the South were a loyal and patient citizenry that had nothing but respect for their white neighbors. Though Washington made some pleas for the easing of economic restraints, he promised that social equality was not on the minds of black Americans. This position on race relations stands in obvious opposition to Griggs's central theme of black political unity leading to full American citizenship.

In *Imperium in Imperio,* Griggs seems to parody Washington's speech and white America's reaction to it. The book begins with the schoolboy days of the two main characters, Belton Piedmont, who is the dark-skinned son of an ex-slave, and the light-skinned Bernard Belgrave, who was born into a certain amount of privilege. The boys, though friends, compete in an oratory contest on the day of their high school graduation, and the speech given by Piedmont, entitled "The Contribution of the Anglo-Saxon to the Cause of Human Liberty," reaches many levels of irony and humor. That a black youth in the South whose own mother had been a slave would write and perform such a speech is ironic, but the real humor lies in the description of how taken his white audience is with his words: "The white people who sat and listened to his speech looked upon it as a very revelation to them, they themselves not having had as clear a conception of the glory of their race as this Negro now revealed" (32–33). This "revelation" is evidence of a peculiar phenomenon that often accompanies ethnic American and mainstream American interaction. In this phenomenon, which Dana Nelson terms "the white gaze," Anglo Americans are unable to see or comprehend situations involving individuals of other ethnicities because their perception is clouded by assumptions they hold about those groups.[21] Though the inability to know or recognize the reality of another is inherently damaging both to the viewer and the viewed, at times the subject of the gaze can use this inability to his or her advantage. Piedmont's audience is unconscious to any possible irony or manipulation because he is saying exactly what they want to hear.

The full range of the irony in this scene lies in the relationship between the speech, the speaker, and the audience. The white audience has come to witness the speech contest and commencement exercise at the substandard black school in their town. They are given the front-row seats, indicating that their presence is more valued than the African American members of the community in attendance, including the families of the contestants and graduates. The black citizens, who live with segregation in every aspect of their public lives, are now restricted to the back rows in one of their own institutions. Piedmont's speech reassures the white audience members that, despite these seemingly unjust conditions, they should be proud of themselves as purveyors of human liberty. What the text suggests is that white America has always been more willing to listen to race rhetoric than to evaluate the complex and paradoxical race realities in the United States. The audience is able to disregard who they are and where they are, in terms of their white privilege, and accept the "glory of their race" as revealed by a black high school student.

The irony of the situation continues as the judges (who are all white) convene to discuss who should win the prize for best oratory. Though all were thrilled with Piedmont's topic and admired his presentation, they simply found it inconceivable that the prize could go to the darker contestant. Their deliberations include the assessment that the "black nigger has beat the yellow one all to pieces this time, but we don't like to see nigger blood triumph over any Anglo-Saxon blood" (35). And so the judges, though they presume to recognize themselves as the "contributors to the cause of human liberty" described in Piedmont's speech, unblinkingly perpetuate an injustice against the darker African American by declaring his rival the winner. There is an obvious parallel here to the nation's reaction to Washington's Atlanta Exposition speech. Though lauded far and wide in 1895 as a reasonable answer to racial strife in the South, it was followed in 1896 by the *Plessy v. Ferguson* decision, which made "separate but equal" the law of the land.

Piedmont's boyhood speech is only the first example of Griggs's treatment of Washington's politics and legacy.[22] Though his novels advocate unity at all levels of black society, they clearly indicate that some responses to the oppression of blacks will not serve to coalesce African Americans as a people or lead to their full participation as U.S. citizens. Just as Griggs repeatedly depicts and rejects armed revolt, he also conjures up Washington's model of African American citizenship, only to reveal its inefficacy. The problem with Washington's metaphor for black and white relations—that "in all things purely social we can be as separate as the finger, yet one as the hand in all things essential to human progress"—is that alienation is antithetical to coalition building.[23] The ultimate goal of most of Griggs's plots is a twofold unity: cohesion among African Americans and cooperation between white and black citizens. In all his narratives, separation breeds fear, contempt, and ignorance. Griggs is careful to point out that between African Americans and whites and within black America there are a host of social structures that prevent meaningful contact between peoples.

Griggs also shows that these barriers are not impenetrable. The motif of crossing—that is, passing from one race to another and from one gender to another—becomes a metaphor of the false boundaries existing in the world. In most cases, the act of crossing is indicative of the fluid nature of racial and social constructions; it is also reminiscent of other "passing" novels of the time.[24] In Griggs's fiction, however, an African American's motivation to pass is rarely the mere desire to escape racial oppression. In his novels, blacks pass as white, whites pass as black, and men pass as women to gather information, subvert the order of society, or advance the cause of civil rights.

In *Imperium in Imperio,* for example, Belton Piedmont disguises himself as a woman and goes into domestic service to spy on whites. He finds that they have little knowledge of the discontent, intellectual activity, or aspirations of the African American community as a whole. Conversely, Ramon Mansford, a white northerner in *The Hindered Hand,* darkens his skin and passes into the black community to solve the mystery of his fiancée's murder. Not only does he discover the truth behind her death, but his eyes are also opened to the real injustices faced by blacks on a daily basis. In the same novel, Earl Bluefield, a light-skinned African American, passes as white to join groups of racist Democrats in the South in order to encourage them to reveal publicly their true position as race-haters, causing them to lose all political power. Another African American who is light enough to live as white in *The Hindered Hand* is Mrs. Seabright. Her goal is to organize all who can pass to infiltrate white society and, as she puts it, "to shake the Southern system to its very foundation" (236). However, Mrs. Seabright's plan ends in failure because it is ultimately divisive to the African American community, as she believes that individuals who decide to cross into white life must, to protect their new identities, cut all ties with their visibly black friends and relatives. In *Pointing the Way,* Eina, a dark-complected white woman from the North, chooses to associate herself with black society and to marry Baug Peppers, an African American lawyer. This may be the only example in American literature of a white character passing as black to marry an African American.[25] As these examples demonstrate, very few characters in Griggs's fiction cross social boundaries as a means to escape race. Passing in his novels is a subversive tactic. The few characters who pass because they want to live in white society, like Eunice in *The Hindered Hand,* are destined to cross into the realm of insanity because of their deeply divided psyches.

Perhaps the most singular instance of crossing racial barriers comes in *Overshadowed.* In this novel, Horace Christian, a white politician, has an innocent black man lynched to further his career; he also callously impregnates and abandons a respectable young black girl. Lanier, another white politician, makes a vow to seek revenge in the name of this girl. He convinces Christian to paint himself black so that they can "go among the darky girls and have a good time" (156). After Christian drinks himself into unconsciousness, Lanier glues a wig on his head and puts him in a prison cell in place of a young African American man who is condemned to die the next day. Christian, unsure of what is going on until the very end, acts the minstrel all the way to the gallows. The significance of this instance of crossing is multilayered. On the surface, Griggs is putting a white man in the shoes of a black man, making him the victim of an unjust execution. The act of hanging a white man in blackface also acts as a symbolic punishment of minstrelsy, a condemnation of white appropriation of black identity in order to exploit it. The scene also serves to subvert the southern justification for lynching. In this case, the white man pays for the actual sexual exploitation of a black girl. Finally, the scene revolves around and plays on the "white gaze." The fact that the guards and the gallery at the execution do not realize that they are hanging a white man in blackface stems from their inability or unwillingness to "see" African Americans. Lanier is able to pull off the switch because he is aware of the "species of contempt" that rendered whites "deficient in ability to readily distinguish" black men from one another (169). In this case, the white insistence that "all blacks look alike" comes into play to the detriment of one of their own. Like Captain Delano in Herman Melville's "Benito Cereno," the witnesses at the execution see only what they want or expect to see.[26]

Though each instance of passing has its own signification, the overarching motif of crossing points to the malleability of identity, race, and society. The various ways that people pass in Griggs's novels seem to indicate that in a world in flux, anything can change, anything can happen. By implication, if the reified realm of race can be breached, then other barriers can be crossed to bring about racial harmony in the nation. In several of the novels, for example, white characters decide to join the cause for black civil rights—as does Lanier in *Overshadowed*— despite possible opposition from their own race.[27]

Another stratification that must be crossed in Griggs's fiction is the social hierarchy within the African American community. Where African Americans of differing classes build coalitions, the old-school

black characters, who are often ex-slaves or who have lived their lives in
service to whites, prove to be powerful allies to the more educated black
characters. The best example of this new activism among the older generation is Uncle Jack in *Pointing the Way.* When he is introduced, he
seems to be a stock character of the Uncle Tom tradition. He is loyal to
all he serves and is adept at winning the good graces of whites through
presenting a humorous persona. Since the days of slavery, his way of
conducting himself has been, to paraphrase Ralph Ellison, to "tell the
joke and slip the yoke."[28] However, when the younger generation comes
to him with a proposal to help defeat disfranchisement laws throughout
the country, Uncle Jack is willing to drop the comic veil and become a
martyr to the cause. Through this character, Griggs addresses popular
stereotypes and subverts the depictions of this type or class of African Americans found in white American literature.[29] Unlike Tom in
Harriet Beecher Stowe's *Uncle Tom's Cabin* (1852) and Jim in Mark
Twain's *Adventures of Huckleberry Finn* (1885), Jack's loyalty is to his own
race, and in the end he sacrifices himself for the young generation of
black Americans.

It is significant that Griggs, who was one of the first writers to explore in fiction the reality of the "New Negro," the class of educated
African Americans who had never known slavery, is also one of the
few writers to redeem the image of the "Old Negro." He shows how
many of the characteristics revered by white southerners and despised
by the younger generation of blacks—such as humility and self-depre-
cation—often constituted a protective front that hid, out of necessity, an
individual's real intelligence and pain. This is the "veil" described by Du
Bois in *The Souls of Black Folk* and the disguise of Paul Laurence Dunbar's "We Wear the Mask" (1896).[30] When Griggs lifts this façade with
the character of Uncle Jack, he reveals a harsh fact about Jack's life: that
the Ku Klux Klan had killed his wife and children. Griggs shows that
what others had interpreted as docility or contentment was actually fear
and helplessness. Jack demonstrates to the younger characters that his
generation has just as much, if not more, incentive to act. He plays his
part in the plan to challenge suffrage laws in the South. On election day
he insists on his right to vote, despite his condition as a landless, illiter-
ate black man. His refusal to back down from the fight costs him his

life. The sacrifice that Jack makes for African Americans, and also for his country, indicates the advantage of alliances across classes. For African Americans, power is found not only in numbers but also in claiming all parts of the black experience and community. Such alliances in Griggs's texts suggest that the diverse population that comprises black America could be unified despite educational, generational, and color differences. His narratives of black coalition indicate that African Americans must create a coherent and cooperative body, a nation unto themselves, in order to gain their full rights of American citizenship.

In this sense, Griggs has been identified as a black nationalist.[31] However, to label him as such is to miss the complexity of what his novels actually depict. Inherent in the ideology of black nationalism is racial separatism, and that is where Griggs's novels deviate from the type of pan-African black nationalism that would be espoused by Marcus Garvey or the black separatist movements that would be explored later in the twentieth century by groups such as the Black Panthers. What Griggs seems to champion is a dual nationalism, one in which a black citizen can embrace both a racial solidarity and an American identity. This is not to say that Griggs does not depict separatist movements in his novels. In fact, the genre of the novel allows him to explore the potential and feasibility of a variety of political stances. Armed resistance or emigration to Africa are presented as undesirable alternatives to enduring the hardships of life in America, but they always lurk as possibilities for black citizens should the nation refuse to change its course. However, a careful reading of his texts reveals that the term "black nationalist" does not accurately describe Griggs's fiction. Whenever a true separatist, black national movement is depicted—as in *Imperium in Imperio*—it inevitably fails. Ultimately, there is no true hope depicted for black separatism in the novels of Sutton E. Griggs. The subtext of most of his nationalist plots is that white and black America are irreversibly connected.

Just as Griggs's characters transgress boundaries of class and race to build alliances and work toward the good of race and nation, his plots indicate that many of these boundaries have already been crossed and are always being crossed in one way or another. In seeking to unify black and white America, Griggs points out the fact that the two races are already connected in the most intimate way: by blood. The theme of miscegenation is not unique to Griggs. Since the days of abolitionist literature, writers had represented the relations between slaveowners and their female slaves as a compelling argument against the institution of slavery. Postbellum narratives often dealt with the fate of mixed-race individuals who were light enough to pass for white, pointing out the injustice of the American social system, which discriminated based on the fact of black lineage even when that lineage could not be detected by appearance. Though Griggs excoriates the rapes that were perpetuated against slave women by white masters and also condemns instances where all-but-white characters suffer when their black roots are revealed, his use of the miscegenation theme is most compelling when it becomes a metaphor for the hidden ties that bind white and black America.

In Griggs's fiction, there are several scenarios in which a light-skinned African American character is revealed to be the progeny of a revered white politician. In *Imperium in Imperio*, Bernard Belgrave meets his father for the first time on the night of his graduation from Harvard. In this clandestine encounter, Belgrave learns that he is the son of a U.S. senator whose "name was a household word throughout the nation," and that his mother's father was a governor (87). He is therefore descended from "a long line of heroes whose names are ornaments to our nation's history" on both sides of his family (90). In *Overshadowed*, Erma Wysong, who has to work as a house servant because there are no decent jobs for educated African American women, turns out to be the "daughter of the Hon. Mr. Lawson, Ex-Governor of Virginia, and Ex-Minister to Germany" (120). In *The Hindered Hand*, the light-skinned Eunice and her darker sister Tiara are descended from one of the founding fathers of the nation, as Tiara explains: "In revolutionary times one of your most illustrious men, whose fame has found lodgment in all quarters of the globe, was clandestinely married to a Negro woman" (234). And in *Pointing the Way*, no one can account for the enigmatic Baug Peppers. Everyone who meets him swears that they have seen him before but cannot tell where or when. The mystery of Peppers is solved when he goes to argue for the suffrage rights of African Americans before the Supreme Court. One of the justices immediately sees that Peppers is, in appearance, the exact double of a president of the United States.[32] This "American statesman" whose "name is indelibly written in the life of the nation," whose "likeness adorns all our walls," and whose "picture is in all of our school books" turns out to be Baug Peppers's grandfather. Though Griggs uses this motif more extensively than any other writer, the trope of the mulatto character with ancestral ties to important American politicians is familiar in African American history and literature. Rumors of the affair between Thomas Jefferson and the slave Sally Hemings had been circulating through black oral history from the early days of the nation until 1853, when one of the first African American novelists, William Wells Brown, wrote a fictional account of the fate of their progeny in his *Clotel; or, The President's Daughter.* These oral and fictional accounts, as well as the very real DNA evidence that has recently linked the Jefferson and Hemings families, serve as a powerful metonym of an American reality, representing how black and white America have always been on intimate terms and demonstrating that black America is by all rights an heir to America both by association and by blood.

In all of Griggs's novels, African American and white American characters collaborate in all sorts of ventures, positive and negative, belying the notion that there ever was or could ever be a true separation of the races. Griggs suggests that the lives of blacks and whites in the United States are destined to be closely intertwined, and that for the health of the individual, the region, and the nation, the nature of this closeness had better be a positive one. This entanglement of races is represented in a rather stunning scene in *Overshadowed.* Horace Christian, the politician who has a black man lynched to win an election, feels compelled to go back under the cover of night to view the body of the innocent man he has had killed. As Christian leans close to the victim to read the placard that has been placed around his neck ("Whatsoever a man soweth, that shall he also reap"), he loses his balance. As Christian describes the scene: "I fell forward, and clutching at anything to keep from striking the ground, caught hold of the dead Negro. My weight, added to his, broke the rope, and we fell down together, my head getting caught under his mangled form" (134). This morbid physical entanglement is emblematic of the fate of the South and the nation. America has the choice of building democratic alliances, as in

Pointing the Way, or of falling, like Horace Christian, under the weight of injustice and violence.

In his fiction, Griggs makes it clear that the political oppression, social restrictions, and personal violence that circumscribe the lives of African Americans, especially in the South, have reached a critical state. As the heroes and heroines in his novels watch friends and relatives lose their lives, minds, and spirits to racial oppression, they each make a positive decision to dedicate their lives to solving the race question. Griggs underscores the importance of this issue by having many of his novels revolve around a recurring story line. In *Overshadowed, Unfettered, The Hindered Hand,* and *Pointing the Way,* domestic happiness is impossible until racial harmony is achieved. In three of these novels a female character cannot or will not marry her beloved until race relations are healed, and in *The Hindered Hand* a husband is compelled to bring an end to racial antagonism so that his wife may regain her sanity.

These plot constructions, though seemingly peculiar, speak to the heart of what was at stake for African Americans. Griggs, as a Baptist minister and a social theorist, believed marriage to be the central contract of civilization. In this worldview, just as the foundation of a sound society depends on a stable relationship between a husband and wife, so the basis of a strong marriage depends on a stable society. The fact that Griggs's heroes and heroines cannot make a home until society has been healed of its racial tensions indicates that he saw no hope for a stable African American community without political and social equality, without the full participation of blacks in American life. In all of his novels, characters take the decisive, irrevocable step of dedicating their lives to ending racial division, and in so doing they cross over from personal ambition to political action in order to obtain domestic stability.

The potential of race to cause fragmentation, which is evident in the plots concerning marriage, is further delineated in the recurring depiction of insanity and suicide. In Griggs's novels, all the characters who lose control of their faculties or decide to take their own lives do so because of the state of race relations in America. In his literary world, race drives people crazy. It is not the condition of being black (or white) that makes individuals insane; rather, the disturbing public attitudes about race lead characters into schizophrenia or depression. These examples of madness can also be read as metaphors for a nation that is unstable and dangerous because of its inability to accept and integrate its different parts. Several black characters undergo transitions in their mental health because of racial matters. Their deterioration is obvious to their friends and lovers because their madness leads them into a state that separates them from those around them.

The first African American character in Griggs's novels to succumb mentally to the confusion of race in America is the beautiful Viola Martin in *Imperium in Imperio.* Viola's compelling characteristics are her intelligence, her devotion to the African American community, and her very dark complexion. She is the girlfriend of Bernard Belgrave, who shares all her traits except for the fact that he is light-skinned. Unfortunately for them both, Viola read a book at the impressionable age of eighteen that had stayed with her, eventually leading to her bewilderment and suicide. The book, *White Supremacy and Negro Subordination,* convinced her that "the intermingling of the races in sexual relationships was sapping the vitality of the Negro race and, in fact, was slowly but surely exterminating the race" (173).[33] In order to save African Americans from extinction, Viola dedicates her life to splitting up mulatto couples and convincing black prostitutes to "cease their criminal conduct with white men" (174). In order to prove to those she advises that she is sincere about her crusade, she vows "to never marry a mulatto man" (174). On the night that Belgrave proposes to her, she kills herself, explaining her motives in a suicide letter. The irony is that a woman dedicated to the cause of equality is removed from the collective struggle because of an essentially racist text. Griggs's representation of Viola's fate is significant on another level. He shows how the prevalent racial theories of the day, when taken for truth by the American public in general, become ingrained in the psyche of black Americans and can become a part of their worldview as well. This theme becomes central to African American literature in the twentieth century and is explored in many of the century's most important novels, including Richard Wright's *Native Son* (1940), Ralph Ellison's *Invisible Man* (1952), and Toni Morrison's *The Bluest Eye* (1970), in which the acceptance of racist cant by African Americans is depicted as essentially self-destructive.[34]

Griggs also shows how well-intentioned but wrong-minded agendas can be destructive to the cause of black unity and African Americans' inclusion into American political and social life. In Viola's case, for example, an intelligent, noble, and sympathetic character acts as a splintering force (by attempting to break up couples) before taking her own life. What is meant to be a sacrifice made for her cause is really a waste of a powerful African American advocate. Her actions also lead Belgrave to make a vow to forever separate the races. It is as the eventual leader of the Imperium in Imperio that he adopts the plan for black Americans to split violently from their native country.

In *Overshadowed*, John Wysong is affected so deeply by the prevailing racial milieu that he too is led to extreme behavior. Wysong is a young black man who is depicted as an independent, hardworking, and compassionate citizen. His goal is to make enough money to pay off the mortgage on his family home so that he can sell it and send his sister to college. He does not regret forgoing college himself, for opportunities available to black men with "a literary education" are scarce (92). He is confident that he has made the right choice to learn a trade and take care of his family financially. When he is called into his foreman's office, he is sure that he is about to be promoted. The foreman begins the meeting by praising the young employee's character and work ethic, telling him that "you have been a good faithful workman and we have liked both you and your work, you have been so polite, industrious, punctual, and painstaking" (92). Despite his industry and his popularity in the shop, Wysong has been called in not for a promotion but for a pink slip. The labor union has ordered that he be discharged, declaring that none of its members will work with non-members and that "colored" men cannot join the union. Therefore, Wysong is forced out of his job.

The young laborer's predicament is a comment on both the racial atmosphere of the time and the position of the most visible black leader of the day, Booker T. Washington. John Wysong seems to follow all the advice put forward in Washington's *Up from Slavery*. He is industrious, faithful to his white southern employers, thrifty, and devoted to his family. He even takes up a useful trade, as Washington recommends, and forgoes a liberal education. In the end, however, all these traits and decisions amount to nothing in society, which disallows the advancement of a black man under any circumstances. John and his sister Erma, who had been on their way to accomplishing their modest dreams through thrift and hard work, find themselves "penniless and homeless" (96).

Wysong's dismissal from the shop is only the beginning of a very effective melodramatic tale that portrays the deep psychological effects of racism and disfranchisement on the psyche of the African American male. After he loses his job, Wysong's economic status and mental state are severely altered. Where once he was the happy, confident, competent breadwinner in his family, he now finds himself "being shut out from all of the departments of skilled labor on account of his color, he had been forced to join the large army of unskilled laborers, grabbing here and there in a desultory manner at every little job of work that appeared, having no steady employment" (98). By coincidence (a major element in melodrama), Wysong is hired to drive the carriage of the Master Workman of the Labor Union of the United States in a big Labor Day celebration. As the carriage goes through the streets, the Mayor of the city proudly points out a church that represents the total dispossession of African Americans. The Mayor tells his guest, "That building is a potent example of how well we have the labor situation in hand in the South. That church edifice is one of the very finest in the city, and is being erected by a congregation of poor Negroes, and yet, not a brick is being laid, nor is a nail being driven by a Negro" (99). The fact that poor black citizens are barred from building their own house of worship so that white laborers are assured work gives Wysong insight into how race and power operate in his community.

The Master Workman, who comes from the North, reveals that white supremacy and racial prejudice in the workplace are not limited to the southern states. In his opinion, the difference between blacks and whites is that blacks have "an abnormal respect for authority," while whites will "ignore all laws, defy all constituted authority, overthrow all government, violate all tradition" to get what they want (101). In the Master Workman's final analysis, "The Negro, lacking this spirit, has no place in our ranks" and so will never be allowed equality in the workforce (102). As Wysong sits silently by and listens to this conversation, he slips into madness:

His mind could go no further. It was in a whirl. Over and over the words of
the Master Workman rang in his ears: "If a foe stands in our way and nothing will dislodge him but death, then he must die." The clatter of the horses'
hooves seemed to say this; the revolving wheels of the carriage seemed to
repeat it over and over, and the hum and noise of the city seemed to be but
a loud echo of the sentiment that had fallen into Wysong's already disor-
dered brain. . . . His hands trembled with nervous excitement, and his eyes
were red and wild-looking. (102)

As often happens in Griggs's novels, when the order of the world as
it should be, or as it claims to be, is disrupted, characters cease to be
able to make sense of things. Their madness is a reaction to an insane
world; in order to operate within the maxims of this new order as they
understand it, they often go against everything that they believe is right.
This is what happens to John Wysong. He has already been a victim of a
society that does not operate in accordance with its own rules. He had
believed that hard work, loyalty, thrift, and compassion would result in
advancement in the workplace. His path clearly reflected the views of
Booker T. Washington, which southern whites agreed was the course
that would gain blacks a level of comfort and protection. Wysong, however, had gained nothing by his hard work and dedication; in fact, he
had lost everything simply because of the color of his skin. As he listens
to the leader of the organization that had caused his downfall proclaim
the essential truth of white supremacy, Wysong snaps.

As he slips into insanity, he becomes like the Anglo-Saxon that the
Master Workman describes. As the union leader and the city dignitar-
ies look at the view from the tower of the city hall, "the seed of murder
dropped into his heart," and Wysong, who stands unnoticed behind the
group, quickly shoves the Master Workman out of the window (103).
One man grabs the Master Workman's coat, and for a suspenseful moment all look in horror at the dangling man. But the coat rips, and the
Master Workman falls. His end is vividly described: "Fifty feet from
the top of the tower the body struck a protuberance, bounded outward,
and fell plump upon the iron palings two hundred feet below, and
they ran their narrow shaped heads through his body as unconcern-
edly as though they were stationed there from all eternity to receive
him" (105). Wysong's descent into madness and murder stems from his

continued existence in a world that does not make sense. He has followed the rules set by God and man, and he has listened to the advice
of the most revered black leader of the day, all to no avail. The fact of
race complicates all truth, all reality, and some, like Wysong, eventually
capitulate to it.[35]

In *The Hindered Hand*, Eunice Seabright is also fragmented by race
matters. Eunice inherits a sort of racial ambiguity from her mother,
Mrs. Arabelle Seabright, who has separated the family according to
skin color in order to follow a mad plan of racial inclusion. Mr. and
Mrs. Seabright and their two oldest children, including Eunice, are light
enough to pass as white, but their daughter Tiara is not. Mrs. Seabright
compels the older two children to live as whites in high society and to
cut ties with Tiara. Mrs. Seabright's plan is to have all African Americans who are light enough to pass infiltrate white society and change
public sentiment by championing black equal rights from the other side
of the color line. She forces Eunice to marry a prominent judge, the
Hon. H. G. Volrees, so that Eunice may have influence in the judicial
system. Eunice leaves Volrees shortly after the wedding and hides out
with her sister until she is able to sneak off to another state and marry
the man she really loves. Her new husband is also an African American who is light enough to pass, and they change their names and live
peacefully among the white community in Louisiana.

Eunice's peace is broken and her mind is shattered when she is
called to trial for bigamy after her whereabouts are discovered. At the
trial, Tiara, as a reluctant witness, reveals her mother's plan and her
sister's racial heritage to the court and the large crowd in attendance.
Eunice's reaction to her sister's testimony is to beg for a conviction. If
she is considered "a Negro woman," then her marriage to Volrees would
be unlawful, as there was no legal marriage between races. She prefers
to be considered white, even if it means her conviction as a bigamist,
and so she begs, "I implore you to convict me! Send me to prison! . . .
Let my son know that his mother is a convict, but in the name of
heaven I ask you, send not my child and me into Negro life. . . . My
God! The thought of being called a Negro is awful, awful!" (242). There
is some sympathy for the beautiful suffering girl, but in the end the
jury and the public adhere to the warped notion of race relations that

would "cast away" the offspring of its great men in order to "prevent a lapse that would taint our blood" (244). When the jury pronounces her not guilty, Eunice begins her shift into black life and eventually into madness. When she leaves the courthouse, her world is immediately changed. She is moved to the back of a streetcar, called "nigger," and thrown out of the hotel in which she has been staying. By the time her husband finds her, she is ranting and raving and considering killing herself and her child.

Viola, Wysong, Eunice, and other characters who break apart spiritually and psychologically represent the devastating power of racism in America. The fate of these characters stands in relation to others who are lynched, several of whom are literally torn apart physically for souvenirs. While lynchings are depictions of fragmentation at the most personal level, Griggs also shows how the divisive nature of racial antagonism can shatter stability at every layer of society. In the realm of the family, the intimate bond between a man and a woman may be disrupted because racial repression hinders the potential for an open, secure relationship. The black community is depicted as splintered because its members make invidious and inherently prejudiced distinctions based on class and color. Communication between blacks and whites is often shown to be discordant because of the racial milieu. And, finally, the nation itself is represented as sadly split, separated from its noblest ideals because it refuses justice to African Americans.

Though Griggs depicts the contemporary state of race in America, he does not limit himself to descriptions of his present reality. While exploring many possible approaches to the problems of his day, Griggs returns again and again to the potential of black unity and full African American citizenship. Most of his characters express a sincere pride in their heritage. Those who do not, like Eunice, are destined to crack under the pressure of race. It is much healthier, Griggs implies, to fully accept this heritage than to deny it. Just as individuals must accept their birthright to be strong and whole, so black America must accept all segments of its society to be a strong, unified group. Internal antagonism along lines of class, color, and generation must be overcome. It was clear to Griggs that many white Americans were resistant to welcoming any segment of the black community, no matter how wealthy or light-skinned, into the political or social life of the nation. Therefore, to abandon or reject anyone in the movement for equal rights was tantamount to a loss of strength, both in terms of numbers and moral relevance. His vision was for African Americans to enter into mainstream American life as a collective, as a nation within a nation. In some of his novels, white America eventually welcomes this event, recognizing in its black citizenry what Griggs saw in them: a rich and complex group devoted to both their race and their country.

If scholars have largely overlooked the works of Sutton E. Griggs, it is probably because some of his extreme and even contradictory answers to questions of race are problematic for modern-day readers. But the very independence of his writing makes him worth studying, for he found room for a multiplicity of visions in the form of the novel. This genre gave him the space to explore—through the diverse positions of his characters, through countless changing scenes, and through varied writing styles—the potential for fiction to enact change. His texts may not have altered the course of the nation, but they did, in a way, interrupt the national discourse on race because they were emblematic of the potential of African Americans to imagine citizenship and the nation in creative ways. Through his meditations on social justice, Griggs offered the Supreme Court a new script, one based on the ideals of the country as expressed in its Constitution, and he proposed alternatives to the cycle of violence and corruption that the legal system had spawned. Above all, he presented his audience with a way out of contemporary modes of thinking that had limited the choices available not only to African Americans but to the nation as a whole.

As in other realist works, the acts of Griggs's characters resonate in society. Indeed, Griggs often exaggerates the scope of these acts. Plans laid by two or three people often have the power to change the country, as local movements take on a national significance. If an African American character writes an editorial in a Tennessee newspaper, it turns into a nationwide trend overnight; if a small southern town finds a way to achieve racial harmony, it gains the attention of the president and becomes a model for the country. Griggs, working with ideas in the medium of the novel, does not have to consider how plausible these scenarios are in his historical moment. His novels reflect Houston A.

Baker's "blues matrix" of African American discourse, which expresses "change, movement, action, continuance, unlimited and unending possibility," and which "achieves a resonant, improvisational, expressive dignity."[36] Griggs's failure to adhere to the strict contemporality of realism and naturalism, the dominant literary traditions of his era, may be one reason why he is all but ignored by scholars today.

The same factors that make Griggs an important literary and historical source also may serve to alienate a twenty-first-century audience. The author often resorts to exposition, a method out of sync with the realist movement. And yet Griggs's texts perform the most crucial function of realism, as they reveal a profound awareness of the social, philosophical, literary, and legal trends of his day. His novels often comment directly on legal decisions and allude to the works of other African American writers, including Chesnutt and Du Bois. He argues with Booker T. Washington's ideology in all of his novels. Griggs sometimes crosses into areas of thought that have not panned out, such as then-popular speculations about race that are identified today as essentialist in nature. It is worth exploring, however, the moments where Griggs seems to succumb to the zeitgeist, as well as the moments when he breaks free from contemporary conventions.

Griggs's creative imagination goes into theoretical and geographical territory unexplored by his contemporaries. There are instances in his novels where characters move beyond the borders of America and where he delves into the liberating and threatening possibilities of pan-Africanism; there is even a scene at the end of *Overshadowed* in which a character, convinced that there is no home in the world for an African American, becomes a "Citizen of the Sea"—an expression of the "black Atlantic" one hundred years before Paul Gilroy developed this theory.[37] Ultimately, however, Griggs's answer to the "race question" was not the black Atlantic, pan-Africanism, or even black nationalism. The political position that played itself out to the most satisfactory end in his narratives was a black racial solidarity that was not at odds with an American identity. There are obvious connections to Du Bois's idea of "double consciousness," but there are also important differences. Whereas Du Bois writes about fragmentation, Griggs depicts a healthy duality, one that is beneficial to African Americans.

In a political manifesto at the end of *Unfettered,* the protagonist
writes, "When a society is in a transitional state, men of imagination
are able through clear comprehension of the forces at work, to project
themselves into the new era, and, seeing where the movement tends,
place themselves at the head of the procession" (231). Sutton E. Griggs
was one of these "men of imagination" who clearly wanted to help the
nation cross over to a new era of civil rights. As things turned out, his
works did not gain widespread attention and were not pivotal in the
course of American history, but his novels nevertheless survive as a
testimony to the dedication of a creative and pioneering artist. Though
his writings may lack the literary polish of some of his contemporaries,
they contain imaginative energy and unbounded intellectual power.
At a time when the lives of African Americans were severely circumscribed, his novels achieved a kind of freedom not found in the works
of any other African American author of the day. This freedom may
stem from the fact that, unlike other great writers—such as Chesnutt,
Du Bois, and Dunbar—Griggs was secure with his audience. While his
contemporaries were doing the difficult and crucial work of opening
the doors of white publishing houses and opening the minds of white
readers, Griggs was writing for the African American reader. Hugh
M. Gloster contends that Griggs was more widely read among black
Americans than either Dunbar or Chesnutt,[38] and it may be that his
novels registered at a level that may not be easy to quantify, on a lower
frequency that did not transmit to literary centers but that resonated, at
some level, within black society. At a time described as the nadir of the
African American struggle for justice and equality, Griggs was imagining possibilities that were as yet not being considered by the American
public, such as coalitions between blacks of all walks of life who inspire
white citizens to join their struggle. His vision would become a reality
half a century later, with the rebellion of Rosa Parks and the activism of
Dr. Martin Luther King, Jr.

Sutton E. Griggs's novels occupy an important place in American
literary history. While Dunbar was creating the poetry of the age, Du
Bois the social theory, and Chesnutt the sophisticated realistic fiction
depicting black life, Griggs was projecting the present into the future,
writing black utopian novels that always laid out a plan for a better

tomorrow. He saw that the potential for African American wholeness lay in individuals living lives that fully embraced both their blackness and their American citizenship. His fiction represents both the struggles and the possibilities of an important era of African American history and literature.

CHAPTER FIVE

The Multicultural Perspective
of Sui Sin Far

SUI SIN FAR'S SHORT STORIES are significant contributions to American literature because of their early insights into the possibilities of diversity. Through the cross-cultural scenarios that she creates in her fiction, Sui Sin Far is able to explore how individuals from different backgrounds come to terms with one another, how interracial couples and biracial individuals make their way in society, and how immigrants deal with assimilation. An underlying theme of her collection *Mrs. Spring Fragrance* is that there is (or should be) room for more fluid and multifaceted expressions of identity in America. Though she only depicts characters who are white or Chinese or both, she still disrupts the "white and other" binary by showing the range of personalities and associations that inhere in the intersection of these two cultures. By exploring concepts of diversity within both Chinese and white American communities, Sui Sin Far's narratives invalidate the idea that insurmountable differences exist between Americans of different ethnicities. Her work thus opens up the possibility of Asian American citizenship.

Like other realist writers of the era, Sui Sin Far creates common characters caught in moral conflicts in order to show how ethical dilemmas play out in the everyday lives of men and women. In contrast to the sensational depictions, typical at the time, of Chinese people as exotic heroines and opium-smoking white slave traders, Sui Sin Far's characters are carefully individualized.[1] She writes of husbands and wives, brothers and sisters, parents and children, friends and young lovers. Her fiction is grounded in the familiar setting of the home. She places her characters in situations familiar to merchant-class Chinese immigrants to show the pressures of acculturation as well as the personal and institutional racism with which they had to contend. In her narratives, the key to overcoming these obstacles lies in bridging the distances between individuals. These distances were not always a matter of ethnicity; Sui Sin Far also wrote about the ways in which people of differing classes, genders, and generations could come together to find common ground. In her news articles about Chinese life in North America and in her two autobiographical essays, Sui Sin Far dismisses as absurd the idea that there are fundamental differences between races and cultures. She says more than once that "individuality is more than nationality."[2] Her works demonstrate this conviction by creating a diverse multicultural world to replace the homogenous image of Chinese Americans that had been perpetuated by other writers.

At about the same time that eastern and southern Europeans began to immigrate to the United States in great numbers, the nation's Chinese population was beginning to decline because of federal legislation that banned the entry of all Chinese laborers. The Chinese Exclusion Act of 1882 virtually halted a wave of immigration to the West Coast that had been going on for over thirty years. In 1849, residents in Guangdong, in the southeast region of China on the South China Sea, began to hear about the gold rush in northern California. Several hundred young men left that year to seek their fortunes; in the decades to come, several thousand more would follow. As early as 1851, the Chinese in America had developed a highly organized society, setting up associations, known as tongs, which were alliances based on family and regional connections. These organizations were created as social and political entities that were meant to aid and protect the Chinese in an often-hostile environment, and the first were based in San Francisco's Chinatown. The tongs also helped other Chinese nationals gain passage to America. Because of this network, most Chinese immigrants came from just two regions on the Pearl Delta River, the Saamyup and the Seiyup. According to Marlon K. Hom, "Saamyup natives in America often engaged in mercantile and other business trades; Seiyup natives, mainly laborers, accounted for seventy percent of the total Chinese population in the United States."[3] Many of these workers came to America because they were unable to make a living in China due to a combination of conditions that was making farming a losing proposition in the delta area. Ronald Takaki states that, "forced to pay large indemnities to Western imperialist powers, the Qing government imposed high taxes on peasant farmers; unable to pay these taxes, many of them lost their lands."[4] Violent rebellions over fertile lands, dense population in some areas, and a massive flood in the delta in 1847 also affected Chinese peasants. These events and conditions, and the poverty they produced, led many to head for *Gam Saan,* or "Gold Mountain," as California—and by extension, America—was called.

In the 1850s most Chinese Americans worked in the gold fields of California, and by the mid-1860s the majority were building the transcontinental railroad, which was completed in 1869. All the while, Chinatowns in the West grew as stores and service enterprises catering to the laborers were established. Though some Chinese in America prospered, and many were able to support families back in China with their wages, it was not an easy life. The United States was quick to establish double standards in points of law between the Chinese and white settlers in California. Some of the legislation targeting the Chinese in the West was based on a federal law, enacted in 1790, which stated that only white persons were eligible to become naturalized citizens. For example, in 1852 the California legislature established a foreign miner's tax that extracted a monthly fee of three dollars from any foreign miner who was not seeking citizenship. As the Chinese in California were not able to become citizens, they were the main targets of this tax. In 1855 a San Francisco resident, Chan Yong, applied for citizenship but was denied based on the 1790 law. This bias reflects the fact that the conception of what constituted an American was not broad enough to encompass Asian residents. There was a definite nativist attitude in California in relation to the Chinese during the gold rush, but their presence was more than welcomed by the capitalists of the Central Pacific Railroad. However, in the 1870s, when the transcontinental railroad was complete, there was an intense backlash against their presence in the West, which led to the Chinese Exclusion Act of 1882.[5]

Despite their precarious position as residents in America ineligible for citizenship, the Chinese often worked together to protect the rights to which they were entitled. The Chinese Six Companies, an association of tongs in San Francisco, lobbied the Chinese and U.S. governments to include a clause in the Burlingame Treaty of 1868 that protected the rights of foreign residents to do business in America. The rights of non-citizens to do business, travel, and work in the United States was also assured by the Civil Rights Act of 1870. In 1886, in the case of *Yick Wo v. Hopkins,* a group of Chinese laundry workers in San Francisco successfully fought the discriminatory application of a city ordinance all the way to the Supreme Court, and they won. The court ruled that the law, which required a permit to run a laundry in a wooden structure, was not in itself unfair, but the fact that the Board of Supervisors in San Francisco gave permits to eighty white applicants and denied them to two hundred Chinese applicants was blatantly biased and unjust.[6]

In spite of these victories in the world of commerce, Chinese Americans received little protection under the law when it came to their personal safety. Violent attacks on Chinese individuals and groups were common in the West, and perpetrators literally got away with murder time and again. Andrew Gyory recites a litany of riots against immigrants that left dozens of Chinese dead, the most violent of which was the massacre of twenty-eight men in Rock Springs, Wyoming, in 1885.[7] In addition to these physical attacks, the Chinese were also subject to racial slurs and unfair treatment as they went among white Americans. It is little wonder that they sought protection in numbers in Chinatowns across the West.

These conditions prompted many immigrants to return to China, but many more stayed and established themselves as residents, if not citizens, of the American West. It is estimated that the Chinese population in America was about 132,000 in 1882, the year the Chinese Exclusion Act was passed. Federal census numbers put the nation's Chinese population at less than 90,000 in 1900 and at 71,531 in 1910.[8] Despite this population decline, Chinese American culture thrived. At the turn into the twentieth century, some Chinese Americans were helping to develop California agriculture, and others were working in the fishing industry in such coastal towns as Monterey. However, most lived in

Chinatowns in western cities, where they worked as merchants and in the service industries. These Chinatowns, and especially the one in San Francisco, were cultural hubs where social, business, and literary organizations flourished. Though Chinese women did not come to America in great numbers, some did come as merchant's wives, and they constituted a small but important element in Chinese American society. The proof that family life was taking hold is evident in the fact that there were four thousand Chinese American schoolchildren in California in the early 1900s. These children, unlike their parents, were officially citizens of the nation.[9]

Nevertheless, at the beginning of the twentieth century, the majority of Asian men and women in the United States were still first-generation immigrants whose "lives were engulfed by the duties of childbearing, childcare, and the business of earning a living."[10] Most Chinese in America, both laborers and those of the merchant class, worked hard not only to provide for themselves but also to support family members back in their native country. Given such economic pressures, very little literature came out of these immigrant communities; and, of course, most of the first generation would have acquired written English skills for the purpose of business, not for the pleasure of creative writing. Fortunately, Edith Maude Eaton, a half-Chinese, half-English Canadian who had always had an interest in her mother's people, came to America and began writing stories from a Chinese American perspective. By all accounts, she was the first to do so. Writing under the pseudonym Sui Sin Far, she published her stories from 1896 to 1912 in several mainstream periodicals, such as *Good Housekeeping, The Century,* and *Overland Monthly,* and in 1912 her stories were collected in *Mrs. Spring Fragrance.*

Sui Sin Far, a writer with a Western education who was raised in Canada by an English father and Chinese mother, was not the typical immigrant. She took her subject matter from neighborhoods she came to know as a reporter, and she wrote more about what she observed than what she experienced. It is also significant that she did not depict, and probably was not privy to, the lives of laborers in bachelor communities, who comprised the majority of Chinese in America at the time.[11] Instead, she primarily wrote about merchant-class families. What she observed, however, was worthy of exploration. She depicted realities that were particular to her day, when Chinese and white Americans were coming into close contact for the first time, not only through commerce but also in social situations.

Sui Sin Far's attention to contemporary social themes makes many of her stories admirable examples of American realism. Like many of the realists who came before her, including Mark Twain and W. D. Howells, she began her writing career as a journalist. Because of her bicultural background and interest in her Chinese heritage, she was assigned to write about life in Chinatown by the papers for which she wrote in Montreal, Los Angeles, and Boston. Her training as a journalist is evident in the verisimilitude she achieves in her fiction. Her careful examination of the complicated social dynamics that Chinese immigrants faced at the turn into the twentieth century is similar to the social analysis central to the fiction of other American writers of her day.

Sui Sin Far's writing reveals a conviction that attitudes are in a large part determined by environment. According to Xiao-Huang Yin, "The idea that environment and association can significantly affect one's ethnic consciousness was . . . firmly rooted in her mind and later became an important theme in her writing, especially in the stories that are her major efforts against racial prejudice."[12] However, Sui Sin Far's stories are not naturalistic, in which environment determines fate, for she also believed that people were adaptable and that attitudes could change through relationships and understanding. As she said, "Prejudice can be eradicated by association" (227). Perhaps because of her own unique heritage, Sui Sin Far appreciated personal differences. Her stories contain engaging details of Chinese American society—such as traditions that had been brought to America and the food, dress, and accouterments of everyday life—without sensationalizing those elements. Her articles and stories show life in all its diversity, and she was accurate in her analysis of Chinese American customs and her translations of legends and poems. Her stories and essays indicate that she was proud of her heritage, angered by stereotypes, and wounded by prejudice. She describes herself as a sort of bridge: "I give my right hand to the Occidentals and my left hand to the Orientals, hoping that between them they will not utterly destroy the insignificant 'connecting link.' And that's all" (230). As a person of both Western and Chinese ancestry, she indicates that not only is it her responsibility to facilitate unification between cultures, but that her own survival depended on it.

Much of the criticism of Sui Sin Far's fiction has interpreted her stories as tales of opposition between the Americanized and the tradition-oriented Chinese in the United States. However, a closer examination of her stories reveals a broad spectrum of personalities, some more and some less Americanized; no one character corresponds exactly to another. This can be said of her Asian, biracial, and white American characters. The problem with stereotyping is that it focuses on one image or characteristic and applies that representation to everyone within the stereotyped group. By individualizing characters, Sui Sin Far challenges the notion that a cultural group can be represented by one personality or one attitude. She wrote in response to racist representations, and, according to Annette White-Parks, "One way to counteract such stereotypes is to stress a human essence that prevails across racial constructs. Sui Sin Far does this by individualizing her characters and their relationships with the world so readers of any racial descent can relate to them."[13] This diverse characterization establishes characters as individuals and not as representations of an entire race. When discussing the writings of Sui Sin Far, it is dangerous to talk in generalities because what may be said about one character will probably prove false if applied to another.

This diversity of characters is perhaps most apparent in stories in which individuals—both Chinese and white, male and female—are confronted with the complexities that arise as immigrants begin to adjust to a new society. The theme of assimilation, or Americanization, as Sui Sin Far calls it, runs throughout her stories. As Yin notes, "What really makes her stories attract critics' attention is her portrayal of the conflict caused by cultural barriers between tradition-oriented and Americanized Chinese—an underlying theme which appears in virtually every piece of her work. Indeed, it was her exploration of the transformation of the Chinese American community under the pressure of acculturation that impressed critics in her lifetime."[14] Though it is true that narratives of acculturation predominate in much of Sui Sin Far's fiction, Yin and other critics fall short in their analysis when they discuss Americanized Chinese and traditional Chinese as homogenous, oppositional groups and when they interpret Americanization as an all-or-nothing proposition. Sui Sin Far's stories portray a wide variety of attitudes and positions regarding Chinese and American cultures. The degree to which characters have been "Americanized" depends on their age, whether they were born in America or China, how long they have been in their new country, and on what may be called personal preference: how much and what aspects of Chinese culture individuals want to retain, and how much and what aspects of American culture they want to adopt.

Two stories that exemplify this selective acculturation are "Mrs. Spring Fragrance" and "The Inferior Woman," which work as companion pieces.[15] Mr. and Mrs. Spring Fragrance are a young couple who have been in the United States for five years, and they both speak English, the wife being even more adept at "the American language" than her husband (17). She has developed a taste for Western literature, especially poetry, but her husband prefers Chinese literature and has books sent periodically from Shanghai. The stylized syntax of their conversation indicates that they speak to each other in Chinese, but they have adopted the Western style of dress. He is a good businessman in the American sense, but his business transactions keep him closely connected to their home area in China. Their neighbors, the Chin Yuens, are older and have been in America longer. They "lived in a house furnished in the American style, and wore American clothes, yet they religiously observed many Chinese customs, and their ideals in life were the ideals of their Chinese forefathers" (17). Their daughter has an American name, Laura, which even her parents call her. Laura's boyfriend was born in America, plays baseball, sings popular American songs with her at the piano, and is "as ruddy and stalwart as any young Westerner" (17). However, he goes by a Chinese name, Kai Tzu, which indicates that he maintains ties with his heritage despite his nationality. Another neighbor, Will Carman, is an American of Irish ancestry who shares Mr. Spring Fragrance's interest in Chinese literature; his mother is a close friend and confidante of Mrs. Spring Fragrance.

Through this broad spectrum of characters, Sui Sin Far explores the ways in which some immigrants manage to find harmony in America despite the climate of prejudice that existed at that time. The plurality of personalities and the friendships between Sui Sin Far's white and Asian characters contradict Yin's conclusion that in Sui Sin Far's stories "one culture does not accept the other and the East and West are mutually exclusive. . . . Those who are recognized by American culture will be denied by the Chinese, and any attempt to bring Western values into the Eastern tradition will ultimately be crushed. As people are unable to synchronize the two different cultures, they will have to make a choice between them."[16] The characters in "Mrs. Spring Fragrance" and "The Inferior Woman" demonstrate that this analysis is not necessarily true. What enables them to find common ground is an informed respect for each other as individuals. In stories where characters seem to be "crushed" under "the pressure of acculturation," the dynamics revolve around individual decisions. In Sui Sin Far's stories, acculturation is not a totalizing social force but something that happens within the context of a community.

Two parallel stories that deal directly with the process of assimilation are "The Wisdom of the New" and "The Americanizing of Pau Tsu."[17] Some critics have found in these stories an absolute proposition: characters must align themselves with either China or America, because there is no middle ground between Eastern and Western cultures. However, as White-Parks recognizes, "Sui Sin Far's identity was not either-or but existed on a continuum."[18] In a way, Sui Sin Far's life depended on the finding of peace across cultures because that was the ground on which she stood. Instead of reifying cultural differences, she actually subverts binary oppositions in her fiction. Both "Wisdom" and "Americanizing" are about Chinese men who have achieved success in America and send to China for their wives. Both wives become distressed in their new surroundings. In both stories the husbands have a young white female friend named Adah. However, the stories' outcomes are quite different. While the end of "Americanizing" is optimistic and suggests that tensions between the couple will be resolved, the end of "Wisdom" is anything but happy: the wife kills their only child. Yin sees "Wisdom" in terms of mutual exclusivity. In his analysis,

> the tragic ending is shocking, but it is Sui's deliberate design, since she points out at the beginning of the story that America is a place both of gain and loss. The loss of the son and the family's disintegration thus can be considered a price the husband has to pay for obtaining "The Wisdom of

the New." While this story also dwells on the theme of cultural conflict, it is not made in the same mold as "Mrs. Spring Fragrance." Here Sui has a clear message to put forward through the tragedy: the price of Americanization may be so high that not everyone can afford or is willing to pay it, and it is impossible for Oriental and occidental ideas to reach a compromise.[19]

Such analysis obscures the subtle nuances of Sui Sin Far's work. Though her characters may be victims of institutional racism and prejudicial attitudes, they are not at the mercy of social forces, which would indicate the inevitability of circumstances and the inability to effect change. These stories, as works of realism, examine instead the ethical choices the characters face. Much of the tragedy in cross-cultural relationships could be avoided, Sui Sin Far suggests, if people, both white and Asian, had a sincere interest in the welfare of those around them.

Xiao-Huang Yin is not the only critic to see "Wisdom" as a story of the dangers of acculturation. Amy Ling also interprets it as a story of the mutual incompatibility of Chinese and American culture: "What is apparent and unambiguous . . . is that the two cultures are incompatible and mutually exclusive: the choice of one necessarily results in the rejection of the other."[20] In Sui Sin Far's stories, however, it is the relationships between husbands and wives and between Chinese families and their white friends that are problematic. Sui Sin Far reveals that assimilation is often difficult for individuals not because there is some universal East-West dichotomy but because of people's unexamined attempts to impose their will on the newcomers. This is especially evident when "Wisdom" is considered in conjunction with "Americanizing." Though both stories address the same theme, there are subtle differences between the characters, both male and female, Chinese and white, that make these tales very different psychologically.

"The Wisdom of the New" opens in China, where Wou Sankwei is growing up in a very pampered and sheltered manner. Being the "only son of the man who had once been town magistrate," he is not allowed by his mother to do manual labor, for that would cause the family to lose face (42). However, since the father has passed away, there is no money to send him to school. He is therefore idle, and his "mother and sister waited on him hand and foot," for "was he not the son of the house?" (42). Wou Sankwei's upbringing reveals his assumption about the position of Chinese women: they function as the servants in the background of his life. It is also significant that he started out in America as a laundry worker and only years later became a merchant. His background and history are quite different from those of Wan Lin Fo, the husband in "The Americanizing of Pau Tsu." Wan Lin Fo was not the eldest son, and he thus did not hold the same position of privilege within his family that Wou Sankwei enjoyed. Furthermore, Wan Lin Fo was "a well-educated Chinese youth" who came over to Seattle with his uncle to help him "start a branch of the merchant business which his firm had carried on so successfully in the different ports of China" (83). He therefore begins his life in America with some status.

The respective social positions of these Chinese men upon their arrival in America affect their relationships with their white friends. In fact, the status of these friends is also important. In "Wisdom," Wou Sankwei began his life in the United States as a laundry worker. Mrs. Dean is a white American, who, in her widowhood, takes on the task of educating immigrant Chinese men; in this capacity she becomes Wou Sankwei's teacher and friend. Adah Charlton is Mrs. Dean's niece who is visiting from the East Coast. She is therefore a sojourner, one who is merely participating in the lives of her aunt's students while on vacation. Their philanthropy, though well-intended, is subtly patronizing. In "Americanizing," Adah Raymond and Wan Lin Fo socialize on a more equal footing. Wan Lin Fo is a junior partner in his uncle's firm, and she is the daughter of his firm's silent American partner. They are not in the relationship of benefactress and student. Rather, she acts as an interested friend until the end. Adah Raymond lives in Seattle; she is not just passing through, and she does not come into the community with any intent to improve Wan Lin Fo's life. Her involvement with this family will have consequences, as she will continue to be a part of the community after her confrontation with Wan Lin Fo. In contrast, Adah Charlton will return to her home at some point after her conversation with Wou Sankwei.[21]

Though Adah Charlton is not overtly prejudiced, she and Mrs. Dean seem at times incapable of judging their Chinese friends fairly because of their insistence on maintaining previously held notions of what constitutes the "Chinese character." Their philanthropy is clouded by self-

interest, which is revealed in their lack of respect for those who do not
wish to be Americanized. When Adah Charlton attempts to guide Wou
Sankwei in regard to his conduct, the problem lies not in her advice,
but in the position of superiority from which she speaks. In her writings, Sui Sin Far frequently notes the existence of a variety of attitudes
regarding the Chinese; overt racism is only one of them. Her stories
include a number of characters who associate with Chinese Americans
and who have the best of intentions, but who still regard the newcomers from a position of superiority. A close look at the attitudes of Adah
Charlton and Mrs. Dean reveals the subtle discrimination inherent in
their relationship with their immigrant friends.

Most critics have seen these women as wholly benevolent figures.
White-Parks describes them as "white women characters whose lives
are deeply entangled with those of a Chinese American family and who
serve as guides, mentors, patrons, and friends of the family, as well as
catalysts of its tragic destiny. Only Adah is sensitive to the cultural complexities."[22] However, the selfless missionary who takes on the "white
man's burden" of civilizing the "heathen Chinese" is a stereotype that
Sui Sin Far examines often in her stories. The women in "Wisdom"
are not as destructive as some of the missionary characters who break
up Chinese American homes, as do the women in "Pat and Pan" and
"A Chinese Boy-Girl," but the effects of their actions should not be
overlooked. White-Parks notes that "regardless of the strategic roles
they play . . . the perspectives of neither Adah nor Mrs. Dean become
central in the text; their viewpoints function to assist the reader's understanding of the positions of Pau Lin and little Yen and Sankwei but
remain those of sympathetic outsiders."[23] However, the perspective of
these women is central to the text. Their conversations reveal that their
sympathy is conditional, and their viewpoints are suspect as well. The
position of Mrs. Dean vis-à-vis the Chinese community is representative: "Since the days of her widowhood Mrs. Dean had devoted herself earnestly and whole-heartedly to the betterment of the condition
and the uplifting of the young workingmen of Chinese race who came
to America. Their appeal and need, as she had told her niece, was for
closer acquaintance with the knowledge of the Western people, and *that*
she had undertaken to give them, as far as she was able. The rewards

and satisfaction of her work had been rich in some cases. Witness Wou Sankwei" (52). It is clear that Mrs. Dean sees herself as the dispenser of Western knowledge to a race that needs uplifting. She also believes that this role has given her insight into the "Chinese character." When Adah tells her aunt that Wou Sankwei's long-distance marriage is dreadful to her, her aunt replies that "it is dreadful to our minds but not to theirs. Everything with them is a matter of duty" (45). This explanation—that Chinese people are less prone to emotions than whites—is suspect, since elsewhere Sui Sin Far states that she writes to correct the stereotype that her mother's people are "alien to all other races in that 'they are placed and unfeeling, and so custom-bound that even their tears are mere waters of ceremony'" (234). There is no question that Mrs. Dean cares for Wou Sankwei; yet she is unable to abandon the perception that the Chinese are guided by custom and not by feelings, despite her friendship with a man from that culture.

The real nature of Mrs. Dean's discriminatory attitude is further revealed when she hears rumors that Pau Lin is jealous of the time Wou Sankwei spends with the Americans and that she does not want their son to go to the American school. Mrs. Dean thinks, "Such bigotry and narrow-mindedness! Here was a man who had benefited and profited by living in America, anxious to have his son receive the benefits of a Western education—and here was this man's wife opposing him with her ignorance and hampering him with her unreasonable jealousy" (52–53). Her ruminations highlight the fact that she is more than an outsider and less than sympathetic. Her consideration lies with Wou Sankwei, whom she believes she has succeeded in Americanizing, but not with his wife, who desires to have no part of Mrs. Dean or her niece and what they represent. Mrs. Dean believes that the Chinese need "was for closer acquaintance with the knowledge of the Western people" and sees that as her mission. In Pau Tsu she sees her efforts being rejected, and so she labels the Chinese woman an ignorant bigot. Mrs. Dean simply cannot accept the idea that a Chinese person would not want to assimilate. The more these immigrants are like her, the more acceptable they are. This is an attitude shared by some of the white characters in Sui Sin Far's stories. They try to fit those of other descent into their own realm of understanding, instead of expanding their view of the world to include new perspectives. Mrs. Dean is not very interested in the Chinese; she is interested in Americanizing them. She has, as White-Parks says of the mission woman in "Pat and Pan," a "lack of authentic interest in Chinese culture."[24] For Mrs. Dean, the exchange of cultural knowledge was never meant to be reciprocal.

"And this little Pau Lin," Mrs. Dean goes on to say, "has everything a Chinese woman can wish for" (53). This assertion coincides with her belief that everything with the Chinese is a matter of duty. Mrs. Dean believes that since Wou Sankwei provides for his wife materially, Pau Lin should be satisfied in doing her duty to him as a wife and expect no more from him. She will concede no claim that Pau Lin has on Wou Sankwei, since she believes that "there is no bond of interest or sympathy between them, save the boy" (53). She even resents Pau Lin's intrusion into her relationship with Wou Sankwei, as she perceives that his growing distance from her comes from his wife's influence and not from the fact that he has taken on the responsibilities of a grown man. She laments, "Before the coming of Pau Lin, he would confide in me every little thing that worried him, as if he were my own son. Now he maintains absolute silence as to his private affairs" (53). This passage reveals Mrs. Dean's patronizing relationship with Wou Sankwei, as well as her assumption that her role as friend and benefactress entitles her to have control of his family life.

In the midst of a discussion with her aunt, Adah Charlton has a revelation that Chinese women might have the same feelings as Americans. This epiphany serves to show how these women have felt all along. Adah sees as the problem Wou Sankwei's trying to "live two lives—that of a Chinese and that of an American." And Mrs. Dean replies, "Is it not what we teach these boys—to become Americans? And yet they are Chinese, and must, in a sense, remain so" (54). The women's views on the relationship between East and West coincide with prevailing societal attitudes; both Mrs. Dean and her niece believe there can be no common ground between the cultures. However, in her lecture to Wou Sankwei, Adah Charlton does have a new insight, and her advice for him to spend time with his wife is sympathetic to Pau Lin's position.

In "Americanizing," Wan Lin Fo has a similar confrontation with Adah Raymond, yet there are notable differences between this encounter and its parallel in "Wisdom." In contrast to Adah Charlton, the Adah in "Americanizing" has been consistently sympathetic to the Chinese wife. Another difference in the two stories is in the way the two men take the advice of their American friends. When Adah Charlton tells Wou Sankwei that he must spend time with his wife instead of with her, he feels himself being "exiled from Paradise" (59). But after being confronted by his American friend, Wan Lin Fo finds himself "wondering how he could ever have wished his gentle Pau Tsu to be like this angry woman" (91). In this comparison between his wife and his American female friend, Wan Lin Fo's devotion to and preference for his wife are clear.

Most critics have concluded that the conflict in these stories comes from the wives' unwillingness or inability to assimilate into American culture, as in James Doyle's cursory analysis: "'The Wisdom of the New' and 'The Americanizing of Pau Tsu' deal with Chinese wives who find it impossible to adapt to the free and easy social customs of Americans."[25] What the Chinese wives object to, however, is not American culture per se, but the insensitive way in which their husbands introduce it to them: through the intrusion of single, white, American women. Wan Lin Fo wants Pau Tsu to become Americanized and sees Adah Raymond as a good role model for his wife, so he invites her to his home quite often. Adah comes to understand the suffering of Pau Tsu because she relates to her experience as a woman, despite their cultural differences. Wan Lin Fo, who had wanted his wife to participate with him in the American experience, finally sympathizes with his wife's position and a compromise is reached in light of his new understanding.

Wou Sankwei, in contrast, has no interest in his wife becoming Americanized. He basically rejects her as a partner and spends his time away from home with Adah Charlton. Unlike Wan Lin Fo, who regards Adah Raymond as a family friend, Wou Sankwei's feelings for Adah Charlton may go beyond platonic friendship. White-Parks also notes the strength of his regard: "Though Wou Sankwei's love for Adah Charlton is unacknowledged and undeclared, it is suggested in the respect Sankwei accords the young woman, in the time he continues to spend with her even after his family's arrival, in the American education he wants his son to have."[26] This relationship goes beyond "free and easy social customs" and becomes a sign of disrespect towards Pau Lin, for a married man spending most of his free time with a single woman is not an acceptable social custom in America. Pau Lin, in turn, feels the "humiliation and shame of bearing children to a man who looked up to another woman—and a woman of another race—as a being above the common use of women" (51). Because Wou Sankwei can only see his wife as a household servant, their story ends in tragedy.

In the final analysis, Pau Tsu thinks that her husband is trying to make her into something she is not. In his eagerness to have her participate fully in his American life, he becomes insensitive to her feelings. Pau Lin's situation is much bleaker; she sees herself as being degraded. Her husband is using her as a housekeeper and childbearer, while he seeks companionship with Adah Charlton. While Pau Tsu is denied her personality by her husband, Pau Lin is denied her humanity.

Both Pau Lin and Pau Tsu seem at first glance to be stereotypically passive Chinese wives; both, for example, have been instructed by their mothers-in-law to maintain silence in the home. Nevertheless, Pau Lin expresses her displeasure at the position her husband has put her in by punishing their son for becoming American and by taunting her husband about his white friends. Pau Lin's killing of her son, however, indicates that she is much more than a dissatisfied wife. Her shocking act reflects the mind of a woman who has suffered not only countless acts of disrespect from her husband but also the loss of a two-week-old infant. Pau Tsu, in contrast, rebels by leaving her husband and writing him a note explaining that her departure is motivated by his wish for her to be like the white woman. Pau Tsu's act not only indicates her clear-headed intelligence, but also demonstrates she has been influenced by the independence of American women.

The actions of these women—and men, for that matter—demonstrate Sui Sin Far's intent to show that Chinese people "are one with the other peoples of the earth. They think and act just as the white man does, according to the impulses that control them. They love those who love them; they hate those who hate; are kind, affectionate, cruel or selfish, as the case may be" (234). Sui Sin Far's characters make decisions that negatively affect those around them, but some of them also recognize their mistakes and try to make amends. Her writings focus on the possibilities present in an integrated society, on how minds can be broadened and understanding between individuals can be reached. According to White-Parks, Sui Sin Far's "aesthetics focus on a world vision that is largely communal in its insistence that humans and other living beings must exist in harmony to survive. In this sense, Sui Sin Far's aesthetic is far ahead of her time and is startlingly contemporary. Appropriately, the underlying theme from her first work to her last is that people are not single-faceted."[27] It is not impossible for two cultures to reach compromise, but rapprochement must come from an understanding between individuals. The fault of Wou Sankwei and Wan Lin Fo lay not in their assimilation or even in their desire for their wives to be Americanized, but in not recognizing their wives' autonomy. The fault of Mrs. Dean and Adah Charlton was in not seeing the Chinese Americans as being like themselves. The theme of these stories is not that East and West are mutually exclusive, but that it is necessary to step outside of societally prescribed views to gain a true understanding between cultures, as well as within them.

However, the relationships and communities in Sui Sin Far's stories obviously are not without conflict. Sui Sin Far was primarily a realist writer who used her art to explore the implications of diversity; her work is not utopian. The commonalities shared by characters of differing backgrounds are often qualified by the acknowledgment that people living in the same country can have vastly different experiences. Even in the stories in which Chinese Americans develop sincere relationships with mainstream Americans, the accord they achieve does not shield the newer arrivals from the nuances of prejudice that their white neighbors are unaware of or simply dismiss as unimportant. This uncanny ability of mainstream Americans to see what they want or expect to see when they view people of color—a phenomenon also depicted in Griggs's works—prevents them from understanding the true implications of what it means to be ethnic American. For example, in "Mrs. Spring Fragrance," the title character writes a letter to her husband about a lecture she attended with a white friend. Her description of the evening, though seemingly lighthearted, is biting in its sarcasm:

> The Subject was "America, the Protector of China!" It was most exhilarating, and the effect of so much expression of benevolence leads me to beg of you to forget to remember that the barber charges you one dollar for a

shave while he humbly submits to the American man a bill of fifteen cents. And murmur no more because your honored elder brother, on a visit to this country, is detained under the roof-tree of this great Government instead of under your own humble roof. Console him with the reflection that he is protected under the wing of the Eagle, the emblem of Liberty. What is the loss of ten thousand years or ten thousand times ten dollars compared to the happiness of knowing oneself so securely sheltered? (210)

It is evident from the sarcasm in this letter that Mr. and Mrs. Spring Fragrance have a shared understanding of the ways in which America does not live up to its own stated ideals. The others in the audience do not possess this same understanding, which is why only Mrs. Spring Fragrance is aware of the irony of the lecture. This technique of embedding serious criticism of social and legal injustices within the text indicates that Sui Sin Far was aware of discriminatory political realities, although she most often chose to examine prejudices on a personal level in her fiction.

Later in the same story, a conversation between Mr. Spring Fragrance and Will Carman reveals that even between close friends, white Americans often have little idea of how their government's decisions affect their Chinese neighbors. In this discussion, Will tells Mr. Spring Fragrance that "just as soon as a foreigner puts his foot upon our shores, he also becomes of the nobility" (23). Mr. Spring Fragrance "dryly" asks, "What about my brother in the Detention Pen?" Will is obviously confused at having to confront the paradox of a nation that professes to be a free country but that is not equally free for all. He replies, "Now, you've got me. . . . Well, what a shame. . . . But understand, old fellow, we that are real Americans are up against it—even more than you. It is against our principles," thus making a distinction between himself and those who make and enforce discriminatory laws. As he obviously is considering the reality of detainment for the first time, he is only "really up against it" in principle, not in practice. However, Mr. Spring Fragrance does not let him distance himself from the actions of his government: "I offer the real Americans my consolations that they should be compelled to do that which is against their principles." Will, because he is young and because he cannot see that the matter has any relevance to his own life, dismisses the comment and the whole issue as only an individual free of such cares could. He tells his friend, "Oh,

well, it will all come right some day. We're not a bad sort, you know"
(23). This nonchalance and indifference indicate a rift in the relationship between the Chinese man and his white American friend, a rift of
which the latter is unaware.

The fact that friends and neighbors can be so apathetic about governmental policies underscores how difficult it is for Chinese Americans to deal with disinterested functionaries of the American government. Though most of Sui Sin Far's stories address legal and political
matters only tangentially, one story, "In the Land of the Free," deals
directly with the Chinese Exclusion Act.[28] Even here, however, Sui Sin
Far depicts a moment of indecision to show how the injuries inflicted
on immigrants are often, if not always, the result of ethically question-
able individual choices. The story's opening scene, in which a husband
greets the arrival of his wife and child from China, is disrupted by two
customs officials who debate whether to follow the strict letter of the
law and detain the child. The reflective nature of one official, who regards the couple "pityingly," is in stark contrast to the officious nature
of the other, who insists on taking the child from his parents (94). The
implication here is that arbitrary laws have only the power of individuals who choose to enforce them, or, as revealed in the conversation
between Will and Mr. Spring Fragrance, by those who choose to ignore
them altogether.

"In the Land of the Free" is political and emotional; it both addresses the national position regarding Chinese immigrants and shows
the anguish of a mother over the fate of her infant son, as the "law of
the land" literally breaks her family apart. The promise of America, represented by the mother and child entering the country in perfect trust,
is utterly disrupted by this forced separation. Even after the shock of
having their child taken from them, the merchant couple still has faith
in the American legal system to do the right thing; as the husband says,
"There cannot be any law that would keep a child from its mother" (96).
His words reflect a confidence that, though mistakes are occasionally
made, at heart the United States is a free and just country that protects
its most vulnerable. This trust is broken as time passes and the child is
not returned to the family, and the couple's faith in the system is further
compromised when they are taken advantage of by a greedy lawyer. Sui

Sin Far shows that behind the cold and impersonal legal system, behind the laws that separate families, behind the confusing bureaucracy and paperwork, there are individuals who perpetuate discrimination by their apathy, officiousness, or self-interest. If U.S. law regarding Chinese immigrants is exploitative, it is allowed to be so by the actions or indifference of individual Americans. On a broader level, the story suggests that exclusion from citizenship leaves otherwise productive residents vulnerable to grave injustices.

Just as Sui Sin Far addresses racial issues in her stories, she also depicts other social realities that were helping to shape a new, multicultural society. The dawn of a new century signified a time of change, and many women saw that Victorian mores could give way to new modes of thinking. Ideas of female autonomy and independence were finding their way into American literature, and Sui Sin Far—herself a single working woman—favored that of the New Woman, a popular realist theme that called for the full participation of women in American society. As with all her methods of characterization, however, she never relied on one type to stand for a group. The liberated female characters in her narratives represent the numerous possibilities for women in an age of change. In her stories, female independence does not necessarily mean trading in the roles of wife and mother for a career. Instead, autonomy is achieved when a woman is able to make her own choices about her life. Sui Sin Far carefully delineates the many areas in which a woman should be free to determine her own destiny. Sometimes that choice flows directly from the mainstream ideal of the liberated woman: not only should a woman be free to work and be financially independent, but she should also be able to earn her own living without being judged as unfeminine. Sui Sin Far's depiction of women's alternatives is broad enough, however, to encompass female characters who consider other options. If a woman is more comfortable as a wife and mother and her personality is not suited for the working world, then she should not be forced to work, and she should not be shamed by her decision. In Sui Sin Far's work, the theme of the New Woman is about American society honoring women's choices.

This theme of women's autonomy goes beyond the struggle between traditional gender roles and life in the business world. In many of Sui

Sin Far's stories, female characters are faced with questions of culture that they must resolve according to what they believe is right or wrong. If the woman is an immigrant or biracial, then she must decide how much or which elements of Chinese culture she wants to retain. Often traditional life choices, like marriage, are complicated by issues of race. As Sui Sin Far portrays the dilemmas that women face, she shows how these personal decisions are subject to outside scrutiny. In her stories, the individuals most likely to undermine or override women's personal decisions are men, most often husbands. Female characters are also subject to the criticism of society at large, which can strongly influence a woman's actions and which often judges her cruelly if she does not make the choice that conforms to the status quo.

While Sui Sin Far is careful to show how difficult it is for women to maintain their autonomy and integrity in a society designed to limit their potential, she also demonstrates that in a multicultural nation there is room for change and new opportunities. Although some husbands never allow their wives freedom of choice, others are more open to female independence. For example, in "The Americanizing of Pau Tsu," Wan Lin Fo comes to the realization that his wife is capable of deciding when and how her own acculturation will take place. Pau Tsu's very modern decision to leave her husband makes her an unlikely, yet decidedly, New Woman. Sui Sin Far depicts how the pressures of society can overwhelm a woman and negate her independence, but she also reveals ways in which women find satisfaction in their lives despite their decisions to go against the American grain.

In *Mrs. Spring Fragrance,* the first liberated woman is young Mrs. Spring Fragrance herself. She is a dynamic and compelling character who always acts according to her best judgment and who manipulates all around her into coming to more modern, inclusive decisions in their relationships. The three marriages in "Mrs. Spring Fragrance" and "The Inferior Woman" are products of her behind-the-scene maneuvers. Working within the role of the kind, obedient Chinese wife, she actually subverts passive stereotypes to bring about the happiness of everyone with whom she comes into contact. Through her caring intervention, the parents of both the Chinese American daughter in "Mrs. Spring Fragrance" and the white American son in "The Inferior Woman" make ethical decisions to resist cultural and societal pressures regarding the marriage of their children.

Mrs. Spring Fragrance, as a successful merchant's wife, has the luxury of deciding where she will divert her energies. In "The Inferior Woman," Will Carman's love interest, Alice Winthrop, is another kind of New Woman. She is a careerist who has the admiration of all her co-workers, but she is perceived as lower class by Will's mother. Alice will not consent to marry Will until his mother gives up her belief that she is beneath them. Mrs. Carman's view of Alice is clearly stated in a letter to the mother of the young woman she wishes Will to marry:

> It is incomprehensible to me how a son of mine can find any pleasure what-ever in the society of such a girl. I have traced her history, and find that . . . her environment, from childhood up, has been the sordid and demoral-izing one of extreme poverty and ignorance. This girl, Alice, entered a law office at the age of fourteen. . . . Now, after seven years in business, through the friendship and influence of men far above her socially, she holds the position of private secretary to the most influential man in Washington—a position that by rights belongs only to a well-educated young woman of good family. (35)

Sui Sin Far's depiction of Alice and her counterpart, the more high-born and educated Miss Evebrook, highlights class differences and the ways in which women often play a part in devaluing and excluding females in society. However, Sui Sin Far does not create the opposi-tional dynamic that might be expected. Alice and Miss Evebrook are friends, and Miss Evebrook, unlike Mrs. Carman, recognizes the value of her friend's achievements. Miss Evebrook, also a New Woman, is a suffragist who has vowed to forgo marriage for ten years as she works for the cause. This story of sisterhood between a working woman and a voting rights advocate can also be seen as a comment on the fact that no woman, regardless of race, class, or ethnicity, had the rights of full citizenship at this time.

Another story that examines female rights is "The Story of One White Woman Who Married a Chinese."[29] Though, as is apparent by the title, the main plot involves a cross-cultural relationship, the New Woman theme comes into play in a very interesting way. The narrator's first marriage is to an American man who considers himself a progressive

thinker and an advocate for equality between the sexes, but who is in fact
mentally abusive to her. The way that he denigrates her very existence
proves him to be not only oppressive and patriarchal but a hypocrite as
well. His main complaint—one that may have been viewed as ironic at
the time—was that his wife was not liberated enough. As in the case of
Wou Sankwei in "The Wisdom of the New," James is always holding up
other women as role models for his wife. He also is in the habit of bringing outsiders into their home, which ultimately destroys the marriage.
Unlike Wou Sankwei, however, the females that James finds appealing are
coldly independent businesswomen, such as his coworker, Miss Moran.

In an effort to satisfy her husband's desire for a working woman,
the narrator starts a new job when her newborn baby is only six weeks
old. She denies her own impulses and personality in order to serve her
husband's selfish demands but finds in the end that she is risking the
health of her child and her own mental health for a man who is just
plain no good. When the narrator overhears her husband making a pass
at Miss Moran, she asserts her independence and leaves him, beginning
her journey to self-fulfillment. She will not be like the New Woman
that her husband admires—stiff, mathematical, and businesslike—but
she will take risks that go beyond the scope of the women's movement
of the time. When the narrator meets her Chinese husband-to-be, Liu
Kanghi, their relationship begins as a platonic friendship, as he and his
family help her get on her feet. He gives her work to do for his business
that does not take her away from her child, and in this way he "made
her independent, not only of others, but of himself" (77). In this story
Sui Sin Far creates another vision of female independence. The narrator
is able to support herself, maintain her integrity as a mother, and make
her own decisions based on her own free will.

As "The Story of One White Woman Who Married a Chinese"
segues into its companion piece, "Her Chinese Husband,"[30] the theme
shifts from the narrator's right to determine her own future to her consideration of the fate of those around her. Once the narrator's conflict
of self is resolved—that is, once she is able to live her life on her own
terms—she becomes concerned with the destiny of her family and particularly of her children, who will be raised bicultural in a racist society.
In the stories in which Chinese and white Americans come together in

one family, Sui Sin Far's multiculturalism comes closest to the new frontiers of American diversity. In fact, "The Story of One White Woman Who Married a Chinese" and "Her Chinese Husband" are preceded by another story, "'Its Wavering Image,'"[31] which also portrays interracial relationships. Whereas "White Woman" and "Chinese Husband" are about a white woman and a Chinese man, the relationship in "'Its Wavering Image'" is between a young biracial woman and a white man. Through these relationships, Sui Sin Far portrays a range of subjects that have since become central to multiethnic American literature, such as Orientalism, white reaction to mixed-race relationships, and the status of bicultural individuals in both their communities and American society as a whole.

In "'Its Wavering Image,'" Mark Carson, a roving reporter who comes to Chinatown to see if he can uncover some good stories, seduces Pan, a biracial girl who is comfortable with herself and her life in her Chinese neighborhood. Like Mrs. Dean in "Wisdom," Carson has no real interest in Chinese people or their culture. He is attracted to Pan, but his construct of reality divides the world into white and other, and he is unable to get past his binary way of thinking. After he meets Pan for the first time, he asks his editor, "Is she Chinese or is she white?" indicating that he cannot conceive of an identity anywhere in between (61). As his relationship with Pan develops from friendship to courtship, Carson must convince himself that Pan is not really Chinese at all, and he tries to make her deny it as well. The two grow close as Pan introduces Carson into the world of her community. When he finally publishes his article on Chinatown, however, it is essentialist in nature and degrading to the city's Chinese residents.

Carson's actions reveal an attitude particular to East-West relations that Edward Said would term "Orientalism" some sixty years later. In Said's interpretation, "Anyone employing Orientalism, which is the habit for dealing with questions, objects, qualities and regions deemed Oriental, will designate, point to, fix what he is talking or thinking about, with a word or phrase, which then is considered either to have acquired, or more simply to be, reality."[32] Characters like Mrs. Dean in "The Wisdom of the New" and Mark in "'Its Wavering Image'" think that they "know" Chinese nature because of their association with individuals within that community. What they actually do, however, is come to conclusions based on preconceived notions of differences between East and West. In "'Its Wavering Image,'" Mark Carson enters Chinatown with an unquestioned conviction that Chinese ways and character are inferior to Western ways and character. He may have been representative of other journalists who perpetuated stereotypes of Asians and who fueled the idea of a "yellow peril" popular at the time. At the very least, Carson repays the openness and kindness of Pan and her community with disrespect and a lack of understanding. In his justification for writing his harmful article, Carson dismisses Chinese American life with the ethnocentric comment, "It is mere superstition anyway. These things have got to be exposed and done away with" (65). His motivation was never to bring his white readership into a deeper understanding of the world of their neighbors. His intention was to overthrow this world by denigrating it in the mainstream press.

This is the very attitude Said describes in his analysis of Orientalism. In his seminal article on this phenomenon, Said detects a Eurocentric approach to writing about Asia dating as far back as Napoleon's *Description de l'Egypte,* which he sees as "the archetype of all further efforts to bring the Orient closer to Europe." This book, and later Western texts that address Asian themes, are prone to the "Orientalist projection," which tends "to divide, deploy, schematize, tabulate, index, and record everything in sight (and out of sight); to make out of every observable detail a generalization and out of every generalization an immutable law about the Oriental nature, temperament, mentality, custom, or type; and above all, to transmute living reality into the stuff of texts, to possess (or think one possesses) actuality mainly because as a European nothing in the Orient seems to resist one's powers."[33] For Mark Carson, the effortlessness with which he entered the Chinese American community and the ease with which he won Pan's affection reaffirmed the essentialist Western notion that "nothing in the Orient seems to resist one's powers." His article, a perpetuation of Orientalist discourse, exacerbates the sinophobia in the white community and the distrust of whites in the Chinese community.

In her evaluation of early Chinese American writing, Elaine Kim concludes that the few other Asian American writers at the turn into the twentieth century were apologetic whenever they offered the slight-est criticism of American culture.[34] Sui Sin Far, however, is often scath-ing in her portrayals of white Americans. Yet she does not stereotype all whites as villains; rather, she creates characters who exhibit a broad range of attitudes in their dealings with their Chinese or biracial ac-quaintances. Though some of her stories contain sympathetic white male characters, Mark Carson is a scoundrel in "'Its Wavering Image.'" His character is an interesting variation on the popular Victorian theme of the "cad," who would sexually use a young woman if she allowed herself to be lured by his appeal. In "'Its Wavering Image,'" the love story is connected to the theme of culture, and so Carson's use and betrayal of Pan is based on his disregard for her cultural loyalty, not her virtue. The story's very title holds several meanings. It is in quotation marks because it is taken from a song in the story that Mark Carson sings to Pan. He sings of "the moon and its broken reflection, / And its shadows shall appear, / As the symbol of love in heaven, / And its wa-vering image here" (64). The song is a seduction, and it induces Pan to bestow her first kiss on Carson. The lyrics, however, reveal what neither of them seem to understand: that what they see in each other is but a distorted image. Pan, in her innocence, believes that Carson is a good man who cares about her. Carson, in contrast, seems to be playing with the Madame Butterfly scenario that has as its pretext Orientalist essen-tialism.[35] He believes that the power of his attractiveness as a Westerner will compel Pan to become whatever he wants her to become. Carson's conviction that the weak and passive East will inevitably capitulate to the strong and irresistible West is apparent in the way that he misuses Pan's kindness. The very morning after their first kiss, Carson begins to write the article in which he betrays Pan's trust and portrays Chinatown through the fixed lens of Orientalism.

It is evident that, until she read Carson's article, Pan did not see Carson clearly. After the article is published, however, she considers his attitude towards her biracial identity and his indifference towards her devotion to the Chinese American community: "None knew bet-ter than he that she, whom he had called 'a white girl, a white woman,' would rather that her own naked body and soul had been exposed, than that things, sacred and secret to those who loved her, should be cruelly unveiled and ruthlessly spread before the ridiculing and un-comprehending foreigner" (64–65). Obviously, Carson did not com-prehend the depth of her loyalty to her Chinese neighbors and culture. As she begins to comprehend what Carson has done, she starts to make racial distinctions herself. Her demarcation of white America as the "foreigner" (though she herself was born an American citizen) indicates that she has begun to incorporate oppositional racial categories into her own worldview.

"'Its Wavering Image'" is an insightful depiction of how limited the world is when observed through the essentializing lens of Orientalism. Even as Pan gives Carson room for growth through exposure to a rich and thriving community, he nullifies this opportunity by falling back on essentialist and racist assumptions. The idea that the feelings of the Chinese do not matter to Pan because she is (he thinks) white reflects on how he lives his own whiteness. Other ethnicities are there for his amusement and exploitation. This combination of arrogance and ig-norance, which is deeply rooted in his own racial identity, is what she finds repugnant in the end. She associates it with being white and so, in turn, rejects her own white heritage. Pan, who has lived into her early maturity with a comfortable acceptance of her biracial inheritance, is completely repelled by the utter lack of sensitivity she finds in Carson. When he comes to see her after a few months, he is surprised that she has not forgotten his betrayal, for "why should a white woman care about such things?" (65). He is surprised by her resolute declaration: "I am a Chinese woman" (65). In this narrative, the potential for the biracial character to act as a bridge between cultures is destroyed by blatant prejudice.

This story astutely reveals how differences become solidified and then oppositional. Pan harbors no racial animosity in her heart until she is confronted with it in the man who betrays her affection and trust. In this story, Carson's incapability of seeing beyond the rigid binary of "white" and "Asian" compels Pan to accept that binary in order to pro-tect her Chinese self from those who would destroy it. It does not fol-low, however, that East and West are incompatible, for she herself is the product of a union between a Chinese man and a white woman. The Chinese community, which seems to accept and love her, also welcomes

Carson when she brings him to Chinatown. There is even an indication that not all whites in the story are as caught up in the racial binary as Carson is. When he asks his editor, "What is she, white or Chinese?" the editor tells him, "She is an unusually bright girl" and a good storyteller, emphasizing her personal attributes, not her racial background (61). In the end, Pan retreats back into the Chinatown community after her encounter with the racial realities of America as represented by Carson.

In Sui Sin Far's other stories that depict the Chinese American community from the inside, the richness of culture and family life is evident in the setting of home. In "White Woman" and "Chinese Husband," the narrator's life is enriched and fulfilled through her relationship with Lui Kanghi and her contact with his Chinese family. With their help, the narrator finds the strength to make a decision that would have been very controversial in 1910 America: she decides to marry a Chinese man. The legal implications of this decision are noticeably absent; such a marriage would not have been lawful in California at the time.[36] However, the narrator moves away from the dictates of society and begins to see things with her own eyes. Her experience with Lui Kanghi's family reveals to her that "virtues do not all belong to the whites" (74). As she lived with her Chinese friends and became involved in their lives, she "lost altogether the prejudice against the foreigner in which [she] had been reared" (74). Close association leads to friendship, understanding, and eventually love.

After their marriage, Lui Kanghi is devoted to the narrator's "happiness, health and development." While she thus finds personal fulfillment from her marriage, there is a societal price to pay that affects their relationship: they are faced with "the constant irritation caused by the assumption of the white men that a white woman does not love her Chinese husband, and their actions accordingly; also sneers and offensive remarks" (81). Sui Sin Far examines how society's judgment of the couple affects them emotionally, and what she depicts is the internalization of that judgment by Lui Kanghi himself. The narrator becomes aware of her husband's "acute consciousness that, though belonging to him as his wife, yet in a sense I was not his, but of the dominant race, which claimed, even while it professed to despise me" (81). The narrator's concern is more for her husband's psyche and for their relationship than for what others may think of them. Her inward longing is for a life based on traditional gender roles, where a wife can freely nurture and care for her family and a husband can protect and support his dependents. Lui Kanghi's feelings of insecurity disrupt the structure that the narrator desires. By equating his wife with the power of the national majority, he upsets the balance of power within their marriage. Even in this evidently loving relationship, the reality of racial attitudes in the United States creates friction. The narrator laments, "In spite of all I could do or say, it was there between us: that strange, invisible—what? Was it the barrier of race—that consciousness?" (81).[37] In her depiction of this marriage, Sui Sin Far creates a union in which the characters can look beyond cultural differences to find a place where they can meet based on common goals, interests, and desires. She is also careful to show, however, that racism can permeate even this intimate sphere.

The stories of "White Woman" and "Chinese Husband" are about two adults who find a way to move beyond the social constructs and limitations of race, living together as nurturing and supportive individuals. Yet they remain concerned about how societal influences will affect the lives of their children. There are two children in the stories. The first is a product of the narrator's first marriage, the racially white daughter who will be raised in the Chinese community by the interracial couple; the second is the son that the narrator and Lui Kanghi have together. This child is of special concern to his parents because his experience will not be like anyone else's in his family. He will grow up biracial in America.

The end of "White Woman" expresses the mother's apprehension for her biracial child in a prejudiced society; she perceives that as her son "stands between his father and myself, like yet unlike us both, so will he stand in after years between his father's people and his mother's people. And if there is no kindliness nor understanding between them, what will my boy's fate be?" (77). The anxiety is mainly on the part of the narrator, as her husband "could not see as could I, an American woman, the conflict before our boy" (83). The father has a much more positive outlook; his view is indicative of the possibilities of multiculturalism. He believes that if his son embraces all that he is, both Chinese and white, no one can make him think less of himself. As he tells his wife

"What is there to weep about? The child is beautiful! The feeling heart, the understanding mind is his. And we will bring him up to be proud that he is of Chinese blood; he will fear none, and, after him, the name of half-breed will no longer be one of contempt" (82). The father expresses the ideal relationship between the individual and society in a multicultural world, where being a biracial citizen of the nation is an advantage, not a point of shame.

Another story of a mixed-race family shows interracial relationships from a different perspective. "Pat and Pan" is the story of a white child who is raised in a Chinese family.[38] His mother, who has no white friends, dies and leaves her infant son to the Lum Yooks, who had cared for her in her illness. The boy, Pat, grows up within the culture of his adoptive family. The couple also has a biological daughter, Pan, who is two years younger than Pat. The story begins with the closeness of the siblings, who are literally curled up together when they are sighted by a "Mission woman," Anna Harrison, who will lead to the disruption and eventual end of their relationship. She makes it her mission to do something about the situation she stumbles upon, since she believes that "for a white boy to grow up Chinese is unthinkable" (161). Harrison first induces Pat's adoptive parents to enroll him in her school in Chinatown; later, she talks them into giving him up to a white American family. Thinking that it is in the best interest of the boy that they love, the Lum Yooks agree to give Pat up despite their "sense of injustice and outraged love" (164). When he learns of his fate, the boy, like Pan in "'Its Wavering Image,'" associates himself with the culture that had nurtured and sustained him. After Mr. Lum Yook tells Pat that he must leave them and be separated from Pan because "you are a white boy and Pan is Chinese," Pat cries, "I am Chinese too! I am Chinese too!" (166). At this point, Pat claims the culture that he loves, not the race that will soon claim him.

Despite these protests, over time Pat integrates into the American mainstream. The siblings meet only twice after their separation. In her brief descriptions of these two encounters, Sui Sin Far shows the process of prejudice as Pat distances himself from his former sibling. On their first chance meeting, he begins to make distinctions between himself and his Chinese sister. He remarks on how little she is, compared to the

white girls in his new school. On their second meeting, Pat pulls away
from Pan completely, although she is happy to see him. As she leans in
to talk to the boy she still loves as her brother, one of Pat's schoolmates
mocks Pan's speech, which compels Pat to turn on his sister and yell,
"Get away from me!" (166). In their first encounter, Pat is beginning to
recognize the different physical characteristics of race that had not been
important to him before. By the second encounter, he has apparently
absorbed the racial prejudice of the white community in which he now
lives. The story demonstrates two of Sui Sin Far's prevalent themes: that
ethnic differences are of no significance outside of racist contexts and
that racial impulses are learned, not inherent. In one brief moment, the
opinion of Pat's new white peers outweighs the previous years of love
and devotion to his Chinese sister. The power of prejudice, the author
indicates, can be that strong.

"Pat and Pan" is a simple story that nevertheless invokes the influence of society and institutions over individuals. It also depicts how
races living in close proximity can enrich and sustain one another, and,
conversely, how the separation of races breeds fear and animosity. This
story may demonstrate better than any other the multicultural perspective of Sui Sin Far. Pat and Pan's childhood relationship becomes emblematic of the ways in which prejudice and segregation are harmful
both to the minority being excluded and to mainstream Americans,
who must deny themselves new knowledge and understanding and
must harbor hate and the resulting guilt that hate inevitably breeds.

Sui Sin Far, writing in the tradition of realism, shows how different
the American landscape looks when viewed from a Chinese American
perspective. Her narratives portray how minds can be broadened and
understanding between individuals can be reached; they also depict
the consequences that occur when individuals are unwilling or unable
to achieve a common understanding. Her best stories, like the works
of many other American realists, trace the struggles of merchant-class
figures as they make their way through the complexities of American
society. The decisions of her characters directly affect those around
them, demonstrating that the social forces of discrimination and oppression are not inevitably imposed on individuals from some outside
entity, but are instead created by individuals in the familiar contexts of

home and community. The ethical dilemmas delineated in her fiction give her audience insight into the social dynamics of immigrant life at the turn of the twentieth century.

Though Sui Sin Far's stories are American narratives, her life and work has wider signification. She was never an American citizen; indeed, according to the law of the land, she never would have been allowed citizenship had she applied for it. The fact that the writings of individuals who were excluded from mainstream American culture and even from U.S. citizenship are now claimed as American literature may seem problematic, yet to continue to exclude them would be more so. The ambiguous national status of Sui Sin Far gives her life and works another dimension for consideration. Her biracial heritage takes on a global significance, as her roots reach back to Europe and Asia and her life was lived in North America. These cross-cultural connections point to a reality that is not new (the coming together of nations and peoples is as old as civilization) but that is just beginning to be understood. As Said put it, "One of the great advances in modern cultural theory is the realization, almost universally acknowledged, that cultures are hybrid and heterogeneous and . . . that cultures and civilizations are so interrelated and interdependent as to beggar any unitary or simply delineated description of their individuality."[39] This hybrid and heterogeneous reality is becoming increasingly familiar in an age of accelerated globalization, but it is important to remember that the turn into the twentieth century was an age of globalization as well. Immigration, telegraphs, steamships, railways, and print journalism were bringing people into contact as never before. In her short stories, Sui Sin Far was able to explore this contact in detail through her portrayal of friendships and families. In the course of these stories, she reveals how limiting what Joe R. Feagin calls the "one-way assimilation to an Anglo-Protestant core culture" was for both native-born Americans and immigrants alike.[40]

At a time when American society was often inhospitable to Asians, Sui Sin Far depicts how Chinese immigrants nonetheless went about making a home in the United States. In her short stories, she creates varied individuals, relationships, and situations that reveal the true complexities—and possibilities—of a multicultural society. She does in the world of fiction what Said tried to do in his own analysis of Orientalism,

which "was not so much to dissipate difference itself . . . but the notion that difference implied hostility, a frozen reified set of opposed
essences."[41] Her fictional exploration of the problems and opportunities
of diversity position her at the beginning of the multiethnic tradition
of American literature in the twentieth century. Her emphasis on the
individual as the locus of culture marked the advent of a new way of
considering ethnic American identity and enabled her to imagine Asian
American and biracial citizenship. Some of her characters identify as
traditional, others as Westernized, while still others define themselves
outside of these obvious categories as they attempt to avoid being forced
into an American identity or relegated to a purely Chinese one. Factors
of gender and class further serve to individualize characters. Perhaps of
all Sui Sin Far's characters, Mrs. Spring Fragrance epitomizes the multicultural ideal. She seeks to make her own choices about her culture
and her role as a woman, and she moves about her community with the
friendship of Chinese, white, and biracial Americans. Though at times
Mrs. Spring Fragrance may be misinterpreted by others, she never lets
these interpretations define her; though she retains the traditional traits
of the gracious Chinese wife, she is subservient to no one. Sui Sin Far's
characters represent a synergistic model of acculturation as they move
past stereotypes to embody the varied and unpredictable ways in which
the diversity of cultures come together in America.

CHAPTER SIX

Conclusion: American Narratives

E THNIC AMERICAN WRITERS in the age of realism gave a more balanced picture of their respective cultures than the racist, stereotypical, or romantic depictions of immigrants and people of color found in popular literature and the press. The turn into the twentieth century was an age of social protest and progressivism, and these realist writers portrayed the particular concerns of their communities as they faced legislation or public opinion that threatened to limit their potential and possibilities. Multiethnic writers, in their explorations of identity, also broadened the definition of what it meant to be American, suggesting ways—such as assmiliation, racial cohesion, or multiculturalism—in which ethnic groups could be incorporated into American society. Some, like Zitkala-Ša, chose to express an ambivalence that served to register discontent with the nation itself.[1] As with other realist texts, the writings of these authors reveal their varied inherited myths, traditions, and philosophies, creating a dynamic cultural particularity—a trend that would continue in American works in the twentieth century. This generation of authors also explored subjects that would become important in the years to come: themes of exile, generational conflict, and the roles of memory and the past in the creation of individual and national identity.

The authors' representations of ethnic American identity were influenced by the ways in which their respective groups were being incorporated into or excluded from the life of the nation. Both Zitkala-Ša and

Mary Antin were deeply affected by the national project of assimilation in the late nineteenth century. Mary V. Dearborn's evaluation of this movement in relation to immigrants may also reflect the experience of Native Americans: "In the Americanization process, the immigrant was confronted with an ideal type of American behavior: a model of patriotism bound up with legends of the founding fathers, flag saluting, and celebrations of national holidays. By adopting a new language, new rituals, new heroes, new founding fathers, and thus metaphorical fathers, the immigrant was both to be adopted by and to possess America. These attributes were to replace the immigrants' old values much like a new suit of clothes."[2] Considering that Mary Antin and Zitkala-Ša were introduced to mainstream American customs, values, and expectations in a similar manner—through elementary education that had their acculturation as one of its major goals—the drastic difference in their representations of their experiences may at first seem surprising. However, when their texts are considered in historical context, it is clear why Antin came to portray assimilation in glowing terms while Zitkala-Ša's works seem to be haunted by it. For Antin, America offered something her old country had not: the possibility of acceptance. In Russia, Jews were the perennial outsiders, and their lives were limited by anti-Semitism and government policies. In her new country, schoolteachers presented America's founding fathers as her own and assured her that she was now a member of the nation. Therefore she expresses a sense of belonging and freedom that she had not felt in Russia. Paradoxically, the adult Antin became aware that there were groups in America that considered new immigrants like her inassimilable. To demonstrate that it was possible to assimilate in one generation, Antin in her autobiography disproves the notion that eastern European Jews were utterly alien. In fact, in the course of her narrative she demonstrates how much they have in common with earlier immigrants.

Zitkala-Ša's texts, however, reveal the much longer and more complicated relationship between Native Americans and the United States. While Antin accepts America's values and history as a gift, Zitkala-Ša is aware that America's values and history have resulted in tremendous loss for her people. Antin views the chance to shed elements of her culture as an opportunity to grow and change, while Zitkala-Ša writes of the pain of having her traditional culture stripped from her. In short, for Antin it was a great achievement to assimilate; for Zitkala-Ša it was a heroic effort not to assimilate.

Sutton E. Griggs does not deal with the American educational system in the same manner as Antin or Zitkala-Ša because he writes primarily about adult characters. But his texts do address the dilemma of the limited opportunities for African Americans who achieve a higher education. His novels reveal that there were marked differences between African American reality and that of other ethnicities. Although African Americans had developed a distinct subculture, in a global sense blacks and whites in the United States were very closely connected. Both had shared the same nation, the same religion, and the same language for centuries. In some sense, African Americans did not need to acculturate in the same way that immigrants or American Indians were expected to because they were already a part of American society and had been so for generations. By the turn into the twentieth century, many black Americans had reached the heights of Western culture. W. E. B. Du Bois, for example, enrolled in graduate studies at the University of Berlin and earned a Ph.D. from Harvard in the early 1890s. Nevertheless, at that time and for decades to come, the majority of black citizens remained segregated from white society through Jim Crow laws in the South and through housing restrictions and prejudicial hiring practices in the North. The question of African American education was taken up by the great social theorists of the day. Booker T. Washington publicly advocated industrial education for blacks; in contrast, Du Bois, in *The Souls of Black Folk,* argued that the stability of the nation would be threatened by the attempt to create a permanent laboring class and that, furthermore, the aspiration for higher learning already existed in the black community.[3] Through the educated characters in his novels, Griggs reiterated Du Bois's philosophy that African Americans needed knowledgeable and sophisticated individuals to lead the fight for equality. But Griggs also described the very real social restrictions that limited the opportunities for college-educated black men and women.

Zitkala-Ša was also concerned about the issue of vocational education, for she perceived that institutions like the Carlisle Indian School were more interested in training Native American children for domestic service than for college.[4] There was little controversy, in contrast, about the status of the Chinese in America. The fact that they were denied U.S. citizenship underscored the widespread assumption that they would remain a cheap and efficient labor pool; there seemed to be no expectation that they would become members of the nation. In 1916 Randolph Bourne questioned the relationship between the United States and the new immigrants, and his conclusion also holds true when applied to the national attitude towards African Americans and Native Americans: "If freedom means a democratic cooperation in determining the ideals and purposes and industrial and social institutions of a country, then the immigrant has not been free."[5] As most immigrants and people of color were prevented, through laws or through social prejudice, from full participation in determining the course of the nation, America was not standing by its ideals of liberty, democracy, and equality. As a prescient thinker, Zitkala-Ša may have been right to doubt the motives of Indian education, for—as the educated classes of African Americans demonstrated—acculturation was no guarantee of social acceptance, economic security, or political power.

There may have been many in the United States who hoped that the Americanization of immigrants, blacks, and American Indians would lead to a society in which all enjoyed the same rights and privileges, but it was clear that some people who believed in educating and elevating those groups did not necessarily desire their complete independence or equality. Sui Sin Far represents this patronizing attitude with the figure of Mrs. Dean in "Wisdom of the New," who cannot accept the fact that her pupil, Wou Sankwei, chooses to live his life without her direction and intervention. Mrs. Dean's attitude reflects a common ethos of Americanization, in which ethnic Americans were often viewed as children; she also mirrors the surprise some people felt when former students or wards of the nation asserted themselves against the status quo. For some reformers, the underlying goal of the educational system with regard to immigrant and American Indian students was to produce a certain type of citizen, one who rises to be a competent worker and identifies as an American, but who does not seek public voice or political power. It may have been assumed that those who were offered the American way would respond with nothing but gratitude, as Mary Antin did. This explains why teachers and administrators at the Carlisle Indian School were so offended with the writings of Zitkala-Ša; she had taken the education they gave her and used it as a weapon against the system they represented and believed in. This is an example of what makes multiethnic American writing such an exciting tradition. Once writers from underrepresented groups find their voice, their artistic productions often contain unconventional perspectives that serve to expand both the literature and the conception of the nation.

One issue related to the educational system that all four writers address in their texts is the shame attached to ethnicity because of attitudes expressed in society. Stereotypes in the press, segregation, antimiscegenation laws, restriction acts, prejudicial hiring policies, and racial slurs all suggested to immigrants and people of color that they were somehow less than or inferior to established white Americans. However, what is compelling about Antin, Zitkala-Ša, Griggs, Sui Sin Far, and almost all the ethnic realists is how they represent this shame in their texts. Most of their narratives depict negative or dismissive public attitudes, such as the Orientalist remarks of Mark Carson in "'Its Wavering Image,'" by Sui Sin Far, or the gawking white visitors in "An Indian Teacher among Indians," by Zitkala-Ša. But even as these writers portray the presence of assumptions of ethnic inferiority, they counter these ingrained beliefs with exemplary characters of their race and assertions of the value of their own cultural traditions.

The realists who wrote on racial issues demonstrated how artistic expression could serve a social purpose. J. Hillis Miller describes two possible functions of narratives: they "can propose models of selfhood or ways of behaving that are then imitated in the real world," and they are also "a relatively safe or innocuous place in which the reigning assumptions of a given culture can be criticized."[6] The works of Griggs, Sui Sin Far, Antin, and Zitkala-Ša fulfill these two basic roles as they focus on the relationship of immigrants and people of color to American society. Each of their texts includes scenes that demonstrate how white Americans should and should not treat their ethnically diverse neighbors; each of their texts also contains rhetoric that indicts the nation for not having yet learned these lessons. There are differences, however, in how these four authors chose to tell their stories. Though three of the four wrote short stories, the fact is that all four writers excelled in separate literary forms. Mary Antin is best known for her autobiography, Zitkala-Ša for her personal essays, Sui Sin Far for her stories, and Griggs for his novels. Though there are connections between these genres, there are also differences in the ways that they shape a narrative and reach an audience. Each of these forms also represents a separate tradition within the history of American literature.

Mary Antin wrote three good stories that were published in major literary magazines, but her most thoughtful and sustained work is *The Promised Land*. In an age of social criticism and journalistic exposé, autobiography may have been appealing to readers because it seemed to reveal the unmediated truth. However, because some facts of Antin's life are concealed and others altered, the narrative is not objective history but an artistic and often pragmatic reconstruction of her early life. In many ways, as is demonstrated by the production of the book itself, Mary Antin was not the typical Jewish immigrant; yet through her descriptions of life in the Pale of Russia and her experiences in America she gives her audience a picture of immigrant life. Through her story, she fulfills the "affirmative culture-making function of narrative" by writing eastern European Jews into American life, and she speaks to the "critical or subversive function" of narrative by addressing prejudices against the new immigrant.[7] Antin's book is also an important link to three critical movements in American autobiography. This genre in American letters had its beginnings with the Puritan spiritual autobiography, in which writers examined the details of their lives to understand God's plan and to chart their own paths to salvation. By the early days of the republic, literary emphasis had shifted from the personal and spiritual to the civic and rational. The quintessential American narrative of this era, and perhaps the most well-known personal transformation story, is the *Autobiography of Benjamin Franklin* (1791). In the mid-nineteenth century the abolitionist movement supported a wave of personal narratives written by former slaves that described the oppression of blacks under the system of slavery. These stories often included the moral and intellectual growth the authors experienced after gaining their freedom. The best of these is the *Narrative of the Life of Frederick Douglass* (1845).

Antin, writing in the early twentieth century, seems to incorporate the dominant tropes of all these movements into her own autobiography. She is reborn in a secular sense as an American, but a secondary motif in the text is her move from the religion of her youth to an all-encompassing transcendentalism that connects her to the universe as well as to an American spiritual tradition. Antin's autobiography encompasses a Franklinesque belief in diligence and self-sufficiency that leads to her rise above her humble beginnings. As Frederick Douglass did before her, Antin ascribes her success first to gaining her physical freedom (in her case, freedom from the limiting world of the Pale) and then attaining literacy and an education that led to her complete liberation. The life experiences of people of color and immigrants are often new stories in the history of the nation and so do not need the mediating artistry of fiction to create interest. Autobiography is an exceptional medium for exploring the implications of ethnicity, identity, and nationality, in that these elements intersect in the life of the individual. As with Antin, the supposedly direct relation of the author's experience gives the texts a certain relevancy, to the extent that they are considered as nonfiction and so somehow more true to life than fictional forms.

While shorter works, like the essays Zitkala-Ša published in the *Atlantic Monthly,* cannot achieve the depth of detail and analysis found in full-length personal narratives, they have another sort of immediacy when they are disseminated to a wide audience through periodicals. In the journalistic medium, textual messages and experiences are conveyed all at once, which has its advantages in a fast-paced world. Personal nonfiction prose has developed into a strong subgenre in American literature, as writers of color continue to shed light on American realities through the meditation on their own (or their families') experiences. In a way, essays are an ephemeral form; they are popular in journals and magazines but often do not gain wide distribution when they are collected into books. Fortunately, editors of many recent literary anthologies recognize the importance of autobiographies and frequently include personal essays, giving them a wider audience and increasing the potential for their critical consideration.

Short stories also have the intellectual immediacy that comes with their appearance in periodicals. The magazine boom at the turn into the twentieth century resulted in the publication of a great number of stories by writers from all walks of life. The contemporary American short story had its roots much earlier, however, in the sketches of Washington Irving and the tales of Nathaniel Hawthorne and Edgar Allen Poe. It was Poe, in fact, who developed a theory of the "short prose narrative," which he saw as having "a certain unique or single *effect*" because it could deliver "the fullest satisfaction" with few details. It could also be read in one sitting.[8] The brevity and selective detail in a story of Chinese American life by Sui Sin Far had the potential to give the early twentieth-century reader a glimpse of the world and art of a little-understood group. The appearance of such stories in national magazines may have served, in a small way, to legitimize the Chinese presence in the country. Though the short story often explores the same themes as the autobiographical essay, the short-story author is more free to vary characters, settings, and details, and, perhaps more importantly, to design the work around a definite plot. In the tradition of realism, plot most often involves a moral dilemma, and in their stories the realists who wrote about ethnicity demonstrated that ethical codes often do not change across cultures. Their mainstream readers would find that, despite superficial differences, the characters in tales by immigrants and people of color were not unlike themselves.

Though individual stories have an immediate, concentrated effect, when gathered in a collection they create a textual world that is more complex in its variation. Each of Sui Sin Far's short works in magazines served to introduce her readers to a new perspective, but when she assembled many tales of Chinese American life in *Mrs. Spring Fragrance,* the impact of all the stories in relation to each other gave the work as a whole a broader significance.

The most popular form of American literature is the novel, Sutton E. Griggs's genre of choice. Although the novel cannot achieve the temporal immediacy of the short story, by its very length it has the ability to delineate plot, theme, and character in more depth, to "tell the whole story," so to speak. This narrative form allowed Griggs to explore a variety of scenarios and possibilities for his African American characters and to reflect in depth on the condition of American society. According to Miller, "In a novel, alternative assumptions can be entertained or experimented with—not as in the real world, where such experimentations might have dangerous consequences, but in the imaginary world where, it is easy to assume, 'nothing really happens' because it happens only in the feigned world of fiction."[9] Some of the situations that Griggs depicts—such as armed revolt, underground conspiracies, or even interracial relationships—could not be openly contemplated outside of fiction at the time due to the prevailing racial climate. In a society that sharply limited the possibilities of black citizens, Griggs used the form of the novel to experiment, to plan, and to dream of a new future. Another element of the genre that enabled Griggs to populate his narratives with an astonishing variety of points of view is its inherent multiplicity. Mikhail Bakhtin defines the novel as "a diversity of social speech types . . . and a diversity of individual voices, artistically organized."[10] Griggs and other writers of color used this multivocal space to portray the variation within their communities.

Like the host of multicultural writers who were to follow, Antin, Zitkala-Ša, Sui Sin Far, Griggs, and the other ethnic realists explored the use of genre to represent cultural identity and American citizenship. These authors can be categorized as a group because of their concentration on these themes at their particular moment in American literary history. In some ways, however, it is difficult to maintain a sense of simultaneity when thinking about this group of writers and their works. Any connection between the disparate realities of Chinese living on the West Coast, immigrants on the East Coast, American Indians on the Plains, and black Americans in the South may seem at best subjective. Nevertheless, when considered in conjunction with each other, the links between their works are apparent. All were in some way portraying the ability or inability of immigrants, African Americans, and American Indians to create a space of existence and acceptance in American society. These groups often experienced both social and physical division from mainstream American society. They congregated into ethnic enclaves in the cities, as Jewish and Chinese immigrants did; they were segregated by law, as were African Americans in the South; or they lived far from the centers of mainstream American life, as did many American Indians. An ideological space between white and ethnic Americans also was created by the perpetuation of demeaning or misleading stereotypes in the press. The insistence that people of color and immigrants were not just different but were inferior to other Americans served to separate groups and individuals.

These separations reinforced racial and social stratifications to an extent that they have been historically difficult to overcome. The lives and works of these four writers, however, demonstrate that these walls were high but not insurmountable. Mary Antin, for example, found her way out of the Jewish ghetto of Boston into the parlors of her educated and philanthropic white neighbors—but, as she acknowledges in her autobiography, none of her relatives or immigrant neighbors were able to do the same. In her literary writing, Zitkala-Ša is adamant about the incompatibility of white and Native American cultures, yet she herself was able to negotiate successfully for American Indian rights in Washington, D.C.. Perhaps the most profound portrayal of the social barriers that prevent interaction and understanding among people is found in the novels of Sutton E. Griggs. No other group in America faced the type of Jim Crow society that blacks confronted in the South. The fact that legislation was enacted to prevent social contact between whites and blacks clearly shows how ingrained racial prejudice against African Americans was at the time. Yet even while presenting these realities in fiction, Griggs created some white characters who choose a common humanity over racial separatism, and he included friendships between the races in almost all of his novels. The most optimistic portrayal of the possibilities of harmonious race relations, however, can be found in Sui Sin Far's short stories. Her ability to imagine and depict a multicultural world may stem from the locality about which she wrote. Much of her fiction is set in the Pacific states, a region with a diverse and burgeoning population. California in particular has always been a multicultural region. White hegemony, though it has periodically asserted itself in the politics of the state, has always been somewhat tenuous. As ethnic communities developed in cities and in rural areas, few places in California have been exclusively white, and the state as a whole was never a homogenous place. The fact that these four writers addressed regional, historical, and cultural differences between ethnicities living in the United States at the turn into the twentieth century enabled them to give different perspectives on some of the pressing concerns of the day—such as exclusion and prejudice—that affected all ethnic groups in some way. When viewed together, the works of these writers broaden the social and literary landscape at the turn into the twentieth century.

In many ways the works of writers such as Antin, Zitkala-Ša, Griggs, and Sui Sin Far laid the groundwork for the literary and social writing on ethnicity and citizenship that was to follow. By 1903 W. E. B. Du Bois already saw that "the problem of the Twentieth Century is the problem of the color-line."[11] These four authors belong to the first generation to explore race relations at length, and so their narratives constitute an important nexus in what would become a national conversation that would last a century and more. Their perspectives at the turn into the twentieth century were precursors to a sea change in racial theory. Whereas late nineteenth-century conjecture on ethnicity and national identity published by white writers was often based on the premise of a hierarchy of cultures, early twentieth-century theorists began to look at race relations in another way.

In 1915, Horace M. Kallen, a Jewish American who had emigrated with his family from Prussia at the age of five and who had earned a Ph.D. in philosophy from Harvard, wrote "Democracy versus the Melting Pot," which was published in *The Nation*. This essay marked a shift in the way that U.S. diversity was viewed. Kallen questioned whether the current paradigm of American identity, in which other ethnicities conformed to the Anglo-Saxon ideal, could not be replaced by a more inclusive model: "What do we will to make of the United States—a unison singing the old Anglo-Saxon theme 'America,' the America of the New England school, or a harmony, in which that theme will be dominant, perhaps, among others, but one among many, not the only one?"[12] Kallen suggested that instead of pressuring everyone within the United States to conform to an Anglo-Saxon, Protestant ideal, the nation should foster cultural difference as something in and of itself American. Kallen would go on to develop this idea and to coin its defining term, "cultural pluralism," in *Culture and Democracy in the United States: Studies in the Group Psychology of the American People* (1924). "Democracy versus the Melting Pot," however, stands as Kallen's first national call to respect diverse cultures on their own terms, a courtesy that realist writers of ethnicity portrayed as more or less lacking among their fellow Americans.

Randolph Bourne was another intellectual to reconsider the implications of a multiethnic country. His "Trans-National America" (1916) is even more emphatic than Kallen's *Nation* article in its insistence that the melting-pot ideal is biased against descendants of non-English cultures and that its premise is in fact detrimental to the nation. Bourne states that the "failure of the melting-pot" is evident in the many immigrant communities that insist on preserving their cultures and, moreover, that the nation would grow stronger if it gave up the idea of assimilation altogether.[13] One limitation of both these articles is that they only consider European cultures in their analysis of American diversity. Still, the publication of these essays ushered in a new stage of cultural discourse in the United States, making ethnic realist writers important pioneers of racial theory as they explored the implications of multiethnic experience without being privy to the modern thought and terminology that were to come.

The writers who explored issues of ethnicity and citizenship in the age of realism were working at a time when no contemporary racial theory actually reflected or considered their experience, so while they often addressed and refuted common misrepresentations and stereotypes in their works, they were free to create a world in their literature unencumbered by ideas of what ethnic American texts should be, do, or say. For example, there could never be such a heartfelt or unselfconscious narrative of assimilation as *The Promised Land* after Kallen, Bourne, and others began to examine and criticize the idea of Americanization. As each generation added to the discussion on race and nation, perspectives on the multiethnic tradition of American literature changed.

In fact, the exploration of ethnic identity can be seen as a particularly American subject, one that is central to American literature in the twentieth century. These themes are compelling because, like all good literary subjects, they speak to the human condition; they reflect the paradoxical human longings for independence and belonging, both for freedom and a sense of connectedness. The United States can claim to have the first national literature to explore the multiple sites of personal identification, as it has had to grapple from its inception with the reality of its multiethnic populace. In a way, it is the mere fact of difference that connects the nation at some level. According to Mary V. Dearborn,

"As Americans we partake of a national identity, a communally deter-mined and accepted sense of self; at the same time, as Americans and ethnics all, we define ourselves ancestrally."[14] It is the American divide between ethnicity and nationality that creates limitless space in terms of literary material.

As a society the United States has always been drawn to this space, and interest in these issues has not abated since the realist era, though the discourse has shifted several times in the last hundred years. Issues of cultural and national affiliation continue to be at the heart of a great deal of American literary production, just as race matters continue to be the subject of debate and fascination in the news and entertainment media. Despite the advance of civil rights and the desire of some Amer-icans for the elimination of the consciousness of racial difference—that is, for a "colorblind society"—the fact is that cultural differences still matter in the lives of individuals and in the life of the nation as well. Race matters in the negative sense, in that forms of personal and in-stitutional discrimination continue to be revealed despite the progress towards equality that was achieved in the second half of the twenti-eth century. But race also matters in another, more positive, way. An individual's heritage and cultural affiliations are significant, important, and should not be devalued. It is just such complexity, which parallels America's paradoxical history of freedoms and repressions, that keeps the themes of ethnicity and citizenship compelling and new generation after generation.

In the simplest terms, ethnic realist works represent the fact that America means different things to different people. Antin portrays it as almost a religion, in which immigrants, like converts, can transcend their past and make a new life for themselves. Griggs, similarly, observes that the nation has its own moral codes of inclusion and justice. Within these principles lies the hope of salvation if the United States can move beyond its prejudice about difference. Antin portrays that hope in the possibilities of assimilation, while Griggs, aware of the racism that pre-vented blacks from being incorporated into American society, depicts the power of racial cohesion. Zitkala-Ša, in contrast, expresses suspi-cion toward a nation that has not dealt fairly with her people; her narra-tives waver ambivalently between a traditional and a national affiliation.

Sui Sin Far, who described herself as a bridge in her autobiographical writing, creates connections—or at least the potential for them—in all of her stories. Those of her characters who take advantage of opportunities for shared cultural understanding demonstrate the possibility for growth and enlightenment inherent in a multiethnic world.

Eric J. Sundquist has written that coming to terms with the literary heritage of the United States "implies the necessity of living with the paradox that 'American' literature is both a single tradition of many parts *and* a series of winding, sometimes parallel traditions that have perforce been built in good part from their inherent conflicts."[15] Mary Antin, Zitkala-Ša, Sutton E. Griggs, and Sui Sin Far represent a group whose writings coincided to produce an important tradition in American letters, a tradition that, in part, was based on their ability to make art out of conflict. Priscilla Wald contends that "the status of an individual in the community" is determined by America's official stories, which "change in response to competing narratives of the nation that must be engaged, absorbed, and retold: the fashioning and endless refashioning of 'a people.'"[16] Individually, these authors and their works may have affected the nation in small and incalculable ways; as a group, they represent a rising consensus, an assembly of voices sounding new ways of envisioning "a people." Though each writer had his or her own vision, the collective chorus exclaims that the old model of American citizenship would not suffice. To comprehend this often-overlooked group and to recognize how the themes of ethnic identity and national citizenship were developed in their texts is to come to a fuller understanding of American literature, American history, and the evolution of the concept of "America" itself.

Appendix: Selected List of Realist Texts That Address Ethnicity

Antin, Mary. "The Amulet." *Atlantic Monthly* 111 (1913): 31–41.

———. *From Plotzk to Boston.* Boston: W. B. Clarke, 1899.

———. "The Lie." *Atlantic Monthly* 112 (1913): 177–90.

———. "Malinke's Atonement." *Atlantic Monthly* 108 (1911): 300–19.

———. *The Promised Land.* Boston: Houghton Mifflin, 1912.

Boyesen, Hjalmar Hjorth. *Vagabond Tales.* Boston: Lothrop, 1889.

Brown, Gertrude Dorsey. "A Case of Measure for Measure." *Colored American Magazine* 10 (1906): 253–58, 301–94, and 11 (1906): 25–28, 97–100, 167–72, 281–84.

———. "Scrambled Eggs." *Colored American Magazine* 8 (1905): 31–38, 79–86.

Burgess-Ware, Mrs. M. Louise. "Bernice, the Octoroon." *Colored American Magazine* 6 (1903): 607–26, 652–57.

Cahan, Abraham. *The Imported Bridegroom and Other Stories.* Boston: Houghton Mifflin, 1898.

———. *The Rise of David Levinsky.* New York: Harper, 1917.

———. *Yekl: A Tale of the New York Ghetto.* New York: D. Appleton, 1896.

Callahan, S. Alice. *Wynema: A Child of the Forest.* Chicago: H. J. Smith, 1891.

Chesnutt, Charles W. *The Colonel's Dream.* New York: Doubleday, Page, 1905.

———. *The Conjure Woman.* Boston: Houghton Mifflin, 1899.

———. "Dave's Neckliss." *Atlantic Monthly* 64 (1889): 500–08.

———. "A Deep Sleeper." *Two Tales* 5, no. 3 (1893): 1–8.

———. *The House behind the Cedars.* Boston: Houghton Mifflin, 1900.

———. "Lonesome Ben." *Southern Workman* 29 (March 1900): 137–45.

———. *The Marrow of Tradition.* Boston: Houghton Mifflin, 1901.

———. "Tobe's Tribulations." *Southern Workman* 29 (1900): 656–64.

———. "A Victim of Heredity; or Why the Darkey Loves Chicken." *Self-Culture Magazine* 11 (1900): 404–09.

———. *The Wife of His Youth and Other Stories of the Color Line.* Boston: Houghton Mifflin, 1899.

Cotter, Joseph. *Negro Tales.* New York: Cosmopolitan Press, 1912.

De Cora, Angel. "Angel De Cora—An Autobiography." *The Red Man* (March 1911): 279–85.

——— [Hinook-Mahiwi-Kilinaka]. "Gray Wolf's Daughter." *Harper's New Monthly Magazine* 99 (1899): 860–62.

——— [Henook-Makwewe-Kelenaka (*sic*)]. "The Sick Child." *Harper's New Monthly Magazine* 98 (1899): 446–48.

Du Bois, W. E. B. *The Quest of the Silver Fleece.* Chicago: A. C. McClurg, 1911.

———. *The Souls of Black Folk.* Chicago: A. C. McClurg, 1903.

Dunbar, Paul Laurence. *The Sport of the Gods.* New York: Dodd, Mead, 1902.

Dunbar-Nelson, Alice. *The Goodness of St. Rocque and Other Stories.* New York: Dodd, Mead, 1899.

——— [Mrs. Paul Lawrence Dunbar]. "Hope Deferred." *Crisis* 8 (1914): 238–42.

Dunne, Finley Peter. *Dissertations by Mr. Dooley.* New York: Harper, 1906.

———. *Mr. Dooley in the Hearts of His Countrymen.* Boston: Small, Maynard, 1899.

———. *Mr. Dooley in Peace and War.* Boston: Small, Maynard, 1898.

———. *Mr. Dooley Says.* New York: Scribners, 1910.

———. *Mr. Dooley's Opinions.* New York: Russell, 1901.

———. *Mr. Dooley's Philosophy.* New York: Russell, 1900.

———. *Observations by Mr. Dooley.* New York: Russell, 1902.

Earle, Victoria. "Aunt Lindy (A Story Founded on Real Life)." *A.M.E. Church Review* 5 (1889): 246–50.

———. "Eugenie's Mistake: A Story." *A.M.E. Church Review* 8 (1892): 262, 267.

Eastman, Charles A [Ohiyesa]. *From Deep Woods to Civilization: Chapters in the Autobiography of an Indian.* Boston: Little, Brown, 1916.

———. "The Madness of Bald Eagle." *Southern Workman* 34 (1905): 141–43.

Fauset, Jessie. "Emmy." *Crisis* 5 (1912): 79–87, and 5 (1913): 134–42.

———. "'There Was One Time!': A Story of Spring." *Crisis* 13 (1917): 272–77, and 14 (1917): 11–15.

Gillman, Nathaniel I. *Circumstantial Affection: A Realistic Romance of the New York Ghetto.* New York: F. T. Neely, 1900.

Griggs, Sutton E. *The Hindered Hand; or, The Reign of the Repressionist.* Nashville: Orion, 1905.

———. *Imperium in Imperio.* Cincinnati: Editor, 1899.

———. *Overshadowed.* Nashville: Orion, 1901.

———. *Pointing the Way.* Nashville: Orion, 1908.

———. *Unfettered.* Nashville: Orion, 1902.

Harper, Francis E. W. *Iola Leroy, or Shadows Uplifted.* Philadelphia: Garrigues Brothers, 1892.

Hopkins, Pauline E. "'As the Lord Lives, He is One of Our Mother's Children.'" *Colored American Magazine* 6 (1903): 795–801.

———. "Bro'r Abr'm Jimsom's Wedding: A Christmas Story." *Colored American Magazine* 4 (1901): 103–12.

———. *Contending Forces: A Romance Illustrative of Negro Life North and South.* Boston: The Colored Co-operative, 1900.

———. "General Washington: A Christmas Story." *Colored American Magazine* 2 (1900): 95–104.

——— [Sarah A. Allen]. "Hagar's Daughter: A Story of Southern Caste Prejudice." *Colored American Magazine* 2 (1901): 337–52, 431–45; 3 (1901): 24–34, 117–28, 185–95, 262–72, 343–53, 425–35; 4 (1901): 23–33, 113–24; and 4 (1902): 188–200, 282–91.

———. "Of One Blood; or, The Hidden Self." *Colored American Magazine* 6 (1902): 29–40, 102–13, 191–200, 264–72, 339–48, 423–32, 492–501, 580–86, 643–47, 726–31, 802–07.

———. "Talma Gordon." *Colored American Magazine* 6 (1902): 271–90.

——— [Sarah A. Allen]. "The Test of Manhood: A Christmas Story." *Colored American Magazine* 5 (1902): 114–19.

———. "Winona, A Tale of Negro Life in the South and Southwest." *Colored American Magazine* 5 (1902): 29–41, 97–110, 177–87, 257–68, 348–58, 422–31.

Johnson, James Weldon. *The Autobiography of an Ex-Colored Man.* Boston: Sherman, French, 1912.

Jones, J. McHenry. *Hearts of Gold.* Wheeling: Daily Intelligencer Steam Job Press, 1896.

Kelly, Myra. *Little Aliens.* New York: Scribners, 1910.

———. *Little Citizens: The Humours of School Life.* New York: McClure, Phillips, 1904.

———. *Wards of Liberty.* New York: McClure, 1907.

La Flesche, Francis. "The Story of a Vision." *Southern Workman* 30 (1901): 106–09.

McCary, Annie. "Breaking the Color Line." *Crisis* 9 (1915): 193–95.

McClellan, George Marion. *Old Greenbottom Inn and Other Stories.* Louisville: George M. McClellan, 1906.

McIntyre, John Thomas. *The Ragged Edge: A Tale of Ward Life and Politics.* New
    York: McClure, Phillips, 1902.
Micheaux, Oscar. *The Conquest.* Lincoln: Woodruff Press, 1913.
———. *The Forged Note.* Lincoln: Western Book Supply, 1915.
———. *The Homesteader.* Sioux City: Western Book Supply, 1917.
Mossell, Gertrude. "Mizeriah Johnson: Her Arisings and Shinings." *Colored
    American Magazine* 4 (1902): 229–33.
Oskison, John M. "Only the Master Shall Praise." *Century Magazine* 59 (1900):
    327–35.
———. "The Problem of Old Harjo." *Southern Workman* 36 (1907): 235–41.
———. "'The Quality of Mercy': A Story of the Indian Territory." *Century Mag-
    azine* 68 (1904): 178–81.
———. "When the Grass Grew Long." *Century Magazine* 62 (1901): 247–50.
Pokagon, Simon. *O-gi-maw-kwe mit-i-gwa-ki (Queen of the Woods).* Hartford,
    Mich.: C. H. Engle, 1899.
Posey, Alexander. "Fus Fixico Letters." In *The Indian Journal.* N.p.: Eufaula,
    Indian Territory, 1902–1908.
Ries, Adeline F. "Mammy: A Story." *Crisis* 13 (1917): 117–18.
Riis, Jacob. *Out of Mulberry Street: Stories of Tenement Life in New York.* New
    York: Century, 1897.
Sanda [W. H. Stowers and W. H. Anderson]. *Appointed: An American Novel.*
    Detroit: Detroit Law Printing, 1894.
Shackelford, Otis M. *Lillian Simmons, or The Conflict of Sections.* Kansas City:
    Burton, 1915.
Sinclair, Upton. *The Jungle.* New York: Doubleday, Page, 1906.
Stewart, Georgia F. "Aunt 'Rias Ten Dollars." *Colored American Magazine* 3
    (1901): 105–08.
———. "The Wooing of Pastor Cummings." *Colored American Magazine* 3
    (1901): 273–76.
Sui Sin Far. "Leaves from the Mental Portfolio of an Eurasian." *Independent* 66
    (1909): 125–32.
———. *Mrs. Spring Fragrance.* Chicago: A. C. McClurg, 1912.
Todd, Ruth D. "Florence Grey: A Three-Part Story." *Colored American Maga-
    zine* 5 (1902): 307–13, 391–97, 469–77.
———. "The Folly of Mildred: A Race Story with a Moral." *Colored American
    Magazine* 6 (1903): 364–70.
———. "The Octoroon's Revenge." *Colored American Magazine* 4 (1902): 291–95.
Walker, Thomas H. B. *Bebbly, or the Victorious Preacher.* Jacksonville: Pepper,
    1910.

Washington, Booker T. *Up from Slavery.* Garden City: Doubleday, 1901.

Wing, Yung. *My Life in China and America.* New York: Henry Holt, 1909.

Zitkala-Ša. "Impressions of an Indian Childhood." *Atlantic Monthly* 85 (1900): 37–47.

———. "An Indian Teacher among Indians." *Atlantic Monthly* 85 (1900): 381–86.

———. "The School Days of an Indian Girl." *Atlantic Monthly* 85 (1900): 185–94.

———. "The Soft-Hearted Sioux." *Harper's Monthly Magazine* 102 (1901): 505–08.

———. "The Trial Path." *Harper's Monthly Magazine* 103 (1901): 741–44.

———. "A Warrior's Daughter." *Everybody's Magazine* 4 (1902): 346–52.

Notes

CHAPTER 1. DIVERSITY IN THE AGE OF REALISM

1. Howells praised the early work of both writers. See "Mr. CWC's Stories," *Atlantic Monthly* 85 (1900): 699–701, and "New York Low Life in Fiction," *New York World* 26 (1896): 18.

2. Fred Lewis Pattee, *A History of American Literature since 1870* (New York: Century, 1915), 18.

3. Vernon Lewis Parrington, *The Beginnings of Critical Realism in America, 1860–1920*, vol. 3 of *Main Currents in American Thought* (New York: Harcourt, Brace, 1930), 168.

4. For a comprehensive account of the critical evaluation of American realism, see Donald Pizer, ed., *Documents of American Realism and Naturalism* (Carbondale: Southern Illinois University Press, 1998).

5. Warner Berthoff, *The Ferment of Realism: American Literature, 1884–1919* (New York: Free Press, 1965), 3.

6. Donald Pizer, *Realism and Naturalism in Nineteenth-Century American Literature*, rev. ed. (Carbondale: Southern Illinois University Press, 1984), 8.

7. Amy Kaplan, *The Social Construction of American Realism* (Chicago: University of Chicago Press, 1988), 10.

8. Ibid., 12.

9. Tom Quirk and Gary Scharnhorst, eds., *American Realism and the Canon* (Newark: University of Delaware Press, 1994), 19.

10. Hopefully, the recent republication of Griggs's first novel will serve to incorporate him into the study of American letters. See Sutton E. Griggs, *Imperium in Imperio* (New York: Modern Library, 2003).

11. Paula E. Hyman, *Gender and Assimilation in Modern Jewish History: The Roles and Representation of Women* (Seattle: University of Washington Press, 1995), 13.

12. Sidonie Smith, "Cheesecakes, Nymphs, and 'We the People': Un/National Subjects about 1900," *Prose Studies: History, Theory, Criticism* 17, no. 1 (1994): 121.

13. W. E. B. Du Bois, *The Souls of Black Folk* (1903; reprint, New York: Dover, 1994), 3.

14. Marlon K. Hom, ed., *Songs of Gold Mountain: Cantonese Rhymes from San Francisco Chinatown* (Berkeley: University of California Press, 1987). This collection is made up of poems translated from Chinese, which were originally published as *Jinshan ge ji* (San Francisco: Tai Quong, 1911) and *Jinshan ge erji* (San Francisco: Tai Quong, 1915).

15. Paula Gunn Allen, *The Sacred Hoop: Recovering the Feminine in American Indian Traditions* (Boston: Beacon Press, 1991), 4.

16. Ibid.

17. Jules Chametzky, John Felstiner, Hilene Flanzbaum, and Kathryn Hellerstien, introduction to *Jewish American Literature,* ed. Jules Chametzky, John Felstiner, Hilene Flanzbaum, and Kathryn Hellerstien (New York: W. W. Norton, 2001), 111.

18. See Ruth R. Wisse, *The Modern Jewish Canon: A Journey through Language and Culture* (New York: Free Press, 2000).

19. Elizabeth Ammons, "Men of Color, Women, and Uppity Art at the Turn of the Century," in *American Realism and the Canon,* ed. Tom Quirk and Gary Scharnhorst (Newark: University of Delaware Press, 1994), 24.

20. James Nagel, introduction to *The Portable American Realism Reader,* ed. James Nagel and Tom Quirk (New York: Penguin, 1997), xx–xxi.

21. Mary Antin, *The Promised Land* (Boston: Houghton Mifflin, 1912), 48–49.

22. John T. Flynn, "The Muckrakers," in *John D. Rockefeller: Robber Baron or Industrial Statesman?* (Boston: D. C. Heath, 1949), 1.

23. Nagel, *Portable American Realism Reader,* xxv.

24. Anthroposophy is a spiritual movement that was founded in the early twentieth century by Rudolph Steiner. It entails using the mind, not faith, to get in touch with the spiritual world. The word comes from the combination of "anthropos" (humanity) and "sophia" (wisdom).

25. Evelyn Salz, "Illness and Gould Farm: 1917–1939," in Mary Antin, *Selected Letters of Mary Antin,* ed. Evelyn Salz (Syracuse, N.Y.: Syracuse University Press, 2000), 88.

26. Dexter Fisher, foreword to Zitkala-Ša, *American Indian Stories* (1921; reprint, Lincoln: University of Nebraska Press, 1985), x.

27. This opera, along with previously unpublished stories and poems, can be found in Zitkala-Ša, *Dreams and Thunder,* ed. P. Jane Hafen (Lincoln: University of Nebraska Press, 2001).

28. Fisher, foreword to Zitkala-Ša, *American Indian Stories,* xv.

29. Carol J. Batker, *Reforming Fictions: Native, African, and Jewish American Women's Literature and Journalism in the Progressive Era* (New York: Columbia University Press, 2000), 24.

30. Randolph Meade Walker, *The Metamorphosis of Sutton E. Griggs: The Transition from Black Radical to Conservative, 1913–1933* (Memphis: Walker, 1991), 26.

31. Ibid., 61.

32. Ibid., 29–30.

33. Annette White-Parks, *Sui Sin Far/Edith Maude Eaton: A Literary Biography* (Champaign: University of Illinois Press, 1995), 26. According to White-Parks, the newspaper articles have yet to be located.

34. Ibid., 47.

35. An interesting connection that reflects on Sui Sin Far's struggles and triumphs is the literary career of her younger sister, Winnifred Eaton. Winnifred created a fictional identity and family history, claiming that she was the daughter of an Englishman and a Japanese noblewoman. She took the Japanese-sounding pen name of "Onoto Watanna" and wrote a series of very popular (and very lucrative) novels set in Japan. Though these books represent issues of gender and ethnicity in their own way, they do not have the power, immediacy, or relevancy of Sui Sin Far's writings. Winnifred's decision falsely to claim association with the admired Japanese instead of with the much-maligned Chinese has been seen as a kind of disloyalty to her heritage. When Sui Sin Far died in 1914, an obituary in the *New York Times* perpetuated Winnifred's version of their heritage. According to White-Parks, "scholars have generally held Winnifred to be the author of this obituary" (50).

36. Sui Sin Far, "Leaves from the Mental Portfolio of an Eurasian," in *Mrs. Spring Fragrance and Other Writings,* ed. Amy Ling and Annette White-Parks (Champaign: University of Illinois Press, 1995), 230. Originally published in the *Independent* (January 21, 1909), 125–32.

37. Homi Bhabha, *The Location of Culture* (London: Routledge, 1994), 1–2.

CHAPTER 2. MARY ANTIN AND ASSIMILATION

1. Arthur Hertzberg, *The Jews in America: Four Centuries of an Uneasy Encounter* (New York: Columbia University Press, 1997), 177.

2. Glenn C. Altschuler, *Race, Ethnicity, and Class in American Social Thought, 1865–1919* (Wheeling: Harlan Davidson, 1982), 47.

3. Hertzberg, 188.

4. Hector St. John de Crèvecoeur, *Letters from an American Farmer* (1782; reprint, New York: Penguin, 1986). Crèvecoeur wrote, "*He* is an American, who, leaving behind him all his ancient prejudices and manners, receives new ones from the new mode of life he has embraced, the new government he obeys, and the new rank he holds. He becomes an American by being received in the broad lap of our great Alma Mater. Here individuals are melted into a new race of men, whose labours and posterity will one day cause great changes in the world" (70).

5. Mary Antin, *The Promised Land,* introd. Werner Sollors (1912; reprint, New York: Penguin, 1997).

6. Gert Beulens, "The New Man and the Mediator: (Non-) Remembrance in Jewish-American Immigrant Narrative," in *Memory, Narrative, and Identity: New Essays in Ethnic American Literature,* ed. Amiritjit Singh, Joseph T. Skerrett, Jr., and Robert E. Hogan (Boston: Northeastern University Press, 1994), 91.

7. Werner Sollors, introduction to Antin, *The Promised Land,* xxxi-xxxii.

8. Examples include Sarah Blacher Cohen, "Mary Antin's *The Promised Land:* A Breach of Promise," *Studies in American Jewish Literature* 3 (1977): 28-35, and Susanne A. Shavelson, "Anxieties of Authorship in the Autobiographies of Mary Antin and Aliza Greenblatt," *Prooftexts* 18 (1998): 161-86.

9. Francis A. Walker, "Restriction of Immigration," *Atlantic Monthly* 77 (1896): 822-29 (quotes, 822, 823). Francis Amasa Walker was a renowned economist whose public roles as (among other things) commissioner of Indian affairs and director of the federal census seemed to qualify him as an expert on ethnic American issues. While his ethnocentrism in this essay may shock a twenty-first-century reader, it is representative of the anti-immigration rhetoric circulating at the time. One of his assertions is that native-born (that is, white, Protestant) Americans had fewer children because of the repulsive and intimidating nature of immigrants in their midst, which resulted in the "degradation of our citizenship" (826). He believed the new wave of immigrants from southern and eastern Europe to be especially repugnant: "The entrance into our political, social, and industrial life of such vast masses of peasantry, degraded below our utmost conceptions, is a matter which no intelligent patriot can look upon without the gravest apprehension and alarm. . . . They are beaten men from beaten races; representing the worst failures in the struggle for existence. . . . They have none of the ideas and aptitudes which fit men to take up readily and easily the problem of self-care and self-government. . . . What effects must be produced upon our social standards, and upon the ambitions and aspirations of our people, by a contact so foul and loathsome?" (828).

10. U.S. Immigration Commission, *Children of Immigrants in Schools,* 5 vols. (Washington, D.C.: GPO, 1911), 1:4.

11. These bills were vetoed by Presidents Grover Cleveland, Woodrow Wilson, Robert Taft, and Theodore Roosevelt, but the group finally prevailed with the establishment of the Immigration Restriction Act of 1924. Hertzberg, *Jews in America,* 179-80.

12. An excellent discussion that links Antin's text and other ethnic narratives to the American colonists can be found in Werner Sollors, *Beyond Ethnicity: Consent and Descent in American Culture* (New York: Oxford University Press, 1986). He shows how the themes of a chosen people and a promised land resonate through American literature.

13. Several friendly letters from Roosevelt to Antin can be found in *Selected Letters of Mary Antin,* ed. Evelyn Salz (Syracuse: Syracuse University Press, 2000). In one, Roosevelt tells Antin, "You are an American in whom I so deeply believe" (151-52).

14. Hertzberg, 243.

15. This group, successful as they were, had their own struggles with the Boston Brahmin. See ibid., 165-83.

16. Horace M. Kallen, "Democracy versus the Melting Pot," reprinted in *Jewish American Literature,* ed. Jules Chametzky, John Felstiner, Hilene Flanzbaum, and Kathryn Hellerstein (New York: W. W. Norton, 2001), 207-17. This article was originally published as "Democracy versus the Melting Pot: A Study of American Nationality,"

The Nation 100 (February 18, 1915): 190–94, and (February 25, 1915): 217–20. Though it developed the notion of cultural pluralism, Kallen did not coin the term itself until his book *Culture and Democracy in the United States* (New York: Boni and Liveright, 1924).

17. Altschuler, 75.

18. Michael P. Kramer, "Assimilation in *The Promised Land:* Mary Antin and the Jewish Origins of the American Self," *Prooftexts* 18 (1998): 128.

19. Ronald Takaki, *A Different Mirror: A History of Multicultural America* (Boston: Little, Brown, 1993), 283.

20. In her exploration of cultural patriarchy, Antin stands at the beginning of a literary tradition that would be expanded in the feminist writing of the twentieth century. Just as Antin has been criticized for scorning Judaism when in fact she was rebelling against the position of women within her religion, later women of color have been reproached by men in their ethnic or racial groups for disparaging their shared culture. For example, Frank Chin denounced Maxine Hong Kingston's *The Woman Warrior,* and Ishmael Reed similarly criticized Alice Walker's *The Color Purple.* The problem comes from the inability of these critics to distinguish between two closely related but not synonymous things, the male hegemony of a patriarchic culture and the culture itself.

21. Norma Fain Pratt, "Traditions in Judaism: The Jewish American Woman through the 1930s," *American Quarterly* 30 (1978): 681–702.

22. Kramer, 143.

23. Josephine Lazarus was the sister of Emma Lazarus, the Jewish American poet who wrote the poem "The New Colossus," which is inscribed on the base of the Statue of Liberty.

24. Mary Antin, *From Plotzk to Boston* (1899; reprint, New York: Markus Weiner, 1986). One passage, when Antin looks out to sea from the boat during her trans-Atlantic journey, is reminiscent of the transcendentalism of Thoreau: "My mind would go on working, till I was overcome by the strength and power that was greater than myself. . . . I was conscious only of sea and sky and something I did not understand. And as I listened to its solemn voice, I felt as if I had found a friend, and I knew that I loved the ocean. It seemed as if it were within as well as without, a part of myself" (70–71). Antin comes from Polotzk, which is in Russia, not Plotzk, which is in Poland. The publisher's misspelling in the title of her first book caused some confusion early in her career.

25. Her friends, however, believe she is fifteen. It is also significant that the publication of *From Plotzk to Boston* is not mentioned in *The Promised Land.* The later book trails off after she enters the Latin School. Perhaps a scenario in which Antin gets a book published as a teenager would mark her as too dissimilar from other immigrants, a group that she depicts herself as representing.

26. Shavelson strongly criticizes Antin's decision to write in English and regards this choice as a desire to "leave behind . . . the immigrant community and her own history" (165). She compares Antin unfavorably to Aliza Greenblatt, who wrote in Yiddish, and whom she sees as being more faithful to the Jewish community and religion. In her evaluation of these writers, Shavelson does not take into account important factors like

their respective ages at immigration (Antin immigrates as a child, Greenblatt as a grown woman), their audiences, or the purpose of their writing.

27. Despite Antin's preference for English, it is not quite accurate to say that she abandoned Yiddish completely. As Sollors points out in his introduction to *The Promised Land,* she included words from her native language in all of her writing. He posits that Antin's knowledge of Yiddish is a source of power in that it gives her an authority in her work. On at least two occasions when Antin's editor asked her to eliminate foreign words from her texts, she insisted on leaving in a limited amount of Yiddish and Hebrew. See *Selected Letters,* 52, 58.

28. The name of the teacher, and her insensitivity in serving pork to a student she knows to be Jewish, seem to connect Miss Dillingham to the notorious Dillingham Report.

29. After her initial strong reaction to eating the ham, Antin quickly justifies the act in a vaguely transcendental passage, in which she seems to avoid any further examination of the implications of her decision: "And to think that so ridiculous a thing as a scrap of meat should be the symbol and test of a thing so august! To think that in the mental life of a half-grown child should be reflected the struggles and triumph of ages! Over and over and over again I discover that I am a wonderful thing, being human; that I am the image of the universe, being myself; that I am the repository of all the wisdom of the world, being alive and sane at the beginning of this twentieth century. The heir of the ages am I, and all that has been is in me and shall continue to be in my immortal self" (197).

30. Chapters 14 through 17 touch on the hardships of Antin's late adolescence. They are "Manna," "Tarnished Laurels," "Dover Street," and "The Landlady."

31. As Sollors points out in his introduction to *The Promised Land* (xxvii–xxviii), a version of this occurrence is found in an early draft but did not make it into her autobiography. The same situation and its moral implications are explored in the short story "The Lie," though Antin makes the main character a boy instead of a girl. Mary Antin, "The Lie," *Atlantic Monthly* 112 (1913): 177–90.

CHAPTER 3. AMBIGUITY AND AFFILIATION

1. Gloria Anzaldúa, *Borderlands/La Frontera: The New Mestiza* (San Francisco: Aunt Lute Books, 1987), 77.

2. There seems to be some discrepancy regarding Zitkala-Ša's specific heritage. She was born on the Yankton reservation, which would indicate that she was Nakota Sioux. However, in her autobiographical essays and in some of her stories, her relatives and characters are called "Dakota." Her pen name is Lakota, which means "red bird." To honor all of these affiliations, I most often refer to her as Sioux.

3. James Wilson, *The Earth Shall Weep: A History of Native America* (New York: Grove Press, 1998), 281–85.

4. Takaki, 235. Proceeds from these sales were to be held in trust. The government handling of this money is a matter of investigation and legislation to this day.

5. Wilson, 301–02.

6. Ibid., 304, 308.

7. The General Allotment Act "had given the Indians nothing—except a small portion of their own land." Altschuler, 35.

8. *South Dakota v. Yankton Sioux Tribe*, 522 U.S. 329 (1998).

9. Wilson, xxv.

10. Ibid., 316.

11. Gerald Vizenor, introduction to *Native American Literature: A Brief Introduction and Anthology*, ed. Gerald Vizenor (New York: HarperCollins, 1995), 5.

12. Henry Dawes, "Have We Failed with the Indian?" *Atlantic Monthly* 84 (1899): 281.

13. Frederick E. Hoxie, introduction to *Talking Back to Civilization: Indian Voices from the Progressive Era*, ed. Frederick E. Hoxie (Boston: Bedford/St. Martin's, 2001), 4.

14. Zitkala-Ša, "A Warrior's Daughter" *Everybody's Magazine* 4 (1902): 346–52.

15. Gerald Vizenor, *The Everlasting Sky: New Voices from the People Named the Chippewa* (New York: Crowell-Collier Press, 1972), 12.

16. Zitkala-Ša, "The Trial Path," *Harper's Monthly* 103 (1901): 741–44.

17. As Vine Deloria, Jr., also Sioux, describes the belief in the afterlife that was handed down in his tradition: "In the days of the wisest men, the 'Milky Way' was thought to be the high road of the Spirits, which led them either toward the happy hunting grounds to the right, or to the left and the abode of punishment." *Singing for a Spirit: A Portrait of the Dakota Sioux* (Santa Fe: Clear Light Publishers, 2000), 133.

18. Zitkala-Ša, "The Soft-Hearted Sioux," *Harper's Monthly* 102 (1901): 505–08.

19. Jace Weaver, *That the People Might Live: Native American Literatures and Native American Community* (New York: Oxford University Press, 1997), 38–39.

20. Susan Bernadin, "The Lessons of a Sentimental Education: Zitkala-Ša's Autobiographical Narratives," *Western American Literature* 32, no. 3 (1997): 217.

21. Quoted in Fisher, foreword to Zitkala-Ša, *American Indian Stories*, viii. Originally published in *The Red Man and Helper* (April 12, 1901).

22. Zitkala-Ša, "Why I Am a Pagan," *Atlantic Monthly* 90 (1902): 801–03.

23. When Zitkala-Ša's stories and essays were collected in *American Indian Stories* in 1921, she seemed to back away from defining herself as a "pagan." "Why I Am a Pagan" is renamed "The Great Spirit," and the former ending—"if this is Paganism, then at present, at least, I am a Pagan"—was rewritten. The new ending reads, "Here in a fleeting quiet, I am awakened by the fluttering robe of the Great Spirit. To my innermost consciousness the phenomenal universe is a royal mantle, vibrating with his divine breath. Caught in its flowing fringes are the spangles and oscillating brilliants of sun, moon, and stars" (107). Zitkala-Ša does not soften her criticism of Christianity, however; her references to it as a "bigoted creed" and a "new superstition" remain.

24. Zitkala-Ša, "Impressions of an Indian Childhood," *Atlantic Monthly* 85 (1900): 37–47.

25. According to Royal B. Hassrick, "The Sioux code prescribed that behavior between persons should be governed by the principles of familiarity and respect" in order to "ensure a cohesive, workable society wherein members endeavor to foster harmony and avoid conflict." *The Sioux: Life and Customs of a Warrior Society* (Norman: University of Oklahoma Press, 1964), 107.

26. Zitkala-Ša, "The School Days of an Indian Girl," *Atlantic Monthly* 85 (1900): 185–94.

27. Jane Tompkins, "Indians: Textualism, Morality, and the Problem of History," in *"Race," Writing, and Difference,* ed. Henry Louis Gates, Jr. (Chicago: University of Chicago Press, 1986), 63.

28. Quoted in Dorothea M. Susag, "Zitkala-Ša (Gertrude Simmons Bonnin): A Power(full) Literary Voice," *Studies in American Indian Literatures* 5, no. 4 (1993): 16.

29. Quoted in Wilson, 312.

30. This metaphor echoes a description in "Impressions of an Indian Childhood," when Zitkala-Ša's mother tells her that "we were driven like a herd of buffalos." This mirroring connects the Dawes-era boarding schools to the larger dehumanizing national policy toward Native Americans, which served to disrupt tribal continuity.

31. Martha J. Cutter, "Zitkala-Ša's Autobiographical Writings: The Problems of a Canonical Search for Language and Identity," *MELUS* 19, no. 1 (1994): 36.

32. English-language acquisition, which was often a struggle for American Indian children and their teachers, is discussed in David Wallace Adams, *Education for Extinction: American Indians and the Boarding School Experience, 1875–1928* (Lawrence: University Press of Kansas, 1995). Adams writes that in order to accelerate their students' English-language skills, teachers at Indian schools were advised that "pupils must be compelled to converse with each other in English, and should be properly rebuked or punished for persistent violation of this rule" (140). According to Adams, most students made rapid progress in learning the new language. Several autobiographies by other Native Americans who attended Indian boarding schools also tell of painful misunderstandings having to do with language differences and English instruction. These authors write in English, but their memories reveal that they still associate the language with negative experiences. See, for example, Luther Standing Bear, *My People, the Sioux* (Boston: Houghton Mifflin, 1928), and Charles A. Eastman [Ohiyesa], *From Deep Woods to Civilization: Chapters in the Autobiography of an Indian* (Boston: Little, Brown, 1916).

33. Zitkala-Ša, "An Indian Teacher among Indians," *Atlantic Monthly* 85 (1900): 381–86.

34. Bernadin, 228.

35. Weaver, 27.

36. The last phrase is possibly a reference to the Carlisle Indian School, the newspaper of which was *The Red Man and Helper.*

37. Weaver, 31.

38. Ibid., 39.

39. Dexter Fisher, "The Transformation of Tradition: A Study of Zitkala-Ša and Mourning Dove, Two Transitional American Indian Writers," in *Critical Essays on Native American Literature,* ed. Andrew Wiget (Boston: G. K. Hall, 1985), 206.

CHAPTER 4. RACE AND NATION IN THE NOVELS OF SUTTON E. GRIGGS

1. Bhabha, 7.

2. U.S. Constitution, amend. 14, sec. 1.

3. Ibid., amend. 15, sec. 1.

4. Rayford W. Logan, *The Betrayal of the Negro: From Rutherford B. Hayes to Woodrow Wilson* (New York: Da Capo Press, 1997), 109. An earlier version of this book, originally titled *The Negro in American Life and Thought: The Nadir, 1877–1901,* was published in London by Dial Press in 1954. An expanded edition, *The Betrayal of the Negro: From Rutherford B. Hayes to Woodrow Wilson,* was published in New York by Collier Books in 1965. The work cited here is an unabridged reprint of the 1965 edition.

5. *Plessy v. Ferguson* 163 U.S. 537 (1896), in *Documents of American Constitutional and Legal History,* ed. Melvin I. Urosfsky (Philadelphia: Temple University Press, 1989), 2:246.

6. Ibid., 2:248.

7. Joe William Trotter, Jr., *The African American Experience* (Boston: Houghton Mifflin, 2001), 336. Statistics can also be found in Logan, 192.

8. Logan, 52.

9. Ibid., 58.

10. Sutton E. Griggs, *Imperium in Imperio* (1899; reprint, Miami: Mnemosyne Publishing, 1969).

11. The "nation within a nation" meets at "Thomas Jefferson College," where members both find fault with the U.S. Constitution and use it as a model for their own constitution. The forming of a new government because of the unjust rule of law has many direct parallels with the American Revolution. Perhaps Griggs has his revolutionaries meet at Thomas Jefferson College to underscore this similarity. Ibid.

12. Frederick Douglass employed familiar national rhetoric and symbols in order to compel the United States to recognize and uphold its highest ideals when dealing with black Americans. Most biting, perhaps, is a speech he delivered in 1852, "What to the Slave Is the Fourth of July?" As he answers this question, "To him [the slave] your celebration is a sham; your boasted liberty an unholy license. . . . All your religious parade and solemnity, are to him mere bombast, fraud, deception, impiety, and hypocrisy—a thin veil to cover up crimes which would disgrace a nation of savages." "What to the Slave Is the Fourth of July?" in *My Bondage and My Freedom* (1855; reprint, New York: Dover, 1969), 445. W. E. B. Du Bois reminds white and black Americans that African Americans seek the same rights on which the country was founded: "By every civilized and peaceful method we must strive for the rights which the world accords to men, clinging unwaveringly to those great words which the sons of the Fathers would fain forget: 'We hold these truths to be self evident: That all men are created equal; that they are endowed by their Creator with certain unalienable rights; that among these are life, liberty, and the pursuit of happiness.'" *The Souls of Black Folk* (1903; reprint, New York: Dover, 1994), 35.

13. Sutton E. Griggs, *The Hindered Hand; or, The Reign of the Repressionist* (1905; reprint, Miami: Mnemosyne Publishing, 1969).

14. It is revealed later that this woman is Eunice Seabright, who is also of African American descent.

15. Raymond Hedin, "Probable Readers, Possible Stories: The Limits of Nineteenth-Century Black Narrative," in *Readers in History: Nineteenth-Century American Literature and the Contexts of Response,* ed. James A. Machor (Baltimore: Johns Hopkins University Press, 1993), 198.

16. Sutton E. Griggs, *Pointing the Way* (Nashville: Orion Publishing, 1908).

17. The "tragic mulatto" is most often an all-but-white African American who suffers both psychologically and socially because of the combination of white skin and black heritage. Often the tragedy has to do with the angst that ensues when his or her ethnicity is discovered. An early discussion of white writers' treatment of this character can be found in Hugh M. Gloster, *Negro Voices in American Fiction* (Chapel Hill: University of North Carolina Press, 1948). More recently, Dickson D. Bruce, Jr., has explored how African American writers incorporate the "tragic mulatto" into their fiction, often subverting, as Griggs does, the stereotypes on which the archetype is based. See Bruce's *Black American Writing from the Nadir: The Evolution of a Literary Tradition, 1877–1915* (Baton Rouge: Louisiana State University Press, 1989).

18. Bhabha, 155.

19. Griggs's consideration of black leaders can be seen as a kind of precursor to Ralph Ellison's *Invisible Man* (New York: Random House, 1952), which comments on the leadership of such black figures as Booker T. Washington, Marcus Garvey, and Frederick Douglass.

20. A more famous literary evaluation of the leadership of Booker T. Washington can be found in W. E. B. Du Bois's essay, "Of Booker T. Washington and Others," in *The Souls of Black Folk,* 25–35.

21. Dana Nelson, *The World in Black and White: Reading "Race" in American Literature, 1638–1867* (New York: Oxford University Press, 1992), esp. chap. 6, "'For the Gaze of Whites': The Crisis of Subject in 'Benito Cereno,'" 109–30. Nelson's evaluation of Captain Delano's inability to interpret the slave revolt is helpful in understanding texts involving interracial interaction.

22. Griggs addresses Washington's policies in all five of his novels. In *Imperium in Imperio,* Piedmont continues to mirror the life of Washington as he comes to represent the conservative African American who would "fondly kiss the smiting hand" of whites (262). In *Overshadowed,* Erma Wysong goes to hear Washington speak, and his influence leads her to give her brother some poor advice. In *Unfettered,* a character laments that African Americans "are being taught in certain high quarters that self-repression is the Negro's chiefest virtues" (174). And in *The Hindered Hand,* Earl Bluefield considers industrial training important but wonders "how great an army of carpenters can hammer the spirit of repression" out of national thought (260). Although Griggs resists much of Washington's agenda, such as abandoning the fight for political and social equality, the two men share some points of agreement. Griggs mocks Washington's conciliatory and apologist position in a speech that Piedmont gives at the end of *Imperium,* but Piedmont, despite his conservatism, is an energetic activist and educator devoted to his race, as was Washington. Griggs also seemed to agree with Washington's policy of forming alliances with the class of educated, liberal, white Americans, which is part of the solution to racial antagonism in *Pointing the Way.* Sutton E. Griggs, *Overshadowed* (1901; reprint, Freeport: Books for Libraries Press, 1971), and *Unfettered* (1902; reprint, New York: AMS Press, 1971).

23. Booker T. Washington, *Up from Slavery* (1901; reprint, New York: Signet, 2000), 154.

24. Most notable among these are Frances E. W. Harper, *Iola Leroy: or, Shadows Uplifted* (Philadelphia: Garrigues Brothers, 1892), and Charles W. Chesnutt, *The House behind the Cedars* (Boston: Houghton Mifflin, 1900). Whether the fair-skinned characters choose to pass (as in *House*) or whether they pass because they are unaware of their black ancestry (as in *Iola Leroy*), the implication is that the idea of race is a social construct, not an ineradicable division.

25. It is also significant that Griggs chooses to have a white woman pass to marry a black man. The rhetoric of hysteria that was circulating in the South at the time warned that repression of African Americans was necessary to protect white womanhood, and a depiction of such a relationship carried the weight of those social implications. Griggs counters the racial connotations of such a union by making it a conscious, reasoned choice between two people. The black man does not pursue the white woman; instead, the woman decides on her husband because he has the best qualities of any man in town.

26. Herman Melville, "Benito Cereno," in *The Piazza Tales* (New York: Dix & Edwards, 1856), 109–270.

27. Griggs, however, often complicates white participation in the black struggle by revealing the deep emotional prejudices of even these apparently liberal characters. Lanier, for example, feels he is helping when he suggests that John Wysong go to Africa because he is "not fit for the rigors of civilized life in America" (172). Another example of well-intended but unconsciously prejudiced white attitudes is found at Belton Piedmont's college in *Imperium in Imperio*. Located in Nashville, Tennessee, "Stowe University" is named "in honor of Mrs. Harriet Beecher Stowe, author of 'Uncle Tom's Cabin'" (48). The school is thus a reflection of Stowe and her most famous work, and, in a broader sense, of northern attitudes to black southerners in general. Founded on "Northern philanthropy," the university has only one black professor, who is an inspiration to the African American students. The fact that the other faculty members do not eat at the same table with him is also significant to the student body. In order to secure social equality for this professor, the students "combine" and protest in a way that is totally unexpected by the well-meaning, but still segregatory, white administrators.

28. This is a paraphrase of the title of a Ralph Ellison essay, "Change the Joke and Slip the Yoke," in *The Collected Essays of Ralph Ellison* (New York: Modern Library, 1995), 100–12.

29. Another plantation stereotype that is subverted is the figure of the "mammy" in the character of Aunt Catherine in *Unfettered*. Aunt Catherine is an ex-slave who was nurse to several generations of a white family before the last heir orders her off the estate. She ends up in Chicago, where she finally has to sell her body to medicine in order to find comfort in the hospital in her dying days (140). Although her friend Morlene explains that Aunt Catherine had been in service to others all her life and begs to take her body back to Tennessee so that she may rest in the land of her people, the white doctors deny this request, deciding instead to use the body for their own purposes, as she had been so used in her lifetime.

30. Paul Laurence Dunbar, "We Wear the Mask," in *Lyrics of Lowly Life* (New York: Dodd, Mead, 1896), 167.

31. The debate over Griggs's black nationalism began in 1948 with Gloster's estimation in *Negro Voices in American Fiction* that Griggs was "militant" (56). In 1958 Robert A. Bone challenged the conception of Griggs as a militant political thinker. Because Bone could not reconcile the various movements depicted in Griggs's novels, he misinterprets their complexity and labels Griggs not a militant but an "accomodationist." *The Negro Novel in America* (New Haven: Yale University Press, 1958), 35. Several articles published in the 1970s made important connections between Griggs's fiction and American black nationalist movements. Among these are Robert E. Fleming, "Sutton E. Griggs: Militant Black Novelist," *Phylon* 34 (1973): 73–77, and Wilson J. Moses, "Literary Garveyism: Three Novels of Sutton E. Griggs," *Phylon* 40 (1979): 203–16. In a 1980 essay, Moses comes to the conclusion that "in all of Sutton Griggs's novels separation of the races finally wins in the end." "Literary Myth and Ethnic Assimilation: Israel Zangwill and Sutton E. Griggs," *New Hungarian Quarterly* 21 (1980): 134. Perhaps the best evaluation of Griggs's political stance is found in Arlene A. Elders, *The "Hindered Hand": Cultural Implications of Early African American Fiction* (Westport, Conn.: Greenwood Press, 1978). Elder contends, as I do, that Griggs posits many possibilities for black Americans, including immigration to Africa and military resistance, but does not actually espouse most of them.

32. The text does not actually identify Peppers's grandfather as a U.S. president, but the implication is clear. The justice talks of the man who "became ——— of our nation, and wrought well domestic and international affairs" (224).

33. This book may refer to Frederick L. Hoffman, *Race Traits and Tendencies of the American Negro* (New York: Macmillan, for the American Economic Association, 1896). In this report Dr. Hoffman, a Prudential insurance statistician, predicts the eventual extinction of black peoples living in America.

34. It should be noted that Griggs himself was not immune from this same phenomenon. Though he challenged many of the racial theories that were circulating at the time, it is clear that he accepted several predominant assumptions. For example, though he combated the idea of white superiority with his narratives and with his life, he often resorted to essentialist language to describe racial differences.

35. Wysong's name is an interesting choice, which is related, either intentionally or thematically, to the poem "Sympathy" (1899), by Griggs's contemporary Paul Laurence Dunbar. The final stanza of the poem reads:

I know why the caged bird sings,
    ah me,
When his wing is bruised and
    his bosom sore,—
When he beats his bars and he
    would be free;
It is not a carol of joy or glee,
    But a prayer that he sends from
his heart's deep core,
    But a plea, that upward to Heaven

he flings—
I know why the caged bird sings!

The name "Wysong" may be a reference to "why sing." That is, why should a black man strive and dream if he has no hope of attaining his dreams, if he is restrained and prevented from doing so by all the powers that be in society, if he is "caged" as the bird in Dunbar's poem? Paul Laurence Dunbar, "Sympathy," in *Lyrics of the Hearthside* (New York: Dodd, Mead, 1899).

36. Houston A. Baker, *Blues, Ideology, and Afro-American Literature: A Vernacular Theory* (Chicago: University of Chicago Press, 1984), 8, 13.

37. Paul Gilroy, *The Black Atlantic: Modernity and Double Consciousness* (Cambridge, Mass.: Harvard University Press, 1993).

38. Gloster, 57.

CHAPTER 5. THE MULTICULTURAL PERSPECTIVE OF SUI SIN FAR

1. For a thorough discussion of the ways in which Chinese immigrants have been depicted in literature, see William Wu, *The Yellow Peril: Chinese Americans in American Fiction, 1850–1940* (Hamden, Conn.: Archon Books, 1982). There is also a good overview of the subject in Elaine H. Kim, *Asian American Literature: An Introduction to the Writings and Their Social Context* (Philadelphia: Temple University Press, 1982), 3–22.

2. Sui Sin Far, "A Plea for the Chinaman: A Correspondent's Argument in His Favor," and "Leaves from the Mental Portfolio of an Eurasian," in *Mrs. Spring Fragrance and Other Writings*, ed. Ling and White-Parks, 192, 230. "Plea for the Chinaman" was originally published in the *Montreal Daily Star* (September 21, 1896); "Leaves" was originally published in the *Independent* 66 (January 21, 1909): 125–32. All citations of Sui Sin Far's articles and stories in this chapter come from the Ling and White-Parks edition.

3. Marlon K. Hom, introduction to *Songs of Gold Mountain: Cantonese Rhymes from San Francisco Chinatown* (Berkeley: University of California Press, 1987), 56.

4. Takaki, 192.

5. For a thorough discussion of the political history of the act, see Andrew Gyory, *Closing the Gates: Race, Politics, and the Chinese Exclusion Act* (Chapel Hill: University of North Carolina Press, 1998).

6. *Yick Wo v. Hopkins* 118 U.S. 356 (1886), in *Documents of American Constitutional and Legal History*, ed. Urosfsky, 2:241–44.

7. Gyory, 94, 96–97, 173–74, 176–77, 287 n. 4, 307 n. 46

8. Hom, 12–13.

9. Ibid., 67.

10. Amy Ling, *Between Worlds: Women Writers of Chinese Ancestry* (New York: Pergamon Press, 1990), 13.

11. The term "bachelor community" refers to male laborers who lived and worked together in North American Chinatowns. Many of these "bachelors" actually had wives in China. See Takaki, 218–20.

12. Xiao-Huang Yin, "Between East and West: Sui Sin Far—The First Chinese American Woman Writer," *Arizona Quarterly* 47, no. 4 (1991): 55–56.

13. White-Parks, 118.

14. Yin, 60.

15. "Mrs. Spring Fragrance" was originally published in *Hampton's* 24 (January 1910): 137–41. "The Inferior Woman" was originally published in *Hampton's* 24 (May 1910): 127–31.

16. Yin, 65.

17. Both "The Americanizing of Pau Tsu" and "The Wisdom of the New" were originally published in *Mrs. Spring Fragrance*.

18. White-Parks, 3.

19. Yin, 64.

20. Ling, 143.

21. The character of Adah Charlton is possibly a subtle social satire. The name Charlton appears earlier in the writings of Sui Sin Far. As Edith Eaton, she wrote an inflamed article for the *Montreal Daily Star* calling for the fair treatment of the Chinese in Canada and America. "A Plea for the Chinaman" suggests that "the people who are persecuting them send one of themselves, nay a dozen of themselves, men who are just as prejudiced as their constituents, just as worked up over fancied wrongs and just as incapable of judging fairly. They are all, Mr. Maxwell, *Mr. Charlton,* Mr. Mcinness, Mr. Smith, etc., etc., equipped with a self-interest which is the strongest of weapons" (192; emphasis added). It is revealing that the character of Adah Charlton has the same surname as a man to whom Sui Sin Far took such offense. There is also a possible reference to another historical figure in association with Adah Charlton. When she advises Wou Sankwei to go spend time with his wife, "he felt himself exiled from Paradise, yet it did not occur to him to question, as a white man would have done, whether the angel with the flaming sword had authority for her action" (59). At the time Sui Sin Far was writing, there was a figure in San Francisco's Chinatown who was known for her work with young Chinese prostitutes. Frank Chin writes of "Donaldina Cameron, celebrated in Christian Chinatown history as 'Chinatown's avenging Angel.'" According to Chin, the purpose of her Cameron House for Chinese girls was to convert the prostitutes and send them back to China to "spread the Gospel and discourage Chinese migration to America." Sui Sin Far's reference to "avenging angel" may thus suggest that the motives of those who choose to intervene in the lives of Chinese immigrants should not go unquestioned. Frank Chin, "Come All Ye Asian Writers of the Real and the Fake," in *The Big Aiiieeeee! An Anthology of Chinese American and Japanese American Literature,* ed. Jeffrey Paul Chan, Frank Chin, Lawson Fusao Inada, and Shawn Wong (New York: Meridian, 1991), 16.

22. White-Parks, 223.

23. Ibid.

24. Ibid., 224.

25. James Doyle, "Sui Sin Far and Onoto Watanna: Two Early Chinese-Canadian Authors," *Canadian Literature* 140 (Spring 1994): 56.

26. White-Parks, 142.

27. Ibid., 3.

28. "In the Land of the Free" was originally published in the *Independent* 67 (September 2, 1909): 504–08.

29. "The Story of One White Woman Who Married a Chinese" was originally published under the title "A White Woman Who Married a Chinaman" in the *Independent* 68 (March 10, 1910): 518–23.

30. "Her Chinese Husband" was originally published in the *Independent* 69 (August 18, 1910): 358–61.

31. "'Its Wavering Image'" was originally published in *Mrs. Spring Fragrance*.

32. Edward Said, "Orientalism," *Georgia Review* 31 (1977): 185–86.

33. Ibid., 199.

34. Kim, 30.

35. "Madame Butterfly" was originally a short story written by John Luther Long and published in *Century* 55 (January 1898): 274–92. Long and Broadway playwright David Belasco made the story into a play, which was seen by composer Giacomo Puccini in London in 1900. Puccini developed the play into his very popular *Madama Butterfly*, which premiered in Milan in 1904 and in New York in 1907. The tale's protagonist is Cio-Cio San, a Japanese woman who renounces her friends, family, and religion to marry Pinkerton, an American, who in turn abandons her for an American wife. In the end Cio-Cio San commits suicide, leaving the child she had with Pinkerton to the American couple. With the popularity of *Madame Butterfly*, the trope of the submissive Asian entered the public consciousness. This figure has been used and subverted in many Asian American texts in the twentieth century. Sui Sin Far's sister, Winnifred Eaton, took on the pen name Onoto Watanna and wrote several novels set in Japan that addressed this theme. More recently, playwright David Henry Hwang's *M. Butterfly* won a Tony Award in 1988.

36. The California antimiscegenation law "prohibited marriages between a white person and a 'negro, mulatto, or Mongolian.'" Takaki, 205.

37. This parallels the race and marriage theme in Griggs's novels, where relationships often are fragmented due to America's continuing racial tyranny.

38. "Pat and Pan" was originally published in *Mrs. Spring Fragrance*.

39. Edward Said, "*Orientalism:* An Afterword," *Raritan* 14, no. 3 (1995): 53.

40. Joe R. Feagin, "Old Poison in New Bottles: The Deep Roots of Modern Nativism," in *Critical White Studies: Looking behind the Mirror*, ed. Richard Delgado and Jean Stefancic (Philadelphia: Temple University Press, 1997), 352.

41. Said, "*Orientalism:* An Afterword," 57.

CHAPTER 6. CONCLUSION

1. Though most texts by immigrants or writers of color during this period represented race relations in America in some way, other texts did not incorporate these themes. Some immigrant authors created narratives that were not set in America at all. For example, *Los de Abajo* (*Those from Below*), a novel by Mariano Azuela about *La Revolución* that was going on in his native Mexico, was written and published in the

United States in 1915. After its publication, Azuela returned to Mexico, where, by the time of his death, he was considered one of the greatest men of Mexican letters. Lamed Shapiro, a Jewish immigrant who migrated to America as an adult, wrote a series of Yiddish narratives in the first decade of the twentieth century—including *Der kush* (*The Kiss,* 1907) and *Der tseylem* (*The Cross,* 1909)—that describe pogroms in eastern Europe. Some works by ethnic American writers primarily involve assimilated white characters, as does *The Uncalled* (1898) by Paul Laurence Dunbar. At least one writer, Onoto Watanna (Winnifred Eaton), created texts in which the main characters were of a different ethnicity from her own. Of Chinese and English descent, she wrote many popular novels that were set in Japan and featured Japanese women as protagonists. Her first was *Miss Numè of Japan,* which was published in 1899. Mariano Azuela, *Los de abajo* (El Paso: El Paso del Norte, 1915); Lamed Shapiro, *Di yidishe melukhe un andere zakhn* (New York: Naytsayt, 1919); Paul Laurence Dunbar, *The Uncalled* (New York: Dodd, Mead, 1898); Onoto Watanna, *Miss Numè of Japan* (New York: Rand, McNally, 1899).

2. Mary V. Dearborn, *Pocahontas's Daughters: Gender and Ethnicity in American Culture* (New York: Oxford University Press, 1986), 86.

3. In "Of the Training of Black Men," Du Bois states, "This is certain, no secure civilization can be built in the South with the Negro as an ignorant, turbulent proletariat. Suppose we seek to remedy this by making them laborers and nothing more: they are not fools, they have tasted the Tree of Life, and they will not cease to think, will not cease attempting to read the riddle of the world." In *The Souls of Black Folk,* 64. For a well-documented explanation of how black education in the south at this time was designed to produce "submissive, nonpolitical, cheap black laborers" (89), see James D. Anderson, "Education and the Race Problem in the New South," chap. 3 in *The Education of Blacks in the South, 1860–1935* (Chapel Hill: University of North Carolina Press, 1988), 79–109.

4. A discussion of Zitkala-Ša's reaction to the school's servant placement program can be found in Bernadin, 212–38.

5. Randolph Bourne, "Trans-National America," *Atlantic Monthly* 118 (1916): 90.

6. J. Hillis Miller, "Narrative," in *Critical Terms for Literary Study,* 2d ed., ed. Frank Lentricchia and Thomas McLauglin (Chicago: University of Chicago Press, 1995), 69.

7. Ibid.

8. Edgar Allan Poe, "Review of *Twice-Told Tales* by Nathaniel Hawthorne," in *The Complete Works of Edgar Allen Poe,* ed. James A. Harrison (New York: AMS Press, 1902), 108. Originally published in *Graham's Magazine* 20 (May, 1842): 298–300.

9. Miller, 69.

10. Mikhail Bakhtin, "Discourse in the Novel," in *The Dialogic Imagination: Four Essays,* ed. Michael Holquist, trans. Caryl Emerson and Michael Holquist (Austin: University of Texas Press, 1981), 262.

11. Du Bois, 9.

12. Horace M. Kallen, "Democracy versus the Melting Pot," in *Jewish American Literature,* ed. Jules Chametzky, John Felstiner, Hilene Flanzbaum, and Kathryn Hellerstein (New York: W. W. Norton, 2001), 214. Originally published as "Democracy versus the

Melting Pot: A Study of American Nationality," in *The Nation* 100 (February 18, 1915): 190–94, and (February 25, 1915): 217–20.

13. Bourne, 84.

14. Dearborn, 3.

15. Eric J. Sundquist, *To Wake the Nations: Race in the Making of American Literature* (Cambridge, Mass.: Belknap Press, 1993), 18.

16. Priscilla Wald, *Constituting America: Cultural Anxiety and Narrative Form* (Durham: Duke University Press, 1995), 2.

Works Cited

Adams, David Wallace. *Education for Extinction: American Indians and the Boarding School Experience, 1875–1928.* Lawrence: University Press of Kansas, 1995.

Allen, Paula Gunn. *The Sacred Hoop: Recovering the Feminine in American Indian Traditions.* Boston: Beacon Press, 1991.

Altschuler, Glenn C. *Race, Ethnicity, and Class in American Social Thought, 1865–1919.* Wheeling: Harlan Davidson, 1982.

Ammons, Elizabeth. *Conflicting Stories: American Women Writers at the Turn into the Twentieth Century.* New York: Oxford University Press, 1992.

———. "Expanding the Canon of American Realism." In *The Cambridge Companion to American Realism and Naturalism.* Ed. Donald Pizer. Cambridge: Cambridge University Press, 1995. 95–114.

———. "Men of Color, Women, and Uppity Art at the Turn of the Century." In *American Realism and the Canon.* Ed. Tom Quirk and Gary Scharnhorst. Newark: University of Delaware Press, 1994. 22–33.

———, ed. *Short Fiction by Black Women, 1900–1920.* New York: Oxford University Press, 1991.

Ammons, Elizabeth, and Annette White-Parks, eds. *Tricksterism in Turn-of-the-Century American Literature: A Multicultural Perspective.* Hanover, N.H.: University Press of New England, 1994.

Anderson, James D. *The Education of Blacks in the South, 1860–1935.* Chapel Hill: University of North Carolina Press, 1988.

Antin, Mary. *From Plotzk to Boston.* New York: W. B. Clark, 1899. Reprint, New York: Markus Weiner, 1986.

———. "The Lie." *Atlantic Monthly* 112 (1913): 177–90.

———. *The Promised Land.* Boston: Houghton Mifflin, 1912. Reprint, New York: Penguin, 1997.

———. *Selected Letters of Mary Antin,.* Ed. Evelyn Salz. Syracuse, N.Y.: Syracuse University Press, 2000.

———. *They Who Knock at Our Gate: A Complete Gospel of Immigration.* Boston: Houghton Mifflin, 1914.

Anzaldúa, Gloria. *Borderlands/*La Frontera*: The New Mestiza.* San Francisco: Aunt Lute Books, 1987.

Azuela, Mariano. *Los de abajo.* El Paso: El Paso del Norte, 1915.

Baker, Houston A. *Blues, Ideology, and Afro-American Literature: A Vernacular Theory.* Chicago: University of Chicago Press, 1984.

Bakhtin, Mikhail. *The Dialogic Imagination: Four Essays.* Ed. Michael Holquist. Trans. Caryl Emerson and Michael Holquist. Austin: University of Texas Press, 1981.

Batker, Carol J. *Reforming Fictions: Native, African, and Jewish American Women's Literature and Journalism in the Progressive Era.* New York: Columbia University Press, 2000.

Bernadin, Susan. "The Lessons of a Sentimental Education: Zitkala-Ša's Autobiographical Narratives." *Western American Literature* 32, no. 3 (1997): 212–38.

Berthoff, Warner. *The Ferment of Realism: American Literature, 1884–1919.* New York: The Free Press, 1965.

Beulens, Gert. "The New Man and the Mediator: (Non-) Remembrance in Jewish-American Immigrant Narrative." In *Memory, Narrative, and Identity: New Essays in Ethnic American Literature.* Ed. Amiritjit Singh, Joseph T. Skerrett, Jr., and Robert E. Hogan. Boston: Northeastern University Press, 1994. 89–113.

Bhabha, Homi. *The Location of Culture.* London: Routledge, 1994.

Bone, Robert A. *The Negro Novel in America.* New Haven: Yale University Press, 1958.

Bourne, Randolph. "Trans-National America." *Atlantic Monthly* 118 (1916): 86–97.

Brooks, Van Wyck. *The Confident Years: 1885–1915.* New York: E. P. Dutton, 1952.

Brown, William Wells. *Clotel; or, The President's Daughter: A Narrative of Slave Life in the United States.* London: Partridge and Oakey, 1853.

Bruce, Dickson D., Jr. *Black American Writing from the Nadir: The Evolution of a Literary Tradition, 1877–1915.* Baton Rouge: Louisiana State University Press, 1989.

Callahan, S. Alice. *Wynema: A Child of the Forest.* Chicago: H. J. Smith, 1891.

Chametzky, Jules, John Felstiner, Hilene Flanzbaum, and Kathryn Hellerstien, eds. *Jewish American Literature.* New York: W. W. Norton, 2001.

Chesnutt, Charles W. *The House behind the Cedars.* Boston: Houghton Mifflin, 1900.

Chin, Frank. "Come All Ye Asian Writers of the Real and the Fake." In *The Big Aiiieeeee! An Anthology of Chinese American and Japanese American Literature.* Ed. Jeffrey Paul Chan, Frank Chin, Lawson Fusao Inada, and Shawn Wong. New York: Meridian, 1991. 1–92.

Cohen, Sarah Blacher. "Mary Antin's *The Promised Land:* A Breach of Promise." *Studies in American Jewish Literature* 3 (1977): 28–35.

Crane, Stephen. *Maggie: A Girl of the Streets.* New York: Appleton, 1896.

Crèvecoeur, J. Hector St. John de. *Letters from an American Farmer.* London: Thomas Davies, 1782. Reprint, New York: Penguin, 1986.

Cutter, Martha J. "Zitkala-Ša's Autobiographical Writings: The Problems of a Canonical Search for Language and Identity." *MELUS* 19, no. 1 (1994): 31–44.

Dawes, Henry. "Have We Failed with the Indian?" *Atlantic Monthly* 84 (1899): 280–85.

Dearborn, Mary V. *Pocahontas's Daughters: Gender and Ethnicity in American Culture.* New York: Oxford University Press, 1986.

Deloria, Vine, Jr. *Singing for a Spirit: A Portrait of the Dakota Sioux.* Santa Fe: Clear Light Publishers, 2000.

Douglass, Frederick. *My Bondage and My Freedom.* New York: Miller, Orton, and Mulligun, 1855. Reprint, New York: Dover, 1969.

———. *Narrative of the Life of Frederick Douglass, An American Slave.* Boston: Anti-Slavery Office, 1845.

Doyle, James. "Sui Sin Far and Onoto Watanna: Two Early Chinese-Canadian Authors." *Canadian Literature* 140 (Spring 1994): 50–58.

Dreiser, Theodore. *Sister Carrie.* New York: Doubleday, Page, 1900.

Du Bois, W. E. B. *The Souls of Black Folk.* Chicago: A. C. McClurg, 1903. Reprint, New York: Dover, 1994.

Dunbar, Paul Laurence. *Lyrics of the Hearthside.* New York: Dodd, Mead, 1896.

———. *Lyrics of Lowly Life.* New York: Dodd, Mead, 1896.

———. *The Uncalled.* New York: Dodd, Mead, 1898.

Dunbar-Nelson, Alice. *The Goodness of St. Rocque and Other Stories.* New York: Dodd, Mead, 1899.

Dunne, Finley Peter. *Observations by Mr. Dooley.* New York: Russell, 1902.

Eastman, Charles A [Ohiyesa]. *From Deep Woods to Civilization: Chapters in the Autobiography of an Indian.* Boston: Little, Brown, 1916.

Elder, Arlene A. *The "Hindered Hand": Cultural Implications of Early African-American Fiction.* Westport, Conn.: Greenwood Press, 1978.

Elliot, Michael A. *The Culture Concept: Writing and Difference in the Age of Realism.* Minneapolis: University of Minnesota Press, 2002.

Ellison, Ralph. *The Collected Essays of Ralph Ellison*. Ed. and introd. John F. Callahan. New York: Modern Library, 1995.

———. *Invisible Man*. New York: Random House, 1952.

Feagin, Joe R. "Old Poison in New Bottles: The Deep Roots of Modern Nativism." In *Critical White Studies: Looking behind the Mirror*. Ed. Richard Delgado and Jean Stefancic. Philadelphia: Temple University Press, 1997. 348–53.

Fisher, Dexter. "The Transformation of Tradition: A Study of Zitkala-Ša and Mourning Dove, Two Transitional American Indian Writers." In *Critical Essays on Native American Literature*. Ed. Andrew Wiget. Boston: G. K. Hall, 1985. 202–11.

Fleming, Robert E. "Sutton E. Griggs: Militant Black Novelist." *Phylon* 34, no. 1 (1973): 73–77.

Flynn, John T. "The Muckrakers." In *John D. Rockefeller: Robber Baron or Industrial Statesman?* Ed. Earl Latham. Boston: D. C. Heath, 1949. 1–6.

Franklin, Benjamin. *The Autobiography of Benjamin Franklin: A Genetic Text*. Ed. J. A. Leo Lemay and P. M. Zall. Knoxville: University of Tennessee Press, 1981.

Gilroy, Paul. *The Black Atlantic: Modernity and Double Consciousness*. Cambridge, Mass.: Harvard University Press, 1993.

Gloster, Hugh M. *Negro Voices in American Fiction*. Chapel Hill: University of North Carolina Press, 1948.

Griggs, Sutton E. *The Hindered Hand; or, The Reign of the Repressionist*. Nashville: Orion, 1905. Reprint, Miami: Mnemosyne, 1969.

———. *Imperium in Imperio*. Cincinnati: Editor, 1899. Reprints, Miami: Mnemosyne, 1969, and New York: Modern Library, 2003.

———. *Overshadowed*. Nashville: Orion, 1901. Reprint, Freeport: Books for Libraries Press, 1971.

———. *Pointing the Way*. Nashville: Orion, 1908.

———. *Unfettered*. Nashville: Orion, 1902. Reprint, New York: AMS Press, 1971.

Gyory, Andrew. *Closing the Gates: Race, Politics, and the Chinese Exclusion Act*. Chapel Hill: University of North Carolina Press, 1998.

Harper, Frances E. W. *Iola Leroy: or, Shadows Uplifted*. Philadelphia: Garrigues Brothers, 1892.

Hassrick, Royal B. *The Sioux: Life and Customs of a Warrior Society*. Norman: University of Oklahoma Press, 1964.

Hedin, Raymond. "Probable Readers, Possible Stories: The Limits of Nineteenth-Century Black Narrative." In *Readers in History: Nineteenth-Century American Literature and the Contexts of Response*. Ed. James L. Machor. Baltimore: Johns Hopkins University Press, 1993. 180–206.

Hertzberg, Arthur. *The Jews in America: Four Centuries of an Uneasy Encounter.* New York: Columbia University Press, 1997.

Hoffman, Frederick L. *Race Traits and Tendencies of the American Negro.* New York: Macmillan, for the American Economic Association, 1896.

Hom, Marlon K., ed. *Songs of Gold Mountain: Cantonese Rhymes from San Francisco Chinatown.* Berkeley: University of California Press, 1987.

Howells, William Dean. "Mr. CWC's Stories." *Atlantic Monthly* 85 (1900): 699–701.

———. "New York Low Life in Fiction." *New York World* 26 (1896): 18.

———. *The Rise of Silas Lapham.* Boston: Ticknor, 1885.

Hoxie, Frederick E., ed. *Talking Back to Civilization: Indian Voices from the Progressive Era.* Boston: Bedford/St. Martin's, 2001.

Hurston, Zora Neale. *Their Eyes Were Watching God.* Philadelphia: J. B. Lippincott, 1937.

Hyman Paula E. *Gender and Assimilation in Modern Jewish History: The Roles and Representation of Women.* Seattle: University of Washington Press, 1995.

James, Henry. *The Ambassadors.* New York: Harper, 1903.

Jinshan ge erji. San Francisco: Tai Quong, 1915.

Jinshan ge ji. San Francisco: Tai Quong, 1911.

Johnson, James Weldon. *The Autobiography of an Ex-Colored Man.* Boston: Sherman, French, 1912.

Kallen, Horace M. *Culture and Democracy in the United States: Studies in the Group Psychology of the American People.* New York: Boni and Liveright, 1924.

———. "Democracy versus the Melting Pot." The Nation 100 (February 18, 1915): 190–94, and (February 25, 1915): 217–20. Part 2 reprinted in *Jewish American Literature.* Ed. Jules Chametzky, John Felstiner, Hilene Flanzbaum, and Kathryn Hellerstein. New York: W. W. Norton, 2001. 206–17.

Kaplan, Amy. *The Social Construction of American Realism.* Chicago: University of Chicago Press, 1988.

Kelly, Myra. *Little Aliens.* New York: Scribners, 1910.

———. *Little Citizens: The Humours of School Life.* New York: McClure, Phillips, 1904.

Kim, Elaine H. *Asian American Literature: An Introduction to the Writings and Their Social Context.* Philadelphia: Temple University Press, 1982.

Kramer, Michael P. "Assimilation in *The Promised Land:* Mary Antin and the Jewish Origins of the American Self." *Prooftexts* 18 (1998): 121–48.

Lee, Yan Phou. *When I Was a Boy in China.* Boston: D. Lothrop, 1887.

Ling, Amy. *Between Worlds: Women Writers of Chinese Ancestry.* New York: Pergamon Press, 1990.

Logan, Rayford W. *The Betrayal of the Negro: From Rutherford B. Hayes to Woodrow Wilson.* New York: Da Capo Press, 1997.

Long, John Luther. "Madame Butterfly." *Century* 55 (January 1898): 274–92.

Melville, Herman. *The Piazza Tales.* New York: Dix and Edwards, 1856.

Miller, J. Hillis. "Narrative." In *Critical Terms for Literary Study.* 2nd ed. Ed. Frank Lentricchia and Thomas McLauglin. Chicago: University of Chicago Press, 1995. 66–79.

Moses, Wilson J. "Literary Garveyism: Three Novels of Sutton E. Griggs." *Phylon* 40 (1979): 203–16.

———. "Literary Myth and Ethnic Assimilation: Israel Zangwill and Sutton E. Griggs." *New Hungarian Quarterly* 21 (1980): 131–36.

Nagel, James. *The Contemporary American Short-Story Cycle.* Baton Rouge: Louisiana State University Press, 2001.

Nagel, James, and Gwen L. Nagel, eds. *Facts on File Bibliography of American Fiction, 1866–1918.* New York: Facts on File, 1993.

Nagel, James, and Tom Quirk, eds. *The Portable American Realism Reader.* New York: Penguin, 1997.

Nelson, Dana. *The World in Black and White: Reading "Race" in American Literature, 1638–1867.* New York: Oxford University Press, 1992.

Norris, Frank. *The Octopus: A Story of California.* New York: Doubleday, Page, 1901.

Omi, Michael, and Howard Winant. *Racial Formation in the United States from the 1960s to the 1980s.* New York: Routledge, 1986.

Parrington, Vernon Lewis. *The Beginnings of Critical Realism in America, 1860–1920.* Vol. 3 of *Main Currents in American Thought.* New York: Harcourt, Brace, 1930.

Pattee, Fred Lewis. *A History of American Literature since 1870.* New York: Century, 1915.

———. *The New American Literature, 1890–1930.* New York: Century, 1930.

Pizer, Donald, ed. *The Cambridge Companion to American Realism and Naturalism.* Cambridge: Cambridge University Press, 1995.

———, ed. *Documents of American Realism and Naturalism.* Carbondale: Southern Illinois University Press, 1998.

———. *Realism and Naturalism in Nineteenth-Century American Literature.* Rev. ed. Carbondale: Southern Illinois University Press, 1984.

Plessy v. Ferguson 163 U.S. 537 (1896). In *Documents of American Constitutional and Legal History.* 2 vols. Ed. Melvin I. Urosfsky. Philadelphia: Temple University Press, 1989. 2:244–48.

Poe, Edgar Allan. "Review of Hawthorne's *Twice-Told Tales.*" In *The Complete Works of Edgar Allen Poe.* Ed. James A. Harrison. New York: AMS Press, 1902. 104–13.

Pratt, Norma Fain. "Traditions in Judaism: The Jewish American Woman through the 1930s." *American Quarterly* 30 (1978): 681–702.

Quirk, Tom, and Gary Scharnhorst, eds. *American Realism and the Canon.* Newark: University of Delaware Press, 1994.

Riis, Jacob. *How the Other Half Lives.* New York: Charles Scribner's Sons, 1890.

———. *Out of Mulberry Street: Stories of Tenement Life in New York.* New York: Century, 1897.

Said, Edward. "Orientalism." *Georgia Review* 31 (1977): 162–206.

———. "*Orientalism:* An Afterword." *Raritan* 14, no. 3 (1995): 32–59.

Shapiro, Lamed. *Di yidishe melukhe un andere zakhn.* New York: Naytsayt, 1919.

———. *The Jewish Government and Other Stories.* Trans. Curt Leviant. New York: Twayne, 1971.

Shavelson, Susanne A. "Anxieties of Authorship in the Autobiographies of Mary Antin and Aliza Greenblatt." *Prooftexts* 18 (1998): 161–86.

Sinclair, Upton. *The Jungle.* New York: Doubleday, Page, 1906.

Smith, Sidonie. "Cheesecakes, Nymphs, and 'We the People': Un/National Subjects about 1900." *Prose Studies: History, Theory, Criticism* 17, no. 1 (1994): 120–40.

Solberg, S. E. "Sui Sin Far/Edith Eaton: First Chinese-American Fictionist." *MELUS* 8, no. 1 (1981): 27–39.

Sollors, Werner. *Beyond Ethnicity: Consent and Descent in American Culture.* New York: Oxford University Press, 1986.

———. "Introduction." In *The Promised Land,* by Mary Antin. New York: Penguin, 1997. xi–l.

South Dakota v. Yankton Sioux Tribe. 522 U.S. 329 (1998).

Standing Bear, Luther. *My People, the Sioux.* Boston: Houghton Mifflin, 1928.

The Statutes at Large of the United States of America, from December 1881 to March 1883, and Recent Treaties, Postal Conventions, and Executive Proclamations (Washington, D.C., GPO, 1883), 22:58–61.

Stowe, Harriet Beecher. *Uncle Tom's Cabin.* Boston: John P. Jewett, 1852.

Sui Sin Far. *Mrs. Spring Fragrance and Other Writings.* Ed. Amy Ling and Annette White-Parks. Champaign: University of Illinois Press, 1995.

———. *Mrs. Spring Fragrance.* Chicago: A. C. McClurg, 1912.

Sundquist, Eric J. *American Realism: New Essays.* Baltimore: Johns Hopkins University Press, 1982.

———. *To Wake the Nations: Race in the Making of American Literature.* Cambridge: Belknap Press, 1993.

Susag, Dorothea M. "Zitkala-Ša (Gertrude Simmons Bonnin): A Power(full) Literary Voice." *Studies in American Indian Literatures* 5, no. 4 (1993): 3–24.

Takaki, Ronald. *A Different Mirror: A History of Multicultural America.* Boston: Little, Brown, 1993.

Tompkins, Jane. "Indians: Textualism, Morality, and the Problem of History." *"Race," Writing, and Difference.* Ed. Henry Louis Gates, Jr. Chicago: University of Chicago Press, 1986. 59–77.

Trotter, Joe William, Jr. *The African American Experience.* Boston: Houghton Mifflin, 2001.

Twain, Mark. *Adventures of Huckleberry Finn.* New York: Webster, 1885.

U.S. Department of Interior and Indian Affairs. *Annual Report of the Department of the Interior.* Washington, D.C.: GPO, 1874–1902.

U.S. Immigration Commission. *The Children of Immigrants in Schools.* 5 vols. Washington, D.C.: GPO, 1911.

Vizenor, Gerald. *The Everlasting Sky: New Voices from the People Named the Chippewa.* New York: Crowell-Collier Press, 1972.

Vizenor, Gerald, ed. *Native American Literature: A Brief Introduction and Anthology.* New York: HarperCollins, 1995.

Wald, Priscilla. *Constituting America: Cultural Anxiety and Narrative Form.* Durham: Duke University Press, 1995.

Walker, Francis A. "Restriction of Immigration." *Atlantic Monthly* 77 (1896): 822–29.

Walker, Randolph Meade. *The Metamorphosis of Sutton E. Griggs: The Transition from Black Radical to Conservative, 1913–1933.* Memphis: Walker Publishing, 1991.

Washington, Booker T. *Up from Slavery.* Garden City, N.J.: Doubleday, 1901. Reprint, New York: Signet, 2000.

Watanna, Onoto. *Miss Numè of Japan.* New York: Rand, McNally, 1899.

Weaver, Jace. *That the People Might Live: Native American Literatures and Native American Community.* New York: Oxford University Press, 1997.

Wharton, Edith. *The House of Mirth.* New York: Scribners, 1905.

White-Parks, Annette. *Sui Sin Far/Edith Maude Eaton: A Literary Biography.* Champaign: University of Illinois Press, 1995.

Wilson, James. *The Earth Shall Weep: A History of Native America.* New York: Grove Press, 1998.

Wisse, Ruth R. *The Modern Jewish Canon: A Journey through Language and Culture.* New York: The Free Press, 2000.

Wu, William. *The Yellow Peril: Chinese Americans in American Fiction, 1850–1940.* Hamden, Conn.: Archon Books, 1982.

Yick Wo v. Hopkins 118 U.S. 356 (1886). In *Documents of American Constitutional and Legal History*. 2 vols. Ed. Melvin I. Urosfsky. Philadelphia: Temple University Press, 1989. 2:241–44.

Yin, Xiao-Huang. "Between East and West: Sui Sin Far—The First Chinese American Woman Writer." *Arizona Quarterly* 47, no. 4 (1991): 49–84.

Zangwill, Israel. *The Melting Pot: A Drama in Four Acts*. New York: Macmillan, 1909.

Zitkala-Ša. *American Indian Stories*. Washington, D.C.: Hayworth, 1921. Reprint, Lincoln: University of Nebraska Press, 1985.

———. *Dreams and Thunder*. Ed. P. Jane Hafen. Lincoln: University of Nebraska Press, 2001.

———. "Impressions of an Indian Childhood." *Atlantic Monthly* 85 (1900): 37–47.

———. "An Indian Teacher among Indians." *Atlantic Monthly* 85 (1900): 381–86.

———. *Old Indian Legends*. Lincoln: University of Nebraska Press, 1985.

———. "The School Days of an Indian Girl." *Atlantic Monthly* 85 (1900): 185–94.

———. "The Soft-Hearted Sioux." *Harper's Monthly* 102 (1901): 505–08.

———. "The Trial Path." *Harper's Monthly* 103 (1901): 741–44.

———. "A Warrior's Daughter." *Everybody's Magazine* 4 (1902): 346–52.

———. "Why I Am a Pagan." *Atlantic Monthly* 90 (1902): 801–03.

Index

acculturation: pressures of, 119, 124, 126; rewards of, 39–40; selective acculturation, 125, 126; synergistic model of, 150. *See also* assimilation

Adams, David Wallace, 178n32

Addams, Jane, 32

African American literature: and abolitionist texts, 15, 105, 156; and development of American realism, 1, 3–4, 14; Griggs's place in, 12, 25, 161; oral tradition of, 12

Alexie, Sherman, 87

Alger, Horatio, 17, 35

Allen, Paula Gunn, 11

Altschuler, Glenn C., 32, 39

ambivalence, towards citizenship, 7, 9–10, 11, 22, 67, 70, 81, 82, 86, 87–88, 151, 163

American Indian boarding schools: and assimilation, 21, 58, 67, 77–79, 84, 152, 178n30; conditions of, 58–59; and English language skills, 79–80, 178n32; graduates of, 1, 11, 12; and Zitkala-Ša, 21, 22, 58, 59, 61, 68, 70, 72, 75–80, 82–87, 88, 151, 152, 153–54

American Indian cultures: American perceptions of, 55, 56, 85; and Christianization, 58, 65, 66, 67, 68–70, 73–75, 77–78, 86; and government policies, 57–59, 79, 84, 85–86; and tribal enlightenment, 59; and Zitkala-Ša, 60, 63-64, 65, 66, 67, 71–72, 74, 75, 78, 82, 84, 88, 177nn17, 25

American Indian lands, 57–58, 71, 82, 176n4, 177n7

American Indian literature: and boarding school graduates, 1, 11, 12; and development of American realism, 1, 3–4, 5; Zitkala-Ša's place in, 11, 22, 87–88, 161

American Yiddish literature, 46, 186n1

Ammons, Elizabeth, 6, 14

anthroposophy, 20, 172n24

Antin, Mary: and Americanization, 30, 33–34, 36, 41, 152–53, 163; background of, 18–21; challenging of immigrant inferiority, 7, 47, 155; critics' recognition of, 3, 19–20; English language skills of, 34–35, 46, 49; and open immigration, 20, 21, 33; place in American literature, 164; place in Jewish American literature, 12, 13, 161; portrayal of assimilation, 21, 30; and public education, 20, 21, 34, 39, 45, 51, 52–53, 54, 154–55; and realism, 1–2, 6, 10, 14, 16–17; use of transcendentalism, 15–16, 35, 45, 50, 51, 157, 175n24, 176n29; and Yiddish language, 46, 176n27

Antin, Mary, works: *From Plotzk to Boston*, 19, 45, 46, 52, 175n24; "The Lie," 176n31; "Snow," 46; *They Who Knock at Our Gates*, 20, 47. *See also The Promised Land* (Antin)

anti-Semitism: in American society, 32, 48–50; in Russia, 49, 152

Anzaldúa, Gloria, 55

Asian American literature: and development of American realism, 5; Sui Sin Far's place in, 13, 18, 27, 122, 161

199